PRESIDENTIAL
RECONSTRUCTION
IN MISSISSIPPI

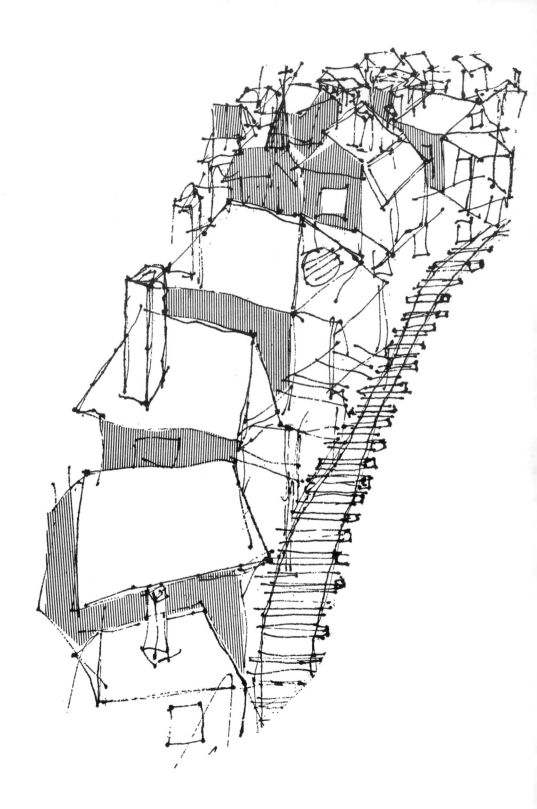

PRESIDENTIAL RECONSTRUCTION IN MISSISSIPPI

William C. Harris

LOUISIANA STATE UNIVERSITY PRESS

BATON ROUGE

TO MY AUNTS

Preface

PROBABLY NO PERIOD or aspect of nineteenth-century Southern history has been so neglected as Presidential Reconstruction in
the individual states. Historical accounts of postwar developments
usually pass over the period immediately after the war with a few
comments concerning the destructive effects of the war in the South,
the transition from slave to free labor, and the Presidential plan for the
restoration of the states to the Union. Presidential Reconstruction is
treated as an interregnum that, despite its noble features, only retarded
the restoration of these states. Thus, in the flow of history, this period,
historians seem to suggest by their neglect, really has little significance.
And after they have chronicled the triumph of Congress over the
President, they rush on to relate the story that they really set out to
tell in the first place—the story of Congressional or Radical Reconstruction.

It is true that a great deal has been written concerning the power
struggle between the President and Congress; but, by their nature,
these studies have focused on the political scene in Washington and
have almost incidentally included affairs in the Southern states.
Furthermore, when developments in the former Confederate states are
mentioned, the attitudes and policies which created or caused these
developments are treated in most of the reconstruction studies as if
the former Confederates of the South were monolithic in their ap-

proach to postwar adjustment. This traditional emphasis upon the struggle between President Andrew Johnson and the Radicals has probably been a major reason why many historians have continued to look at this period from a national standpoint and have neglected the less panoramic local view.

Notwithstanding this neglect, and yet probably to some extent because of it, a study of this period focused on the state level rather than on Washington can be extremely meaningful. White Southerners in 1865 and 1866, for the only time during the reconstruction era, were generally free to react naturally to the problems of adjustment after the Civil War, the results of which had included the shattering of a labor and social system which had pervaded all aspects of life in many areas of the South before 1865. When military rule was reimposed upon the South, less latitude was available for local divisions and for the candid expression by Southerners of attitudes and opinions regarding the postwar settlement.

Donald H. Breese in his dissertation, "Politics in the Lower South during Presidential Reconstruction," attempts to fill, in part, this void in Southern historiography; however, the scope of his study does not extend beyond the election of the home rule or restoration governments in 1865. His work, then, deals primarily with a period when the shock of defeat and quasi-military rule still profoundly conditioned the reactions of the people to many of the problems of postwar adjustment.

Many significant questions can be answered, at least in part, by a state study of the period of Presidential Reconstruction. Specifically, what were the psychological and physical effects of the war on the people of the state? What were some of the immediate problems facing a people who had suffered military defeat in a devastating war? Which groups or parties controlled the state under the provisional government and which under the restoration government? What policies did these leaders promote toward the freedmen and toward resolving the serious economic and political problems of reconstruction? Were their policies influenced by past experiences and antagonisms, or did the Civil War provide them with an opportunity for a clean break with the past? Did the restoration government attempt seriously to meet the issues of postwar adjustment, or was it diverted by popular emotions or constrained by tangential or even irrelevant forces? Did the acts of the government reflect a white monolithic view of these problems and especially of the place of the Negro in the society of the state? And were the leaders of 1865–67 devising a formula for restoration acceptable to the bulk of the Northern people when the military reconstruction acts of 1867 were passed?

A study of any of several former Confederate states might produce meaningful answers to these questions or might provide significant insights into problems of defeat and readjustment, as well as into the Southern culture from which had to be drawn the means or resources for coping with these problems. Of these states, Mississippi offers a very fertile area for such historical investigation. Mississippi in the decade of the 1860's was not just typical of the states of the cotton South; in some ways its characteristics and experiences were an extreme form of those common to other states of the region. Mississippi experienced a great deal of physical destruction during the Civil War; it was partially occupied by Federal troops for an extended period of time; it had been the largest cotton producing state in 1860; it depended upon Negro labor more than any other state except perhaps South Carolina; it had an influential and vocal group that had opposed the policies of the dominant party before 1865 and was anxious to challenge the acts of the past two decades; it was the first state to hold a reconstruction convention under the Presidential plan of reconstruction; and it was the first state to attempt to define the place of the Negro in its postwar society.

This study represents an attempt to answer the above questions, and others as well, and an attempt to portray the forces at work in Mississippi society that conditioned the responses of the people to the problems of postwar adjustment. By the nature of the problems of reconstruction, the emphasis in this study is on political and economic developments in the state. Events and developments in Washington and in the North are only generally mentioned, and only to the extent that they had a direct influence on affairs in Mississippi.

Without the assistance of many persons this book could not have been written. I wish especially to express my appreciation to Professor Thomas B. Alexander of the University of Alabama, who encouraged me in this project and who often rallied my spirits with his enthusiasm for the study. He spent countless hours reviewing the manuscript, conferring with me, and recommending numerous changes to the work. I am deeply indebted to Professors James F. Doster and Robert E. Johnson, also of the University of Alabama, for their painstaking reading of the manuscript and for their helpful suggestions in both style and content. Aid and advice was also rendered by Professors Ross H. Moore of Millsaps College, David N. Young of Carson-Newman College, Will Holmes and Harold M. Hollingsworth of Arlington State College. I would indeed be remiss if I did not express my appreciation to Millsaps College, and especially Dean Frank M. Laney and Professor Moore, for giving me an opportunity during the summer months for uninterrupted research and writing on this book.

A debt of gratitude is owed to Mrs. Corneil Caldwell, Mrs. Laura Harrell, and Mrs. Jane Melton of the staff of the Mississippi Department of Archives and History. They gave abundantly of both time and assistance to the research on this study. The staffs of the libraries at the universities of Alabama, Mississippi, and North Carolina, Chapel Hill, and Duke University, along with those of the Library of Congress and the National Archives, also made their books, manuscript materials, and newspaper files easily accessible to me. Miss Mary O'Bryant and her assistants in the Millsaps College Library contributed greatly to this study by securing for me important materials from other libraries.

Finally, I wish to acknowledge the assistance of my wife Betty G. Harris. Somehow she managed to take time from her duties on the faculty of the School of Nursing of the University of Mississippi and her responsibilities as a mother to type drafts of this manuscript and to help with innumerable other tasks connected with it.

W.C.H.

Contents

Illustrations

Maps

PRESIDENTIAL
RECONSTRUCTION
IN MISSISSIPPI

1

Background: Defeatism in Confederate Mississippi

ON MAY 21, 1865, the "old and maimed" Confederate governor, Charles Clark, quixotically resisted the demands of Federal Brigadier General Embury D. Osband for custody of the public records and offices of the state. However, at seven o'clock on the day designated for the surrender, May 22, the governor, still strongly protesting against any such usurpation of his authority, notified Osband that he would not attempt to resist the assumption of control of the state government by the armed forces of the United States. At nine o'clock on the same morning Captain J. Warren Miller and a squad of Federal troops entered the Mississippi state capitol at Jackson and without incident escorted Governor Clark from the executive office.[1] Thus ended Mississippi's Confederate experiment.

Although the final collapse of the Confederacy was deferred until May, 1865, Mississippians were certainly not confronted in that month with an unexpected crisis, nor were they wholly unprepared for what might be expected of them in the period of adjustment to follow surrender. Throughout the latter half of the war there had been numerous and ever increasing evidences that defeat for Confederate forces was recognized as a distinct possibility if not a probability. War weariness and many associated factors must have turned the minds of a great many Mississippians to the alternatives to continued resistance to Federal forces. An embattled people are far from free to express their defeatism openly and candidly as long as the government under which they live maintains military posture and fails to acknowledge

[1] Clark to Osband, May 22, 1865, in Mississippi Governors' Correspondence, File E-68, Mississippi Department of Archives and History, Jackson, hereinafter cited as Governors' Correspondence, with file designation.

defeat. Nonetheless, clues to the developing readiness for defeat and its consequences are numerous; and an understanding of attitudes of Mississippians in May, 1865, can be furthered by noting such clues, which began to appear as early as mid-war.

A few influential Mississippians had favored an end to the war as early as 1863, but apparently it was not until 1865 that the peace movement had become significant and widespread in the state.[2] The desire for peace, the opportunity to restore the means of livelihood, and, for many, simply survival, were by late 1864 the critical factors in the state of mind of a great many Mississippians. Loyalty to the Confederacy or to the Union was of secondary importance to a people who were tired of bloodshed, disillusioned, almost destitute, and anxious for a government that would protect their lives and remaining possessions and give them a chance to produce and market their crops.[3] Raked by military raids and by lawless bands often pretending to act for either the Union or the Confederacy, many areas of the state faced virtual anarchy by late 1864. Courts were closed, and incompetent law enforcement officers, often old men or young boys, were powerless to cope with the disorders. Many people had come to realize that, as repugnant and publicly unpopular as it might be, only federal authority would be in a position any time soon to provide security for life and property.

Law and order began to deteriorate with Major General Ulysses S. Grant's campaign against the river towns in 1863. At the same time the northeast counties became a battle area. Unionists, seeking to avenge the past misdeeds of their secession antagonists, roamed at will in one of these counties, Tishomingo, and pillaged the countryside.[4] As the Federal armies advanced into the interior after the fall of Vicksburg, Confederate soldiers, particularly unwilling conscripts and

[2] The most useful secondary source for conditions in Mississippi during the Confederate period is John K. Bettersworth, *Confederate Mississippi: The People and Policies of a Cotton State in Wartime* (Baton Rouge: Louisiana State University Press, 1943).

[3] For manifestations of this war weariness, see Charles W. Ramsdell, *Behind the Lines in the Southern Confederacy* (Baton Rouge: Louisiana State University Press, 1944), 113, and Mary Elizabeth Massey, *Ersatz in the Confederacy* (Columbia: University of South Carolina Press, 1952), 172.

[4] Petition of citizens of Tishomingo County to Milton Brown, president of the Mobile and Ohio Railroad, undated, in Governors' Correspondence, E-68; Orlando Davis to Provisional Governor William L. Sharkey, June 28, 1865, *ibid.*, E-69; Bettersworth, *Confederate Mississippi*, 204–205, 216.

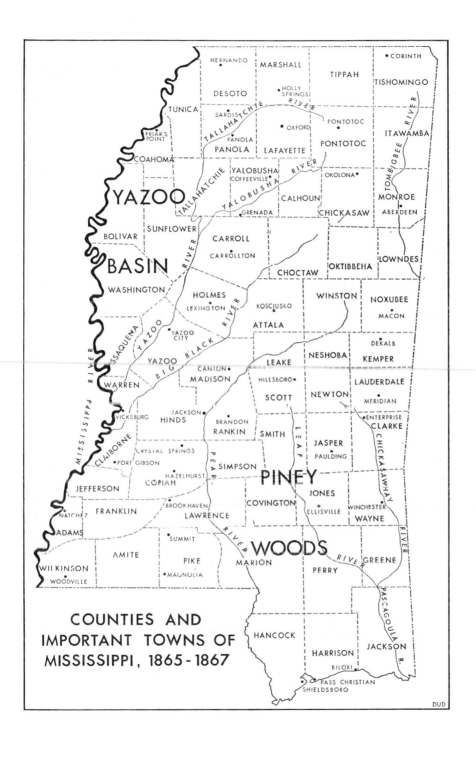

COUNTIES AND
IMPORTANT TOWNS OF
MISSISSIPPI, 1865-1867

those who had been lukewarm on the secession issue from the beginning, deserted by the hundreds. Hounded by state and Confederate cavalry, such men formed bands for protection and often left their hiding places in the woods to plunder their vulnerable neighbors.[5]

Cotton and livestock were appealing objects for plunderers and military raiders. During one Federal raid up the Yazoo River in early 1865, 1,728 bales of cotton were indiscriminately taken. Private cotton in many cases was burned by Confederate forces to prevent it from falling into the hands of the enemy.[6] Confederate Senator John W. C. Watson wrote that periodically north Mississippi was raided for horses and mules until, before the end of the war, people there "had, to a considerable extent, adopted the habit of keeping their horses and mules in such bad order as to render them undesirable to soldiers." Yet livestock that escaped seizure by raiders was often impressed by Confederate authorities.[7]

One bright spot in this story of insecurity in the state was that Negroes did not generally engage in these nefarious operations nor did they attempt mass violence against their masters.[8]

State and local officers found themselves almost completely helpless to combat the near anarchy prevailing in much of the state by late 1864. Local officials were too inefficient and weak to return deserters and fugitives from conscription to the army and to bring law violators to justice. Furthermore, many of these officers tended to sympathize with such men. Robert S. Hudson, a circuit judge in central Mississippi, wrote Governor Clark twice in May, 1865, that not one of the civil officers in his area was attempting to discharge his duty of ap-

[5] Bettersworth, *Confederate Mississippi*, 208–209, 236–38; H. W. Walter to Confederate Senator John W. C. Watson, December 29, 1864, in *The War of the Rebellion: A Compilation of the Official Records of the Union and Confederate Armies* (Washington: Government Printing Office, 1880–1901), Ser. 4, Vol. III, 976, hereinafter cited as *Official Records, Armies.*

[6] New York *Times*, June 18, 1865; A. Sellew Roberts, "The Federal Government and Confederate Cotton," *American Historical Review*, XXXII (1927), 262; Ephraim S. Fisher to Governor Clark, February 14, 1865, in Governors' Correspondence, E-68; J. T. Hollingsworth to Reverdy Johnson, May 25, 1865, in Andrew Johnson Papers, Manuscripts Division, Library of Congress.

[7] Watson to Sharkey, July 11, 1865, in Governors' Correspondence, E-70; petition of citizens of Noxubee County to Clark, April 24, 1865, *ibid.*, E-68; Orlando Davis to Sharkey, June 28, 1865, *ibid.*, E-69.

[8] Bell I. Wiley, *Southern Negroes, 1861–1865* (New Haven: Yale University Press, 1938), 37–38.

prehending deserters, despite the fact that the counties were full of such men, who were frequently committing crimes. The majority of these officers, Hudson averred, were "absent from their counties and districts one half their time, engaged in extortionary speculations." Their neighbors, and often their own sons, were fugitives, whom they met, and sometimes fed and entertained, "without attempting to arrest or even to reprimand them." [9]

Although cavalry units had been sent during 1864 to track down deserters, it had become all but impossible by 1865 for Confederate authorities to provide men for such operations in view of the tottering fortunes of the armies. The result was that brigands and deserters became bolder in sallying forth to commit depredations upon communities. Lieutenant General Richard Taylor, Confederate commander of the department, demanded that Governor Clark call out the militia for employment in arresting deserters.[10] Even though the legislature authorized its use for this purpose, the governor, at the same time arguing with Confederate authorities over the disposition of state troops in the general military service, did not call out the militia to restore order until March 27, 1865.[11]

Skeleton militia units, however, were unable to apprehend brigands. In Winston and Neshoba counties predators threatened to annihilate the militia and to burn the homes of its members if an attempt were made to arrest them. Conditions were so deplorable in the northern part of the state that Confederate and Federal officers agreed to cooperate in the suppression of marauding deserters.[12]

Destitution in many areas and the economic debacle that confronted the state if the war continued also served to convince many by early 1865 that peace should be arranged as soon as possible. Areas that

[9] James W. Silver (ed.), "The Breakdown of Morale in Central Mississippi in 1864; Letters of Judge Robert S. Hudson," *Journal of Mississippi History*, XVI (1954), 104.

[10] Ephraim S. Fisher to Clark, February 14, 1865; Taylor to Clark, February 26, 1865; petition of citizens of Warren County to General Taylor, March, 1865, all in Governors' Correspondence, E-68.

[11] Charles A. Lewers to Clark, March 29, 1865; Thomas E. B. Pegues to Clark, March 30, 1865; James T. Gresham to Clark, April 15, 1865, all *ibid.*

[12] New Orleans *Picayune*, March 29, 1865. In fact, it was reported that some deserters were serving as officers in the militia in Neshoba and neighboring counties. W. McDonald to Colonel E. Surget, April 19, 1865, in Governors' Correspondence, E-68.

were the scene of military campaigns suffered an especially concentrated devastation. This was particularly true of counties overrun by Major General William T. Sherman's Meridian expedition of early 1864, after which he declared that he had "made a swath of desolation 50 miles broad across the State of Mississippi which the present generation will not forget."[13] Communities in his path remained without means of support for the remainder of the war, since labor and provisions were not available to restore their productivity.

Counties in the northeastern part of the state, which had endured periodic military raids for two years, were denuded of the means of producing the necessities of life; and some, if not many, of the inhabitants faced critical malnutrition or starvation by 1865. One farmer wrote that the shipment of provisions to this section "cannot long be delayed without great suffering to the people, many of whom are now on short rations of bread, while very few have any forage at all, not even fodder or shucks to feed their work horses and mules or any other kind of stock, most of which of necessity must perish, before the winter [of 1864–65] is over, from starvation."[14] An arrangement was made with Federal and Confederate military authorities to ship food into the area, but officials of the Mobile and Ohio Railroad refused to undertake such a project. The officers of the road gave as their reason for refusal that, even if the necessary repairs were made on the railroad above Okolona and trains were run into the area, Federal troops might violate their pledge, molest the crewmen, and destroy the rolling stock.[15]

Even many of those who were not destitute found that the economic dislocation of the state had made it virtually impossible for them to secure the necessary provisions to plant a crop. Credit to obtain supplies was simply not available in districts where commercial conditions were insecure. In cases where they were able to obtain supplies on credit, their purchases only added to their already heavy indebted-

[13] George Barnes to Clark, April 13, 1865, in Governors' Correspondence, E-68; Stephen D. Lee, "Sherman's Meridian Expedition from Vicksburg to Meridian, February 3rd to March 6th, 1864," *Publications of the Mississippi Historical Society*, IV (1901), 46–47.

[14] C. A. Taylor to Clark, undated, in Governors' Correspondence, E-68.

[15] Robert A. Hill to General Nathan Bedford Forrest, February 1, 1865; Forrest to Hill, undated; petition of citizens of Tishomingo County to Milton Brown, president of the Mobile and Ohio Railroad, undated; Lee Fleming to Clark, February 15, 1865, all *ibid.*

ness.[16] Only in areas near the Mississippi River, where Federal troops maintained control, had the normal flow of commerce been restored. Confederate authorities during the late months of the war, however, permitted needy farmers of the interior to trade with Memphis, Vicksburg, and other Northern-occupied commercial centers; but the Richmond government took one third of the proceeds of the farmer's cotton for granting this privilege. As planters and farmers of the interior of the state became more desperate, illegal trade with the river towns increased.[17]

Civil disorders, economic collapse, and destitution evidently contributed greatly to the deterioration of morale and the desire for peace during the latter months of the war. Furthermore, the hope for an end to hostilities was accentuated by the Confederate government's conscription policy and the "Twenty Negro law," which created a feeling of dissatisfaction and resentment that became more intense as the fortunes of the Confederacy waned.[18] Property impressment measures were never popular and during the latter months of the war were causing great discontent, even among the staunchest Confederates.[19] Many farmers were hoping to retain property, especially cotton, with which to finance a new start after the war. But the arbitrary activities of impressment authorities dimmed their hopes. A war fought to retain liberties now appeared to many to be one in which liberty, property, and perhaps life were in great jeopardy every day it continued.

Prolonged inconveniences and irritations caused by a lack of necessities added to the demoralization of the people. The impossibility of securing salt in some counties because of seizures by raiders of both armies meant that meat, except while fresh, ceased to be a part of the

[16] H. W. Walter, touring the state at the end of 1864, believed that only one half of the farmers and planters of Mississippi would be able to plant a crop in 1865. Walter to John W. C. Watson, December 29, 1864, in *Official Records, Armies*, Ser. 4, Vol. III, 978.

[17] Fisher to Clark, February 14, 1865, in Governors' Correspondence, E-68.

[18] Albert B. Moore, *Conscription and Conflict in the Confederacy* (New York: The Macmillan Company, 1924), 354, 359. The "Twenty Negro law" provided for the exemption from conscription of one white man on each plantation with twenty slaves or more.

[19] Bettersworth, *Confederate Mississippi*, 196, 199. The unpopular tax in kind, speculation, and trade with the Federal-occupied towns worked also to demoralize the people.

diet.[20] An observer in central Mississippi during the fall of 1864 wrote that although the wheat crop was plentiful, "so great has been the demand from consumers and speculators, principally from the Southern portion of the State and even from East Louisiana, that but little wheat is to be had now. It is commanding $20 a bushel, and, as to flour, the mills have in a great measure ceased selling it at home." [21] Even the great planters of happier days did not have the means to secure the common items of the household. Susan Dabney Smedes, the daughter of Thomas Dabney, one of the planter aristocrats of the antebellum period, describes the means her family employed in order to continue a semblance of their old way of life: "We had coffee made of blackberry-leaves, and green tea made of holly leaves. . . . We had scarcely any clothes. . . . Our shoes were made of the skins of oxen, roughly tanned by the plantation shoemaker, and manufactured into covering for the feet by him." [22]

The shortage of food and supplies, along with the instability of Confederate currency, brought a marked inflation in prices. The speculator arose as both a cause and an effect of this inflation.[23] People were unable to procure essential commodities, except at grossly inflated prices, and this fact played an important part in the desire for peace in Mississippi.

The disruption of transportation and communications during the latter part of the war added to the general hopelessness and demoralization of the people. Counties and communities found it virtually impossible to secure the labor necessary for the proper maintenance of the roads and to patrol the highways against brigands.[24] Yet planters and farmers understood that the restoration of their fortunes depended upon their ability to ship cotton to market as soon as hostilities had ceased. Already markets were opening for farmers

[20] J. R. M. DuBerry to Clark, February 1, 1865; petition of Police Court of Calhoun County to Clark, February 13, 1865, both in Governors' Correspondence, E-68.

[21] Correspondent to Meridian *Clarion*, October 18, 1864, in Jason Niles Scrapbook, Vol. XLI (MS in Southern Historical Collection, University of North Carolina Library, Chapel Hill).

[22] Susan Dabney Smedes, *A Southern Planter* (4th ed.; New York: James Pott and Co., 1890), 224.

[23] Massey, *Ersatz in the Confederacy*, 163; Robert S. Hudson to Jefferson Davis, November 25, 1864, in *Official Records, Armies*, Ser. 1, Vol. XLV, Pt. 1, pp. 1247–48.

[24] Fisher to Clark, February 14, 1865, in Governors' Correspondence, E-68.

within or near the Federal lines. The longer the war continued the more the roads would deteriorate and the greater would be the difficulty in reviving the cotton and provisions trade. The prospects of the war's being concluded soon on terms recognizing the independent status of the Confederate States appeared so unlikely that the only realistic hope of escaping destitution lay with the reconstruction of the state in the Union.

Judge Robert S. Hudson, disclaiming any intention of being an alarmist, as early as March, 1864, painted a distressing picture of morale and loyalty in central Mississippi. Hudson wrote President Jefferson Davis:

> Mississippi is in a most deplorable condition. . . . Very many of the middle class, a large number of the more intelligent, and nearly all of the lower class of her people are drifting to the Yankees. . . . These are facts that can be proved beyond all question. Desertion from the army, trading with the enemy, and the removal of deserters and their families into the lines and the supposed lines of the enemy is now the order of the day, and the citizen who opposes these things stands almost alone and in great personal danger.
>
> Many of the men not liable to military service and nearly all the women are openingly [sic] at work to weaken our army, procure desertion, and assail the Confederacy.
>
> The state is now under the tacit rule of deserters, thieves, and disloyal men and women. The lower and middle tier of counties are vastly rotten.[25]

In November, 1864, Hudson wrote President Davis that the people blamed their misfortunes on the Confederate government and that they were disposed "to rise up in opposition to the powers that be, declare for reconstruction, or anything else but the things that are." [26]

Thus it is not surprising to find active peace movements in the state several months before the end of the war. What is surprising is the fact that the Unionist cause did not triumph before the collapse of the Confederacy. The river counties were generally under Federal control by 1864 and therefore could have served as formidable bases for loyalist activities. At Natchez, Lorenzo Thomas, adjutant general of the United States Army, found in October, 1863, "quite a Union feel-

[25] Hudson's letter to Davis may be found in *Official Records, Armies*, Ser. 1, Vol. XXXII, Pt. 3, pp. 625–27.
[26] *Ibid.*, Ser. 1, Vol. XLV, Pt. 1, p. 1248.

ing," but he thought that it was not the place to begin a reconstruction movement, since "the other counties have usually looked upon Adams County (Natchez) with a jealous eye."[27] Plans, however, were already being made to begin the movement in adjoining Wilkinson County. Natchez Unionists hoped to be able to persuade William L. Sharkey, former chief justice of the high court, to lead the movement, and they worked to secure his appointment as military governor for the occupied portion of the state. Although Sharkey had consulted with General Sherman at Jackson in July, 1863, regarding the possibility of securing the restoration of Mississippi to the Union, he declined to participate in any such movement at this time and suggested that the undercurrent of Unionism be given an opportunity to show itself more distinctly throughout the state before implementing plans for reconstruction.[28] Armistead Burwell, a loyalist of Vicksburg, was more optimistic concerning Unionist strength in the state. He wrote Abraham Lincoln in August, 1863: "There are thousands in Miss: who desire most ardently the restoration of the United States Government. . . . If you wish to hear Jeff: Davis, Wigfall, Toombs, Floyd, etc. etc., cursed from the bottom of the heart, and with the whole soul, go disguised to Vicksburg, and converse with the men of Mississippi. . . . There are many bold and talented men, once men of wealth and influence, who at all hazards were [and are] willing to raise the old standard, and follow it to the death." Burwell asserted, somewhat wishfully, that "there are more unconditionally loyal or Union men in that state [Mississippi], in proportion to population than in the state of Ohio or New York."[29]

The peace movement did not succeed, for one reason, because of the disagreement among its supporters as to the terms and procedure

[27] Adjutant General Lorenzo Thomas to Secretary of War Edwin M. Stanton, October 24, 1863, in *Official Records, Armies*, Ser. 3, Vol. III, 916–17; Major General William T. Sherman to Major General Ulysses S. Grant, July 21, 1863, *ibid.*, Ser. 1, Vol. XXIV, Pt. 2, pp. 530–31.

[28] Sherman to Grant, *ibid.*, 531.

[29] Frank W. Klingberg, *The Southern Claims Commission* (Berkeley: University of California Press, 1955), 198. The term "loyalist" will be used in this study to describe a person who remained a persistent or unconditional Unionist and who never recognized the legitimacy of the Confederate States. The description of a person as an "original Unionist" indicates that he sought to prevent secession but after the Confederacy had been established he acknowledged its authority and, in many cases, actively supported its war effort. Most "Union Whigs" evidently were original Unionists, not loyalists.

for reconstruction. One group, led by Confederate Whigs, favored an honorable peace and restoration which would permit them to retain many of their old privileges. On the other hand, loyalists, embittered by a long period of persecution and proscription at the hands of the "rebels," desired a thoroughgoing reconstruction of the type that Parson William G. Brownlow was by early 1865 leading in Tennessee. A moderate group of original loyal men desired only the return of their state to the Union. In fact, Burwell, a moderate, urged upon Lincoln a plan of speedy restoration similar to the one which the President adopted.[30]

Cut off from communications with the interior by Federal occupation of the river counties, reconstructionists of the Vicksburg-Natchez area were unable to coordinate their activities with Unionists of the back country. Without a newspaper, loyalists had no means for widely disseminating information even if communication lines could be opened, and as a result the restoration movement remained localized until the capitulation of the Southern armies.[31]

Strong disaffection with the Confederate administration, but not necessarily of a disloyal nature, appeared in politics as early as the campaign and election of 1863. Conservatives, many of whom were Whigs, were elected to state and Confederate offices. Charles Clark, a conservative who had deserted the Whigs in the 1850's to become a Democrat, won the governorship; and John W. C. Watson, an ardent Whig, secured the overwhelming vote of the new legislature for Confederate senator. It was at this time that a secret political organization was allegedly formed with the avowed purpose of supporting no candidate for office who was a secessionist or who was serving in the Confederate army. This election, however, represented a resurgence of conservative, old-line Whig policies rather than a manifestation of Unionist sentiment, in spite of the fact that Whig patriarchs Sharkey and William Yerger had collaborated unsuccessfully a few weeks earlier with General Sherman to secure the reconstruction of the

---

[30] See *ibid.*, for Burwell's position. A letter from S. S. Fairfield to President Johnson, May 26, 1865, in Johnson Papers, explains the position of a radical loyalist regarding reconstruction.

[31] "Report of the Joint Committee on Reconstruction," *House Reports*, 39th Cong., 1st Sess., No. 30, Pt. III, 68–69; W. McDonald to Colonel E. Surget, April 19, 1865, in Governors' Correspondence, E-68; Bettersworth, *Confederate Mississippi*, 211.

state.[32] On the other hand, since many Whigs and other discontented persons were known to favor a compromise peace that would restore the Union, the results of the election gave encouragement to the restoration movement.[33] After 1863 conservative Whigs, who had generally opposed secession until it was a *fait accompli,* increasingly worked for the termination of the war. Many still hoped for a peace that would recognize Southern independence, but probably a majority of former Whigs gradually came to accept something less and began to advocate a restoration to the Union on honorable terms.

Despite the strong internal opposition to the Confederate government and the deterioration of morale, it was the military victory of Federal forces over the Southern armies that finally brought about the restoration of the state to the Union. Faced with the grim prospect of the state's continuing as a battleground, the Jackson *Mississippian,* formerly a leading secession journal, during the fall of 1864 called for an "honorable peace," suggesting that this might be accomplished only by restoration to the Union.[34] By March, 1865, Northern newspapers were reporting that state wartime political leaders like Jehu A. Orr, John W. C. Watson, Otho R. Singleton, and William D. Holder were supporting reconstruction. The intrepid Orr, a member of the Confederate Congress, in February, 1865, even appeared before the legislature to denounce President Davis for rejecting Northern peace terms. Meetings were held in Jefferson County and several counties in east-central Mississippi in which resolutions were adopted expressing a readiness to accept the authority of the federal government and asking for Federal troops to subdue jayhawkers. Delegates were selected at the meetings to visit Vicksburg and express these resolutions to the Federal commander there. Reconstructionists even occupied the same platform with implacable foes of surrender and

[32] John K. Bettersworth (ed.), "Mississippi Unionism: The Case of Reverend James A. Lyon," *Journal of Mississippi History,* I (1939), 38; David Donald, "The Scalawag in Mississippi Reconstruction," *Journal of Southern History,* X (1944), 448; John Prestioge to Provisional Governor William L. Sharkey, June 25, 1865, in Governors' Correspondence, E-69; Meridian *Clarion,* October 8, 1865.

[33] Thomas B. Alexander, "Persistent Whiggery in the Confederate South, 1860–1877," *Journal of Southern History,* XXVII (1961), 309.

[34] Bettersworth, *Confederate Mississippi,* 209–10; William Yerger to President Johnson, June 28, 1865, in Records of the Adjutant General, Amnesty Papers, Mississippi, National Archives, hereinafter cited as Amnesty Papers, Mississippi.

debated the momentous issue of peace.[35] In such a meeting at Canton
on March 1, William Yerger, a prominent member of the Mississippi
bar and a Union Whig, decried an "independence or death" speech
by Chief Justice Alexander H. Handy and urged immediate state
action looking to reconstruction. The legislature, however, refused
to discuss the possibility of restoration, probably because its members
were fearful of arrest and fearful of a lasting reputation as quitters if
they debated such a proposition. This repulse meant that the reconstructionists and peace advocates had no statewide forum for ham-
mering out a plan for the restoration of the state.

Demands for Governor Clark to call a reconstruction convention
followed the news of General Lee's surrender at Appomattox. Die-
hards in a final gesture of defiance urged him not to be swayed by talk
of submission. George W. Shelton, a former Whig politician of
Brandon, wrote to the governor that Mississippi would not gain better
terms if a convention were called; nothing would be gained but
"degradation and dishonor. There are many—very many of us here
and elsewhere—who are not yet whipped, and don't intend to be." [36]
Hiram Cassedy, who had been speaker of the state house of representatives during the late 1850's, felt that the South would triumph, in
spite of Lee's surrender. "All that is required now is a persistence in
our determination to be free," he declared. "A little more sacrifice and
we are safe." Yet he admitted that the people, despondent and fearful,
"are as crazy as crickets smoked out of a rotten log in the fire place and
ready to run into the fire for safety." [37]

Notwithstanding the protests of die-hards, a significant effort was
made in late April and in May to call a convention independent of
state authorities. In an address to the people on April 18, loyalist
Armistead Burwell asked the counties to send delegates to a statewide
meeting of reconstructionists at Jackson on June 5. This meeting was

[35] Captain John W. Crane to Brigadier General T. W. Sherman, April 5, 1865,
in *Official Records, Armies*, Ser. 1, Vol. XLIX, Pt. 2, p. 248; James W. Garner,
Reconstruction in Mississippi (New York: The Macmillan Co., 1901), 55–56.
This account does not intend to suggest that there were no leaders or newspapers
who attempted to revive the morale of the people. The Meridian *Clarion*, January
28, 1865, for example, proclaimed to its readers that "the prospect is good, if not
really cheering," for the Southern military campaign of 1865.

[36] George W. Shelton to Clark, April 25, 1865, in John L. Power Papers, Mississippi Department of Archives and History, Jackson.

[37] Hiram Cassedy to Oscar J. E. Stuart, April 29, 1865, in Oscar J. E. Stuart
Papers, Mississippi Department of Archives and History, Jackson.

expected to arrange for the calling of a convention of men "of well-known loyalty," who would abolish slavery and request readmission to the Union. Loyalists asked federal authorities to give their approval to the Burwell proposal, and at the same time they expressed their strong opposition to the present state government or to Confederates sharing in the political restoration of Mississippi.[38] At first the district commander endorsed the movement. However, President Johnson was in the process of formulating a broader plan for reconstruction, the execution of which would not be limited to persistent Unionists. Accordingly, the commander in Mississippi was notified not to permit the meeting of the Burwell convention or any other such convention.[39]

On May 6 near Meridian General Richard Taylor surrendered what remained of the Confederate forces east of the Mississippi River. With this capitulation military resistance to Federal control in Mississippi was at an end. On the same day Governor Clark issued a proclamation to the people informing them of the surrender and urging local officials to be vigilant in the preservation of order and the protection of property. He directed militia organizations to keep their arms and to be alert to arrest marauders and plunderers. "The State laws must be enforced as they are now until repealed," Clark declared. "If the public property is protected and peace preserved, the necessity of Federal troops in your counties will be avoided." Masters were informed that they were still responsible "for the protection and conduct of their slaves, and [that] they should be kept at home as heretofore." [40]

Clark apparently believed that the present state authorities would be permitted to initiate the work of restoration. After meeting with

[38] Ira A. Batterton to President Johnson, May 16, 1865; S. S. Fairfield to Johnson, May 26, 1865, both in Johnson Papers; Natchez *Tri-Weekly Courier*, May 11, 1865. Burwell, however, was a moderate Unionist who apparently had no objections to some Confederates participating in reconstruction. See above, p. 12.

[39] New York *Times*, June 4, 1865. Another group of Mississippi Unionists, meeting at Memphis in early May along with loyalists from Tennessee and Arkansas, called for a reconstruction convention at Vicksburg. This effort to reorganize the state government, like the Burwell movement, proved abortive. Winbourne M. Drake, "The Mississippi Reconstruction Convention of 1865," *Journal of Mississippi History*, XXI (1959), 226; Garner, *Reconstruction in Mississippi*, 59.

[40] Clark's proclamation may be found in Walter L. Fleming (ed.), *Documentary History of Reconstruction, Political, Military, Social, Religious, Educational, and Industrial, 1865 to the Present Time* (Cleveland: Arthur H. Clark Co., 1906–1907), I, 167.

several conservatives at the home of William Yerger in Jackson, he asked the legislature to convene on May 18 for the purpose of calling a reconstruction convention.[41] On the day that the legislature assembled Brigadier General Embury D. Osband arrived in Jackson, but he did not prohibit its meeting since the members told him that "they did not meet as a legislature, but as a committee of public safety." [42] The legislature had been in session less than two hours when the report arrived at the capitol that Osband had received orders from his superior at Vicksburg to disband the legislature and to arrest its members. The body immediately passed three measures and adjourned; and many of the members made haste to leave town. In its brief session, the legislature provided for a convention to meet on July 3, directed the governor to select three commissioners to go to Washington to confer with the President as to his reconstruction policy, and adopted a resolution deploring the death of President Lincoln.[43] With Clark's surrender of the executive offices on May 22 the state was under Federal military rule.

In general, then, it may be noted that in Mississippi a widespread desire for peace had developed before the official surrender of the Confederate forces in the state in May, 1865. Indications of this desire emerging from the officially imposed Confederate posture of continued resistance were numerous and suggestive. Evidently many believed that only if the state were reconstructed in the Union would security to person and property be restored, prolonged irritations and inconveniences be removed, and economic restoration of the state be accomplished. It would stand to reason that even defeat had become widely accepted as the necessary price for ending the war. For these reasons, it might be expected that the attitude of the people toward federal authority during the immediate postwar period would be characterized by a considerable spirit of cooperation, and even by a sincere willingness on their part to renew their allegiance to the United States.

[41] Thomas J. Wharton to John F. H. Claiborne, August 5, 1879, in John F. H. Claiborne Papers, Southern Historical Collection, University of North Carolina Library, Chapel Hill.

[42] Brigadier General Embury D. Osband to Lieutenant Colonel C. T. Christensen, May 22, 1865, in *Official Records, Armies*, Ser. 1, Vol. XLIX, Pt. 2, p. 879.

[43] *Ibid.*; New York *Times*, June 1, 1865.

2

The Aftermath of War

To CONFEDERATE veterans returning home to Mississippi in the spring of 1865 the society and economy of the state appeared disarrayed and prostrate. Property had been destroyed, weeds were covering the fields, roads and railroads were in disrepair, the slave labor system was shattered, many people of all classes were destitute, and local governments were suspended at a time when marauders were boldly roaming the countryside. The cost of secession and war appeared indeed to have been high to those who viewed conditions in the state in early 1865.

Of all the physical evidences of the war in the state, probably the most general was that of destroyed town properties. Where armies had trod or cavalry units had raided, commercial centers and hamlets lay in partial or complete ruin. Towns along the railroads had suffered most at the hands of the armies. Being along lines of communication, they had had tactical and strategic value and had been thus subject to pillage and destruction by Federal forces. Jackson, a town of more than three thousand in 1860, had been a promising commercial center before the war because of its position at the junction of the Southern and the New Orleans, Jackson, and Great Northern railroads. But the town lay in ruins in 1865. In early June a newspaper correspondent described what remained of the town: "Once a beautiful city, it is now a mass of ruins. Piles of brick and mortar cover the once famous retreats of wealth and fashion. Numerous columns, shattered and charred, have suggested for the name of the place 'chimneyville.' The State House, the Governor's Mansion, the City Hall and the Asylum are the only public buildings remaining." [1] Young Whitelaw

[1] As reported in the New York *Times*, June 18, 1865.

Reid, touring the state six months later, found "solitary chimneys and shattered ruins" still in the state capital.[2]

Towns in the path of Sherman's Vicksburg to Meridian expedition of early 1864 had been almost totally destroyed, except for residences—and these were not always spared. At Enterprise, no stores or houses escaped destruction. An officer in Sherman's army reported that at Lake Station "the Signal Corps went through the town like a dose of salts," and as he left he noticed a man attempting to get someone to make an affidavit that a town had existed before the raid.[3] Several of the small towns that were destroyed had already begun to decline as stations along the Southern Railroad rose to handle the bulk of the trade of the area. Sherman's raid only accentuated this decline. Since no economic reason existed for their restoration, the burnt-out and devastated buildings in some of these towns had not been replaced as late as 1867.[4]

Meridian, a small hamlet until it became the junction of the Mobile and Ohio and the Southern railroads during the war, had especially felt the harsh hand of Sherman. Except for two hotels, the army had burned all of the business district.[5] Corinth, at the junction of the Mobile and Ohio and Memphis and Charleston railroads, at the end of the war was "a bruised and battered village surrounded by forts, earthworks and graves," according to one traveler.[6] In the embattled prairie town of Okolona only two or three houses remained standing after the war. Travelers reported burned districts in Crystal Springs, Summit, and Magnolia, towns along the New Orleans, Jackson, and Great Northern Railroad.[7]

Vicksburg, of course, suffered heavily from the bombardment and siege of 1863, although conditions had improved somewhat by the end

[2] Whitelaw Reid, *After the War: A Southern Tour* (Cincinnati: Moore, Wilstach, and Baldwin, 1866), 423.

[3] John B. Walters, "General William T. Sherman and Total War," *Journal of Southern History*, XIV (1948), 471–72.

[4] Meridian *Semi-Weekly Gazette*, April 13, 1867.

[5] William H. Hardy, "Recollections of Reconstruction in East and Southeast Mississippi," *Publications of the Mississippi Historical Society*, VII (1903), 203.

[6] John T. Trowbridge, *The Desolate South, 1865–1866* (New York: Duell, Sloan, and Pearce Co., 1956), 159.

[7] Robert Somers, *The Southern States Since the War, 1870–71* (London: Macmillan and Co., 1871), 144; Jackson *Clarion*, February 23, 1867; New Orleans *Picayune*, November 17, 25, 1865.

of the war.[8] In the Yazoo Basin or Delta, Friar's Point and Prentiss, the small county seat of Bolivar County, were completely destroyed by Federal forces. Yazoo City, Grenada, Greensboro, and other small towns of central Mississippi had been partially burned.[9]

On the other hand, two of the leading towns in the state had escaped destruction by the armies. Natchez, the largest town in Mississippi before the war, had been occupied by Federal troops in 1863 but had suffered very little at the hands of the conquerors. Columbus, the third ranking town in size in 1860, had not been captured or even attacked during the war. Property deterioration and decay, however, represented a heavy loss to owners in these two towns; especially was this the case in Natchez, where citizens had abandoned their town property *en masse* just before the arrival of the Federal army.[10]

The freeing of approximately 400,000 slaves represented a definite economic loss for Mississippians. The value of these slaves was in their capacity to produce, and Negro labor at the end of the war, although generally available, was not as reliable or as efficient as that of the slavery era. Furthermore, with the emancipation of the slaves a valuable credit collateral was destroyed; and, when other forms of security, such as land, declined in value, planters found that they had to pay exorbitant interest on loans in order to continue farming operations.

The destruction and impressment of livestock during the war also represented a sizable loss for Mississippi planters and farmers. The value of livestock in the state was $41,891,692 in 1860 as compared to a Department of Agriculture estimate of $16,815,802 in 1868.[11]

Plantation property and equipment lay in ruin. Storehouses, corn cribs, and meat houses were decayed or destroyed. Few fences were

[8] Peter F. Walker, *Vicksburg: A People at War, 1860–65* (Chapel Hill: University of North Carolina Press, 1960), 222.

[9] Jackson *Clarion*, October 27, 1865; Friar's Point *Coahomian*, October 27, 1865; Franklin A. Montgomery, *Reminiscences of a Mississippian in Peace and War* (Cincinnati: Robert Clark Co., 1901), 265; correspondent to the Canton *American Citizen*, January 10, 1865, in Niles Scrapbook, Vol. XLI.

[10] New York *Times*, July 11, 1866; William L. Lipscomb, *A History of Columbus, Mississippi, during the 19th Century* (Birmingham: *Dispatch* Printing Co., 1909), 122; Carl Schurz, *The Reminiscences of Carl Schurz* (New York: The McClure Co., 1908), III, 198.

[11] *Report of the Commissioner of Agriculture for the Year 1868* (Washington: Government Printing Office, 1869), 44.

left standing by the spring of 1865, and the livestock that remained feasted upon plants in the unfenced fields.[12] Fields in many cases had not been plowed since the early days of the war.[13]

Many landowners who had abandoned their plantations ahead of invading armies returned to discover that Federal officials had leased their property to Northerners. In the Vicksburg area alone, Freedmen's Bureau officials estimated that 136 abandoned plantations were leased, 113 by Northern whites and 23 by Negroes. Although President Johnson soon after the end of the war ordered the restoration of abandoned plantations to their owners, this action did not come in time for the planting season of 1865.[14]

The fertile Delta country suffered more during the war than the farmlands of any other section of the state. Although most of the lowlands underwent little fighting, several overflows of the Mississippi River occurred, the last coming in the spring of 1865. Because of a critical lack of labor as slaves deserted to military camps during the latter part of the war, levee maintenance was neglected, resulting in numerous breaks in the levee system. Large openings were cut by Federal armies to further the inundation of the area, which was an important source of cotton for the Confederacy.[15] The effect of the broken levees was to make the river counties practically a wilderness. Soldiers and planters returning home often worked their way back in

[12] New Orleans Picayune, November 8, 1865; "Affairs in the Late Insurrectionary States," House Reports, 42nd Cong., 2nd Sess., No. 22, p. 875.

[13] For descriptions of this general ruin, see James Lusk Alcorn to his wife Amelia, August 29, 1865, in James Lusk Alcorn Papers, Southern Historical Collection, University of North Carolina Library, Chapel Hill; George C. Osborn (ed.), "The Life of a Southern Plantation Owner during Reconstruction as Revealed in the Clay Sharkey Papers," Journal of Mississippi History, VI (1944), 104–105; and the Raymond Hinds County Gazette, February 2, 1866.

[14] Sam S. Boyd to Provisional Governor Sharkey, July 13, 14, 1865, in Governors' Correspondence, E-70; Friar's Point Coahomian, October 20, 1865; James D. Richardson (comp.), A Compilation of the Messages and Papers of the Presidents (New York: Bureau of National Literature and Art, 1896–1908), VI, 340; Map of Vicksburg District for Leasing Abandoned Plantations, 1864, in Mississippi Department of Archives and History, Jackson. For a distance of approximately seventy-five miles northward, planters had generally deserted their lands with the approach of the Union forces in 1863.

[15] Willie D. Halsell, "Migration into, and Settlement of, Leflore County, 1833–1876," Journal of Mississippi History, IX (1947), 233; Walter Sillers, "Flood Control in Bolivar County," ibid., 6–7; Montgomery, Reminiscences, 258–59; Memphis Appeal, November 23, 1865.

dugouts to the high lands on their plantations.[16] A few months after the conclusion of the war, Brigadier General Andrew A. Humphreys of the United States Corps of Engineers examined the river country and reported that the "greater portion" of the improved lands of the basin was flooded. He estimated that there were one million acres under cultivation and felt that with a reconstructed and improved levee system seven million acres could be made available for farming. He believed that it would cost $1,500,000 to repair the levees in the state; however, local flood-control commissioners disagreed, saying that Humphreys' estimate was entirely too low.[17]

The condition of the railroads of the state at the conclusion of the war offered little hope for the speedy restoration of the commerce of the interior counties or for the rapid transportation of cotton to external markets. In addition to the heavy physical damage suffered by the roads, all of the companies came out of the war with large debts and long overdue bond-interest payments. Working capital in the form of Confederate currency was worthless, and circulating notes of the railroads were vastly depreciated. Furthermore, some of the cotton that several of the companies had collected and stored in warehouses to be converted into cash when peace was restored had been destroyed by military forces.[18]

The two roads which served as a great north-south artery for central Mississippi, and as an important link in the trunkline that extended from Kentucky to New Orleans, sustained seemingly paralyzing damages as a result of the war. In 1862 Federal forces seized control of the lower course of this line, the New Orleans, Jackson, and Great Northern Railroad. This road, extending from the great Louisiana port to Canton, Mississippi, a distance of 206 miles, was controlled only intermittently by company officials for the next three years.[19] As a result of Brigadier General Benjamin J. Grierson's raid in 1863, the

[16] William F. Gray, Imperial Bolivar (Cleveland, Mississippi: Bolivar Commercial Newspaper Co., 1923), 14.

[17] "Report on the Levee on the Mississippi River," Senate Reports, 39th Cong., 1st Sess., No. 126, pp. 1–2; New York Times, June 16, 1866; Benjamin G. Humphreys, Jr., Floods and Levees of the Mississippi River (Washington: n.p., 1914), 36.

[18] Report of President M. Emanuel to the Stockholders of the Southern Railroad Company, March 15, 1866 (n.p., n.d.), 7; "Affairs of the Southern Railroads," House Reports, 39th Cong., 2nd Sess., No. 34, p. 838.

[19] Thomas D. Clark, A Pioneer Southern Railroad from New Orleans to Cairo (Chapel Hill: The University of North Carolina Press, 1936), 115–17.

railroad was virtually destroyed from Brookhaven to Ponchatoula, Louisiana. After this raid by the "railroad wrecker," the New Orleans road ceased operations, except for the fifty-four miles between Jackson and Brookhaven, until the conclusion of hostilities.[20]

Not only did the New Orleans, Jackson, and Great Northern suffer property destruction from military raids, but much of its rolling stock and equipment was carried off by the Federals to serve more strategic lines. From all causes, the company lost over 90 per cent of its rolling stock and motive power. Seventy-eight bridges were completely or partially destroyed by raiders, beginning with Grierson's raid, and large portions of the road not altogether destroyed by these forces were by 1865 deteriorating and crumbling away after months of neglect. Furthermore, when the war ended, the railroad was without operating currency. As in the case of most of the other railroads running through the state, the New Orleans line was controlled by the Federal army when peace was restored.[21]

The Mississippi Central Railroad, controlling the portion of the north-south trunkline from Canton to Jackson, Tennessee, was attacked by both sides during the war. The company claimed that Confederate forces destroyed $366,200 worth of its property, while the damage wrought by Federal troops amounted to $344,500. During the winter of 1864–65 raids occurred in such rapid succession as to leave the Mississippi Central company with only one locomotive in operation. Thus most of the road's rolling stock, machine shops, and bridges were left in a ruined state at a time when the company was ready to commence the work of restoration. Furthermore, when the war ended, the Mississippi Central was $1,589,059 in arrears on its debt of $3,358,117.[22]

[20] For General Grierson's report on the raid see *Official Records, Armies*, Ser. 1, Vol. XXIV, Pt. 1, pp. 522–31. See also the testimony of President C. C. Shackleford in "Affairs of the Southern Railroads," *House Reports*, 39th Cong., 2nd Sess., No. 34, pp. 138–42.

[21] *Commercial and Financial Chronicle: Banker's Gazette, Commercial Times, Railway Monitor, and Insurance Journal*, February 2, 1867, p. 134, hereinafter cited as *Commercial and Financial Chronicle*; John F. Stover, *The Railroads of the South, 1865–1900: A Study in Finance and Control* (Chapel Hill: The University of North Carolina Press, 1955), 52, 158; Jackson *Clarion*, February 2, 1866.

[22] *Annual Report of the President and Directors of the Mississippi Central Railroad Co., to the Stockholders for the Year Ending August 31, 1865* (New Albany, Indiana: Norman and Matthews, Railroad Printers, 1865), 6, 8–11; *Commercial and Financial Chronicle*, August 31, 1867, p. 265. In addition to these losses the

The Mississippi and Tennessee Railroad, running from Memphis to Grenada where it connected with the Mississippi Central, suffered quite as much as its neighboring road. At the surrender the railroad was virtually a wreck, with more than one half of its eighty-five cars requiring repairs and refittings. Only thirty miles of the railroad were in operation on May 1, 1865. The company estimated that Confederate troops destroyed property valued at $132,600, compared to $117,650 destroyed by Union raiders. The finances of the company were "in a most desperate condition," with no available assets with which money could be raised to pay off debts and to reconstruct the road.[23]

Extending north and south through most of east Mississippi, the Mobile and Ohio Railroad suffered heavily from general neglect during the war, from its inability to obtain replacement parts, and especially from military raids.[24] The road was a wreck from Okolona to Union City, Tennessee, a distance of almost two hundred miles. Along this line contending armies destroyed almost all of the bridges, trestle works, warehouses, and depots. In the Meridian area Sherman ruined twenty-one miles of track in 1864. The repair shops at Jackson, Tennessee, were ruined, and all the equipment had been carried away.[25] The company estimated that it had suffered a loss of several million dollars in property destroyed and damaged by military forces and in Southern currency and bonds as a result of the failure of the Confederate States. During the war the Mobile and Ohio company had purchased 3,693 bales of cotton to be applied later to bond payments. Of this cotton 870 bales were destroyed by fire and theft. As in the case of the other railroads, the Mobile and Ohio came out of the war with an empty treasury and owing large interest payments on bonds.[26]

Mississippi Central lost assets totaling half a million dollars as a result of the freeing of its slaves and the voiding of Confederate securities which it held. Ross H. Moore, "Social and Economic Conditions in Mississippi during Reconstruction" (Ph.D. dissertation, Duke University, 1938), 132. The above monetary figures were evidently based on adjusted United States currency.

[23] *Merchants' Magazine and Commercial Review*, May 1867, pp. 342–43; *Commercial and Financial Chronicle*, April 20, 1867, p. 489; Jackson *Clarion and Standard*, June 14, 1866.

[24] Stover, *The Railroads of the South*, 158; Meridian *Semi-Weekly Gazette*, September 25, 1867.

[25] *Merchants' Magazine and Commerical Review*, February, 1867, p. 126.

[26] *Ibid.*, 126–28; Meridian *Semi-Weekly Gazette*, July 21, September 25, 1867;

The condition of the Southern Railroad offers an excellent illustration of the seemingly disabling effect the war had on the railroads of the state. This road, running from Vicksburg to Meridian where it joined with the Mississippi and Alabama and the Mobile and Ohio, was completed in 1861. During the latter part of the war Grant and Sherman burned station houses, warehouses, and machine shops, twisted rails, burned and damaged cars and locomotives, and destroyed eighty-five bridges and trestles. When the war ended the Southern was operating only between Vicksburg and the Big Black River, a distance of twelve miles.[27]

Financially, the Southern Railroad was left, according to President Morris Emanuel, "without a dollar of current money in [its] treasury, with nearly a million and a half of dollars of unpaid debt that had matured during the war, besides upwards of six hundred thousand dollars of unpaid interest coupons." In order to show good faith toward its creditors, the company had purchased $175,820 in cotton in 1863 for use in making an interest payment on its debt immediately after the war. Sherman and other Federal raiders, however, burned one half of the amount.[28]

Steamboat commerce suffered greatly with Grant's campaign against the river towns. But with the Federals in complete control of the Mississippi River, this trade revived, stimulated not only by the Northern desire for cotton but also by Northern efforts to secure the trade of the Mississippi Valley. On June 1, 1865, the Vicksburg *Herald* reported that there was a great deal of cotton on the levee and that boats carried it north and south every day.[29]

The few industrial establishments that existed in the state in 1861 were generally destroyed by Federal raiders during the latter part of the war. Of the four garment factories in Mississippi before the war only one, the relatively large Bankston plant, continued to produce

"Affairs of the Southern Railroads," *House Reports*, 39th Cong., 2nd Sess., No. 34, p. 838.

[27] *Report of President Emanuel, 1866*, p. 1.

[28] *Ibid.*, 1–3, 7. Actually the Southern Railroad was a weak line, and its fundamental difficulties were not caused by the destructive effects of the war. It was built only for local traffic and had an odd four-foot ten-inch gauge. The Memphis and Charleston and the Alabama and Mississippi railroads are only generally considered in this study, since they ran for only a few miles in the state.

[29] Moore, "Social and Economic Conditions in Mississippi during Reconstruction," 113.

goods after the disastrous summer of 1863.[30] This combination woolen and cotton mill, managed by the antebellum industrial promoter James M. Wesson, remained in operation until December, 1864, when it was burned by Federal troops. The only industrial establishments remaining in Mississippi in May of 1865 were munitions plants, grist mills, one spinning mill, and a few small, scattered sawmills.[31]

When the war ended, financial assets in the form of currency, insurance policies, and bonds were almost completely worthless. Banks were closed. The specie that had circulated in the state had been generally taken out of Mississippi during the conflict, or had been seized by Federal forces. A few people, however, had managed to hoard some gold or silver or to place some of their liquid assets in Europe for safekeeping until the end of the war. In the river counties United States greenbacks had circulated since the Federal forces occupied the area in 1862 and 1863, and some greenbacks had entered the large Confederate-held cotton-producing region of central Mississippi through legal and illegal trade with Federal-held towns. Except in the river counties lines of credit, however, had not been restored by May, 1865.[32]

The demise of slavery had a profound effect on all aspects of life in Mississippi. Slavery was fundamental to the state's economic and social life; it was the main reason that many of the whites of the state had fought so desperately. Therefore, the abolition of the institution threatened habits and attitudes of a lifetime and produced social and labor difficulties alike for both whites and Negroes, which greatly complicated the work of political and economic reconstruction.

The labor difficulties that resulted from the freeing of the slaves accentuated the manpower losses suffered by the state during the war. John L. Power, former Superintendent of Army Records for the state, made a careful study soon after the war and found that 30 per cent of the Mississippians who had fought under the Stars and Bars were

[30] Mary Frances W. Dykes, "Mississippi Industrial Legislation, 1865–1880" (M.A. thesis, Mississippi State University, 1953), 21–22. The four antebellum garment mills had a total capital value of only $230,000 in 1860, produced goods worth $176,328, and employed 215 hands. U.S. Bureau of the Census, *Eighth Census of the United States: 1860, Manufactures,* 294.

[31] Dykes, "Mississippi Industrial Legislation," 22–23; Wesson *Weekly Enterprise,* February 1, 1952.

[32] Moore, "Social and Economic Conditions in Mississippi during Reconstruction," 80–81.

dead. By his estimate, 78,000 men served in Confederate and state units, of whom 12,000 were killed or died of wounds and 15,500 died of disease.[33] This loss comprised about one fourth of the white males of age fifteen and above in 1860. An unmechanized agricultural area, like Mississippi, could ill afford to lose such a large percentage of its manhood at a time when farm labor and management were especially needed.

Nowithstanding the crucial need for labor, thousands of white Mississippians did not put their hands to the plow in 1865. Many of the soldiers who returned were diseased or crippled and were therefore unable to perform the heavy manual labor necessary to restore the fields to productivity. A traveler who attended a meeting of three hundred people in Aberdeen in 1865 declared that at least one third of them had lost either a leg or an arm, while one half of the remainder bore evidence of hard campaigning.[34] Disabled Confederates flocked to the towns looking for odd jobs with which to support their families until they could find permanent employment. One observer during the late spring found Jackson full of Confederate soldiers, "gathered in groups on the street, or lounging about the hotels, and talking in an under-tone about the 'situation.'"[35] All were looking for jobs. The Natchez Courier called upon the people of its town to employ the numerous disabled veterans "to paint signs and houses, do plastering or white-washing . . . carpentry, or bricklaying," or any work that they were able to preform.[36]

Many maimed soldiers hoped to secure enough capital to enter the mercantile business, where hard labor was not necessary for success. A popular enterprise for these veterans during the first months after the war was the grocery and distilled liquor business. A surprising number of disabled Confederates were able to secure, either by credit or cash, the necessary assistance to establish such businesses.[37]

[33] John L. Power to Governor Benjamin G. Humphreys, October 29, 1865, in Governors' Correspondence, E-77; Friar's Point Coahomian, December 8, 1865.

[34] Garner, Reconstruction in Mississippi, 123.

[35] New York Times, June 18, 1865.

[36] As quoted in the New Orleans Picayune, November 14, 1865.

[37] Numerous letters from grocery and whiskey storekeepers to Provisional Governor Sharkey, found in the Governors' Correspondence, E-71, indicates the popularity of this type of business. These operators asked the governor to remit to them the state tax on grocery and distilled liquor stores. In spite of his lack of sympathy for the Confederate cause, Sharkey almost invariably complied with

Because of the superabundance of these ventures, many apparently were short-lived. Nevertheless, simultaneous with railroad developments, with the expected expansion of the freedmen consumer market, and with the efforts of Northern jobbers to sell their products, the merchandising business in the state received an important stimulus from veterans who were anxious to try an occupation other than farming.

Some few Confederates, depressed by defeat and uncertain of the course of reconstruction, sought security and better opportunities in Latin America. Organizations were formed in some Mississippi counties to examine the possibilities for settlement. A Copiah County organization dispatched a deputation to Honduras with authority to secure desirable lands for a colony.[38] Published letters from optimistic former Confederate leaders who had gone to Mexico kindled in the minds of many the belief that central Mexico was ideal for agriculture. "I am fully satisfied that any good farmer can make a fortune here in six or ten years," wrote General Joseph O. Shelby.[39]

Although a great deal of publicity and discussion developed, apparently few Mississippians felt the urge to migrate.[40] An active campaign by state newspapers to disabuse farmers of ideas in circulation that Mexico and Brazil were veritable gardens of Eden for cotton growers evidently caused many to reconsider the advantages of migration. Furthermore, the anticipated mass punishment of Confederates by the federal government did not develop. Accounts of growing disenchantment on the part of immigrants in Latin America and reports of the abandonment of the settlement at Carlota, Mexico, practically put an end to migration plans.[41]

---

these requests. Some healthy veterans who returned to farming became dissatisfied with agriculture as a result of the crop failures of 1865–67. The Meridian *Weekly Gazette*, November 13, 1867, thought that "every young man in the country, as a general thing, wants to quit the field and seek employment in some shop, store, or corporation."

[38] Meridian *Semi-Weekly Gazette*, July 18, 1867; Osborn (ed.), "The Life of a Southern Plantation Owner during Reconstruction," 108.

[39] As quoted in the Friar's Point *Coahomian*, January 12, February 16, 1866.

[40] For a list of Southerners in one colony, with the names of their former states included, see Carl C. Rister, "Carlota, a Confederate Colony in Mexico," *Journal of Southern History*, XI (1945), 44.

[41] A. K. Farrar to Sharkey, June 27, 1865, in Governors' Correspondence, E-69; Raymond *Hinds County Gazette*, March 9, August 10, 1866; Friar's Point *Coahomian*, March 9, 1866; *Meridian Semi-Weekly Gazette*, July 18, 1867. For a

Destitution pervaded the whole state in 1865. "Extreme poverty rules in almost every household," a correspondent to the New Orleans *Times* reported.[42] Suffering was acute in the area around Meridian, and many farmers in east Mississippi faced a bleak year without even the means of planting corn, since their mules and horses had been impressed by General Taylor and his troops during the last weeks of the war.[43] Traveling in northeast Mississippi, John T. Trowbridge, a Northern journalist, found extreme destitution. He visited the survivors of a family living in a new house of rough logs, situated in the midst of the ruins of an old house. One division of the house was occupied by Negro servants and the other by two white women. "One of these [whites] was young, the other aged and bent with grief and years. . . . The walls and roof were full of chinks, the wind blew through the room and she [the young woman] crouched shivering over the hearth." [44]

Many had large families to support, without adequate means. A friend wrote Provisional Governor William L. Sharkey that he and his family of sixteen would not have been able to survive had it not been for the rations doled out by Federal officers.[45] Those who survived the war with their health unimpaired were often called upon to aid unfortunate kinsmen. General William S. Featherston, although without immediate means, assumed the responsibility of supporting five families after the war—families of nephews killed in battle.[46]

Of those veterans who sought to return to the occupation of their agrarian fathers, many, if not a majority, arrived home too late in 1865 to participate in spring planting. In most cases, however, the family, with indomitable spirit and the help of faithful servants, had planted a small crop in anticipation of the soldier's return before the summer.

brief but excellent survey of the Southern emigration movement, see John S. Ezell, *The South Since 1865* (New York: The Macmillan Co., 1963), 34–37.

[42] As reported in the New York *Times,* June 18, 1865.

[43] George Barnes to Governor Clark, April 13, 1865, in Governors' Correspondence, E-68; Captain Henry C. Hodges to Lieutenant Colonel C. G. Sawtelle, May 18, 1865, in *Official Records, Armies,* Ser. 1, Vol. XLIX, Pt. 2, p. 835.

[44] Trowbridge, *The Desolate South,* 160. See also S. S. Fairfield to President Johnson, May 26, 1865, in Johnson Papers.

[45] John Prestioge to Sharkey, June 25, 1865, in Governors' Correspondence, E-69.

[46] George H. Gray, Sr., to Sharkey, June 26, 1865; J. A. Horne to Sharkey, June 26, 1865, both *ibid.;* Statement of F. U. Still, November 26, 1866, in Amnesty Papers, Mississippi.

Most Confederates were home by late June, except those from distant Northern prison camps.[47]

If the whites found it difficult to stay alive, the inexperienced freedman's position was worse. Freedom for many slaves had come with Major General Ulysses S. Grant's movement into the state in 1862 and 1863. Hundreds of Negroes had rushed to the camps of the Federal armies and hailed the soldiers as their deliverers.[48] After its fall in July, 1863, Vicksburg had become the great rallying point for the Negro refugees of the state. It is probable that by the spring of 1865 at least one third, and possibly more than one half, of the Negroes of the state had known a form of freedom within the Union lines or through arrangements with their owners. With the end of the war the news and actuality of freedom came gradually to the remaining slaves, particularly slowly in the interior counties. Most of the freedmen remained at work, but there were enough moving about during 1865 to give the impression that a large portion of the Negro population was on the march and to cause planters to doubt, as many already did, that the freedman would ever be a satisfactory worker without compulsion.[49] The greater part of the movement was toward the towns. The "day of jubilee" had come, and many freedmen wanted to see the fabled glories of Vicksburg, Natchez, Columbus, and other towns. As a result, hundreds of Negroes gathered in even black-belt towns that were mere villages.[50]

With little means of support except meager government rations, refugee freedmen in the towns lived in wretched poverty. In Vicksburg they occupied shanties built of such scraps as they could find,

[47] Thomas W. Harris to Sharkey, June 15, 1865, in Governors' Correspondence, E-69; John D. Williams to Sharkey, July 9, 1865, ibid., E-70.

[48] This account largely follows Vernon L. Wharton's excellent study, *The Negro in Mississippi, 1865–1890* (Chapel Hill: The University of North Carolina Press, 1947), 27–57 *passim*. For a description of the Negroes' attraction to military camps, see Thomas W. Knox, *Camp-fire and Cottton-field* (New York: Blelock and Co., 1865), 436.

[49] For impressions held by planters that the whole Negro population was on the move, see Thomas E. B. Pegues to Governor Clark, March 30, 1865, in Governors' Correspondence, E-68; George S. Gaines to Sharkey, July 17, 1865, ibid., E-70; Robert S. Hudson to President Johnson, November 2, 1865, in Johnson Papers; and Thomas C. Billups and George R. Clayton to Major General Benjamin H. Grierson, May 22, 1865, in *Official Records, Armies*, Ser. 1, Vol. XLIX, Pt. 2, p. 878.

[50] Gustave Wilcox and J. S. Vaughan to Sharkey, July 22, 1865, in Governors' Correspondence, E-70.

or lived in the burrows in the hillsides which whites had used during the seige of the town. Reports from Meridian, Jackson, and elsewhere indicated similar appalling conditions. The wretched quarters in these towns were swept by epidemics of cholera and smallpox. The death rate was extremely high.[51]

Freedmen who remained at home generally fared better, but, as one planter complained, the whites "who have negro women and children find it as much as they can do to feed them." [52] Needing labor and desiring to aid their old slaves, most planters apparently furnished the necessities of life for their helpless Negroes.[53]

The numerous reports of destitution and fatal diseases among the freedmen led to the belief in Mississippi that the Negro race could not adjust to freedom and thus would perish. The Meridian *Clarion* in August, 1865, asserted that the Negro would die out within one hundred years.[54] The editor of the Natchez *Democrat* gave the Negro even less time. "The child is already born who will behold the last negro in the State of Mississippi," this editor declared. "With no one to provide for the aged and the young, the helpless incompetent to provide for themselves, and brought unprepared into competition with the superior intelligence, tact, and muscle of free white labor, they must surely and speedily perish." [55] Before the Joint Committee on Reconstruction, Senator-elect and former Provisional Governor William L. Sharkey emphatically declared that the Negroes were "destined to extinction." [56]

The state census of 1866 seemed to sustain these predictions, indicating a decline of more than 12 per cent in the Negro population for the period between 1860 and 1866. One careful student of the Mississippi Negro, however, has concluded that the 1866 figures represent a tremendous undercount.[57] It is impossible to estimate ac-

[51] Wharton, *The Negro in Mississippi*, 53.

[52] Thomas E. B. Pegues to Clark, March 30, 1865, in Governors' Correspondence, E-68.

[53] See, for example, Robert S. Hudson to President Johnson, November 2, 1865, in Johnson Papers, and Smedes, *A Southern Planter*, 228, 247–48.

[54] Meridian *Clarion*, August 17, 1865.

[55] Natchez *Tri-Weekly Democrat*, January 6, 1866.

[56] "Report of the Joint Committee on Reconstruction," *House Reports*, 39th Cong., 1st Sess., No. 30, Pt. III, 136.

[57] Professor Wharton says that the inaccuracy of the 1866 figures was demonstrated by the federal census of 1870, which reported an actual increase of

curately the number of Negroes who died during the first flush of freedom; yet those who survived still constituted a clear majority of the population of the state. At any rate, the loss and the instability of much of the old labor force was a major handicap that had to be overcome if the agricultural economy were to be restored.

All economic groups suffered because of the civil conflict, but none had more to lose, in terms of property value, than the large planter-lawyer class. Their influential social and economic position had been the bulwark of commerce and society in their communities. With few exceptions this class was insolvent by 1865. The case of Judge Alexander M. Clayton, a member of both the secession convention and the Confederate Congress, is illustrative of the plight of the planter-lawyer. Clayton admitted to President Johnson that he had been a rich man in 1861, but during the war his house had been burned, his plantation devastated, and the largest portion of his estate forfeited for inability to pay state and Confederate taxes.[58] A lesser planter, Thomas A. Locke of Charleston, owned $18,000 worth of property before the war, yet he wrote Johnson in 1865 that he had "only a small tract of land and four mules, the latter . . . purchased with the remnant of corn left by the Federal forces. . . . I am very badly in debt and my creditors are pressing me." [59] Although Carl Schurz desired the humiliation of the old slaveholders, whom he somewhat inaccurately associated with the haughty secessionists of 1861, he found a touch of pathos in a scene he witnessed in Natchez of an old planter aristocrat, having lost everything but his house, cutting firewood to sell to the passing steamboats. The old aristocrat laconically explained to Schurz why he was engaged in such hard manual labor: "I must live. My sons fell in the war. All my servants have left me." [60] Unusual means of securing subsistence on the part of members of the

more than seven thousand in the Negro population of Mississippi during the decade. It later became evident that this figure itself was the result of a large undercount, and probably needed to be increasd by between fifty and seventy-five thousand. Wharton, *The Negro in Mississippi*, 54.

[58] Clayton to Johnson, June 12, 1865, in Amnesty Papers, Mississippi.

[59] Copy of a letter from Locke to President Johnson, September 28, 1865, in Governors' Correspondence, E-72. For other examples of planter-lawyer losses during the war, see Samuel H. Lamkin to Johnson, undated, Thomas S. Dabney to Johnson, August 3, 1865, and T. W. Harris to Johnson, September 4, 1865, in Amnesty Papers, Mississippi.

[60] Schurz, *Reminiscences*, III, 198.

planter class were not uncommon in many towns and communities of Mississippi in 1865. Francis W. Henry, an agent for an out-of-state merchant, succinctly described these conditions when he wrote: "Change is written upon the face of almost everything in this country. Men who were wealthy at the commencement of the terrible War [that] we have passed through are now bankrupt." [61]

Merchant losses in many cases were as severe as those of the planters. In arrears on their debts to New Orleans and New York merchants, local businessmen hoped at the end of the war to make at least a payment on these and thus regain their credit standing with out-of-state mercantile houses. But the generally impoverished condition of local debtors made it impossible for these merchants to collect money that was owed to them, and consequently they were not able to settle their accounts.[62] Two years after the conclusion of the war, one merchant's agent in the state hopelessly wrote: "I have not collected a dollar since the close of the war; . . . and to collect now is out of the question." [63] Edwin L. Sabin, a piano dealer of Vicksburg, had not lost one per cent of his accounts annually prior to the war. But of the $56,000 he had on his books in 1861, he was able to collect only $1,220 after the conflict. Henry's and Sabin's experiences were apparently typical of the losses sustained by merchants of the state.[64] A Natchez editor dismally described prospects for these merchants as a result of account losses: "With no means to recommence life now, with credit destroyed, and defrauded of their only means for settling their old debts, they must stand aside and let Northern men and Northern capital come in and do the business of the country." [65]

The fortunes of war made no distinction for loyalties. Unconditional Unionists found with the arrival of peace that their property

[61] Francis W. Henry to B. E. Wofford, April 15, 1867, in Francis W. Henry Papers, Duke University Library.

[62] Natchez *Democrat*, November 14, 1865.

[63] Henry to Wofford, April 15, 1867, in Henry Papers.

[64] Edwin L. Sabin, "Vicksburg and After: Being the Experience of a Southern Merchant and Non-combatant during the Sixties," *Sewanee Review*, XV (1907), 483. Newspaper comments of the period, particularly those of the river towns, suggest that merchants found it extremely difficult to collect any part of the indebtedness that their customers owed them. For example, see the Natchez *Courier*, December 16, 1865, the Natchez *Democrat*, November 14, 1865, and the Vicksburg *Journal*, November 12, 1865.

[65] Natchez *Democrat*, November 14, 1865.

losses were as extensive as those who had served the rebel cause.[66] Besides the usual losses from military destruction, cotton seizures, and property deterioration, many loyalists had voluntarily furnished livestock and grain to the invading Federal armies with the assurance that they would be reimbursed at the end of the war. After peace was restored, however, loyalists found that they had been indicted with their section and that the promises of payment for their goods had been virtually repudiated by the government.

It was not until 1871 that a Southern claims commission was established to adjudicate these quartermaster and commissary claims. At this time 152 Mississippi loyalists, each of whom had claims of over $10,000, asked the commission for a total of $3,824,063 for supplies or stores furnished to the army. Of these, forty-four cases were recognized as valid claims by the Southern claims commission, and the total amount paid was $270,421. Some claimants asserted that their assistance to the Union cause had been quite substantial and had led to their poverty. The widow of William Minor claimed that her husband, a wealthy and influential unconditional Unionist of Natchez, had furnished Federal troops with $64,155 worth of supplies during the war; she received $13,072 from the claims commission. Gray W. Smith, an unconditional Unionist of Marshall County, came out of the war financially ruined and with an indebtedness of $32,000, which had been accumulated largely, he said, as a result of his giving aid to the Federal cavalry. He collected only $7,000 in claims from the government.

Although their claims might not be as large, other loyalists found the government quite as ungenerous in accepting and paying claims as it was in the cases of Minor and Smith. In essence, the persistent Unionists of Mississippi suffered heavily as a result of the war and perceived themselves the victims of ingratitude as well as victims of the general poverty of the state.

The political uncertainties of federal reconstruction in the spring of 1865 were of less concern to Mississippians than the disorder which prevailed in the interior counties of the state. Federal Major General

---

[66] The following account of loyalist losses and their frustrating efforts to secure reimbursement for the provisions that they furnished Federal troops is based on Klingberg, *Southern Claims Commission*, 37, 55, 111, 116, 136, 207. See S. S. Fairfield to President Johnson, May 26, 1865, in Johnson Papers, for an expression of a loyalist's bitterness at having suffered the same ruin as his secession neighbors.

Peter J. Osterhaus reported: "This poverty-stricken and utterly sub-jected people are now only anxious for the restoration of authority of whatever description."[67] With the end of Confederate authority, county governments became virtually nonexistent, notwithstanding Governor Clark's parting instructions to local officials to remain at their posts and to maintain law and order. In cases in which law viola-tors were apprehended, no method existed for bringing them to justice, except through summary punishment by vigilante groups. Few cir-cuit courts were open at the end of the war, and these were held with-in the Federal lines. In some counties courts to try criminal cases had not been held for three or four years. Criminals, if arrested and held for court action, usually found that escape was easy from the dilapi-dated jails, which had been allowed to deteriorate during the war.[68]

With the collapse of local governments and the confusion of authority in 1865, many men, demoralized and faced with poverty, turned to stealing and to plundering their neighbors. In almost all of the interior counties there were marauders who stole cotton, mules, horses, and any other property of value that could be seized with impunity. "People say that they have fought hard four years without pay," a Mississippi correspondent to the New Orleans *Times* wrote, "and now they propose to pay themselves. C.S.A. cotton seems to be an especial object of cupidity." In central Mississippi "the Con-federate authority is not recognized—the Federal has not been estab-lished—and thus the country is suffering all the grief of an interregnum, or more properly, of anarchy."[69] A Clarke County resident reported wryly that in his area thieves were engaged at first in seizing only Confederate cotton and shipping it to market, but after a few suc-cessful enterprises, they "overcame this disposition to discriminate," and considered lawful prize all cotton upon which they could place their hands. Daily there were rumors of thefts, he said.[70]

Some loyalists, embittered by the rancorous treatment meted out to

[67] Osterhaus to Lieutenant Colonel C. T. Christensen, June 14, 1865, in *Official Records, Armies*, Ser. 1, Vol. XLVIII, Pt. 2, p. 878.

[68] New Orleans *Picayune*, November 24, 1865; W. A. Champlin to Provisional Governor Sharkey, June 28, 1865, in Governors' Correspondence, E-09; Carl Schurz to President Johnson, August 29, 1865, in Johnson Papers.

[69] As reported in the New York *Times*, June 18, 1865. See also the petition of members of the bar and civil officers of Pontotoc County to Sharkey, July 17, 1865, in Governors' Correspondence, E-70.

[70] Richard Gray to Sharkey, July 29, 1865, in Governors' Correspondence, E-70.

them by their Confederate neighbors, found during this chaotic period an opportunity to secure vengeance. A veritable civil war broke out in Choctaw County. A secret Union or Loyal League was organized in the county, ostensibly "to suppress crime, keep down rebellion, and keep order and discipline among the negro population." [71] The main purpose of the league, however, was to plunder its old enemies and to secure the election of unconditional Union men to office. After becoming provisional governor, Sharkey ordered the disbandment of the league and the discontinuance of the lawless practices of loyalists in the area. The leader of the league blatantly defied the governor, declaring that to break up the Union League "is a matter of impossibility as it is growing stronger every day . . . and will eventually in my opinion spread all over the state." [72]

Conditions in Mississippi in 1865 appear indeed to have been bleak and discouraging, and only the most optimistic could look forward to the future without misgivings. The interior of the state, a semi-frontier area in 1860, had reverted to frontier conditions by the spring of 1865. Yet dislocation and destruction could have had a greater effect if Mississippi had been an industrial state instead of an agrarian one. Hard work and adequate money or credit for farm provisions, in addition to a degree of political and social stability and a government that could enforce law and order and protect property rights, were the main requisites for the restoration of such an agricultural society. On the other hand, the rebuilding of an industrial system that has been disrupted or destroyed by war is far more complex and difficult. Since industry was practically nonexistent in Mississippi at that time, the economic restoration of the state depended almost entirely on the recovery of agricultural production and commerce.

[71] William M. Pollan to Sharkey, July 20, 1865, *ibid.*

[72] *Ibid.* Apparently Sharkey's admonitions had some effect on the operations of the league, for the organization ceased temporarily its attacks on former Confederates, and these were not revived until the summer of 1866. W. J. Brantley to Governor Benjamin G. Humphreys, August 8, 22, 1866, *ibid.*, E-79.

3

Establishment of the Provisional Government

MISSISSIPPI CONFEDERATES accepted ruefully the collapse and surrender of their armies, despite their desire for peace and despite an early and gradual awareness by many that defeat was inevitable. Although familiar with the hardships and reversals of living in a semi-frontier region, most people were not really prepared for unconditional surrender and the prospect of continued military rule at the hands of the enemy. For many the Southwestern successes in conquering a wilderness and in subduing the enemy, both foreign and domestic, had become a part of the folklore of Mississippians, as Americans. Defeat was no part of this image; and when they realized that they had been vanquished by their enemy, a rationalization of their predicament was a psychological necessity.

Some associated their misfortunes with the will of God, an approach that reflected the strong Calvinistic bent of the people of much of the South. The editor of the Friar's Point *Coahomian* exhorted his readers to accept defeat without murmur, for "remember [that] it was Providence who willed it. It was by his Divine command that the people of the South are now humbled; and if this be true, and no one can question it, then bitter reviling is not only a folly but it is a blasphemy." [1] The Vicksburg *Journal* joined in advising the people to submit themselves to the will of God. "Let us make contentment our companion through life, and carry it with us through all the sorrow of our earthly pilgrimage," the *Journal* editor counseled. [2] The Natchez *Weekly Democrat*, tending to be somewhat more optimistic, probably expressed fairly accurately the philosophy of

[1] Friar's Point *Coahomian*, April 20, 1866.
[2] Vicksburg *Journal*, December 1, 1865.

most Mississippians toward defeat and tragedy. "The gloom of night has been upon the land," the *Democrat* declared. "But we should remember that darkness shows us worlds of light we never saw by day. We should banish all repinings; utter no murmurings; leave sighs to the imbecile; take things as they are; recognize the hand of providence in all things; give our hearts to our work, and our shoulders to the wheel, and the watchman will yet be heard to cry, All is well! All is well!" [3]

Although apprehensive concerning the settlement to be imposed upon them, former Confederate nationalists almost unanimously, as Sharkey later testified before Congress, "were perfectly reconciled to the condition of things, and very anxious to be restored to their former position in the Union. I think that they were sincerely and honestly so; that was the current sentiment beyond all doubt at that time [June, 1865]." Sharkey said that secessionists "admitted that they had made a miserable failure; many of them very sore over it, to think that they had involved the country in terrible calamities. . . ." [4] Another Union Whig reported that "no good citizen will now seek a controversy with his Government under any pretext whatever. Public sentiment is in favor of a speedy resumption and restoration of Civil law and authority." [5] The Union Whig editor of the Natchez *Courier,* who had actively supported the Confederate cause, thought that the victory of the Federal armies should send "a thrill of pleasure to every home in this broad land. Under the Union we prospered [for] many years. There was no anarchy and confusion then. Law, civil law, had its sway, and the people received from the courts ample consideration and justice." [6]

Former Confederate military leaders and secessionists encouraged the people to resume their loyalty to the Union and to commence the work of economic restoration. General Nathan Bedford Forrest set an example for his veterans when he settled on his Coahoma County plantation and energetically cleared the land and planted a crop. Albert G. Brown, probably the most influential "fire-eater" in the state during the sectional controversy, returned to his plantation to farm. Apparently sobered by the fruits of separation and war, Brown

[3] Natchez *Weekly Democrat,* December 9, 1865.

[4] "Report of the Joint Committee on Reconstruction," *House Reports,* 39th Cong., 1st Sess., No. 30, Pt. III, 132-33.

[5] Prosper K. Montgomery to Sharkey, July 10, 1865, in Governors' Correspondence, E-70.

[6] Natchez *Tri-Weekly Courier,* May 11, 1865.

reportedly remarked to former secessionist colleagues in Jackson, "Haven't we played h-ll." [7] A secessionist member of the convention of 1861 declared that since their arms had proved unsuccessful, he felt it to be his duty to return to his allegiance to the United States Government, "and yield to its policy a fair and candid support." [8]

A petition from the members of the reconstruction convention of 1865 to President Johnson undertook to summarize the sentiments of most Mississippians toward the restoration of the state to the Union. "Here, resistance to the authority of the United States is at an end. There is no longer among our people any intention or wish to resist the Government, but an honest determination to return to their peaceful occupations, and to restore the prosperity that once blessed our state." [9]

The war may have subdued the separationist tendencies of many Mississippians, but it did not dispel their antipathy toward Northern abolitionists, whom they linked generally with New Englanders. Benjamin C. Truman, President Johnson's investigator, reported that he heard strong expressions against New Englanders when he visited the state.[10] Editor George W. Harper of the Raymond *Hinds County Gazette* abhorred any thought of the Southern churches reuniting with their Northern counterparts, whose "pulpits are filled with bloody men." It would be impossible, the Friar's Point *Coahomian* asserted, to form a "good society . . . out of such a mongrel crew as they have up there." [11]

Months before the collapse of the Confederacy many whites began to realize that the institution of slavery was staked upon the result of the war. Therefore when the war ended, most planters who had not already freed their slaves unhesitatingly informed their Negroes of

[7] Friar's Point *Coahomian*, February 23, 1866; John A. Wyett, *That Devil Forrest: Life of General Nathan Bedford Forrest* (New York: Harper and Brothers, 1959), 546, 549; Jason Niles Diary (MS in Southern Historical Collection, University of North Carolina Library, Chapel Hill), August 21–24, 1865.

[8] Orlando Davis to Sharkey, June 28, 1865, in Governors' Correspondence, E-69.

[9] Petition of members of the Convention of 1865 to President Johnson for the release of Jefferson Davis and former Governor Clark, August 21, 1865, in Johnson Papers.

[10] New York *Times*, February 4, 1866.

[11] Raymond *Hinds County Gazette*, January 13, 1866; Friar's Point *Coahomian*, January 19, 1866. For another statement showing a spirit of malevolence toward New Englanders, see Ephraim Lewis to Johnson, February 28, 1866, in Johnson Papers.

their new status. In the isolated areas of the interior, however, there was some effort to keep the blacks from learning of their freedom. Some planters believed that President Lincoln's Emancipation Proclamation could not be sanctioned legally and thus could not be enforced.[12] Colonel Samuel Thomas, assistant commissioner of the Freedmen's Bureau for the state, suspected that this disposition on the part of planters was inspired by "the hope that some change will be made, by which they will be allowed the work of these people free of charge, or that some new form of slavery will be substituted for the old, in the reorganization of the State." [13]

The belief that the freeing of the slaves was illegal under the Constitution was particularly strong among the loyalist class. These planters generally felt, as one of them wrote Sharkey, that "slavery is dead, dead, dead, but that is not the question. The question is this, can the U. States take away a loyal citizen's property without compensation?" If the planter freed his slaves because of the political circumstances of the time, he would be surrendering all legal claim for compensation, loyalist planters concluded. They proposed to carry the question to the United States Supreme Court, if necessary.[14] They were soon to be disappointed.

Unaware of President Johnson's plans for reconstruction and with hopes of influencing him to pursue a moderate course, Governor Clark, in his last act before being removed from office by the Union army, appointed Sharkey, William Yerger, and Thomas J. Wharton as state commissioners to confer with federal authorities at Washington. Sharkey and Yerger were Union Whigs, whereas Wharton was a Democrat and had been a disunionist in 1860–61. Wharton, however, wisely declined the appointment in view of the fact that his past separationist activities might endanger the success of the mission.[15]

[12] Wharton, *The Negro in Mississippi*, 47–48.
[13] "Report of the Commissioner of the Freedmen's Bureau," *House Executive Documents*, 39th Cong., 1st Sess., No. 70, p. 167.
[14] B. F. Moore to Sharkey, July 28, 1865, in Governors' Correspondence, E–70. Some loyalists were disturbed by Lincoln's Emancipation Proclamation and immediately turned against the Union. Wilson F. Dillon, a Hinds County planter, later told the Southern Claims Commission that "after the proclamation of President Lincoln in 1862 I thought it a most unjust measure to thousands of Union men who were in the South. I then did not care what the devil became of the country." Klingberg, *Southern Claims Commission*, 108.
[15] Proclamation of Governor Clark, May 22, 1865, in Power Papers; Thomas J. Wharton to John F. H. Claiborne, August 5, 1879, in Claiborne Papers.

Both Sharkey and Yerger had refused to support the Confederate war effort and had worked for a restoration of the state to the Union as early as 1863. It was hoped that the counsels of such moderate and prominent Unionists as these two would have considerable influence on President Johnson, despite the fact that they had belonged to the Whig party, traditionally hostile to the Democratic party, of which Johnson always considered himself to be a member. Firmly imbued with the efficacy and desirability of civil and constitutional government, Sharkey and Yerger probably felt that the main objective of their discussions with Johnson was to mitigate as much as possible the harshness and shorten the duration of military rule.[16]

Loyalists, meanwhile, were writing to Johnson, painting a pessimistic and troubled picture of political conditions in the state. S. S. Fairfield of Grenada declared that the old slave aristocracy was already employing chicanery "to retain something of their ancient dominion." IIe claimed that "the whole *ruling* party together with the whig party that was always kept out of power, but generally being large slaveholders, went over en masse into the rebellion." The true loyalists had never been prominent politically or economically; hence they were "poorly prepared to meet the adverse circumstances of the present crisis, if the rebels" were not restrained from practicing their political sophistries. Fairfield urged Johnson to place the administration of the state in the hands of a military governor "until such time as the loyal citizenry are fully prepared to take charge of and control affairs in the state in spite of opposition."[17]

A more prominent loyalist, John F. H. Claiborne, historian and former Democratic congressman, also believed that a speedy restoration of the state to its constitutional rights and privileges would be disastrous. Confederates "do not yet sufficiently comprehend the force of events, and the duty of accepting them in perfect good faith," he wrote Johnson. "They are not, just now, capable of administering their own affairs, or of adopting a State government adapted to existing facts, and to new social organizations." He proposed the establishment of military rule, evidently without civil functionaries, for a

[16] In a speech before the reconstruction convention in August, 1865, Yerger gave an account of the trip to Washington. *Journal of the Proceedings and Debates of the Constitutional Convention of the State of Mississippi, August, 1865* (Jackson: E. M. Yerger, State Printer, 1865), 146, hereinafter cited as *Convention Journal, 1865.*

[17] Fairfield to Johnson, May 26, 1865, in Johnson Papers.

period of twelve months.[18] In suggesting an authoritarian approach to reconstruction, Claiborne apparently was sincerely apprehensive that secessionists would be restored to power in the state.

When Sharkey and Yerger arrived in Washington, they were notified that they could not be received as representatives of the state, but only as private individuals. President Johnson met with them on June 8 and listened to their description of conditions in the state and to their suggestions concerning reconstruction. Johnson, however, had already decided upon a uniform program for the political restoration of all the Confederate states.[19] He had issued two proclamations on May 29, 1865, which stated the basis of his plan for reconstruction. One proclamation granted amnesty with a general restoration of property, excluding slaves, to all but fourteen excepted classes of former Confederates when they should take an oath of allegiance. The excepted classes were similar to those excluded in President Abraham Lincoln's plan, that is, high Confederate leaders. But a new condition was made: the general pardon did not automatically include those whose taxable property exceeded $20,000. All in the excepted classes, however, might petition the President directly for pardon.[20]

The President's second proclamation appointed William W. Holden provisional governor of North Carolina with "all the powers necessary and proper to enable such loyal people" of the state to restore it to the Union. A convention was to amend the constitution of the state to effect an acknowledgment of the results of the war. For the election of delegates to this convention, only persons who had been qualified voters before the passage of the ordinance of secession could participate, and each must first have subscribed to the amnesty oath of allegiance. Temporarily, civil government was to be administered under the authority of the provisional governor, with the aid of the military. The edict also restored federal functions (courts, postal services, and revenue offices) in the state.[21]

[18] Claiborne to Johnson, May 1, 1865, *ibid.* William M. Pollan, a Mississippian who served in the Federal army during the war, urged the President to pursue not only a harsh policy toward the "rebels" but also a vindictive and punitive one. Pollan to Johnson, June 3, 1865, *ibid.*

[19] *Convention Journal, 1865*, p. 146; John T. Morse, Jr. (ed.), *Diary of Gideon Welles, Secretary of the Navy under Lincoln and Johnson* (Boston: Houghton-Mifflin Company, 1911), II, 524.

[20] Richardson (comp.), *Messages and Papers*, VI, 310–12.

[21] *Ibid.*, 312–14.

During the conference with Sharkey and Yerger, Johnson, showing deference to their opinions, asked the two Mississippians if the terms outlined in the North Carolina proclamation would be acceptable to them. They replied that next to a quick restoration of representative government, his plan would meet the exigencies of reconstruction.[22] A few days later, June 13, Johnson issued a proclamation, similar to the North Carolina edict, to apply to Mississippi. The President appointed Sharkey provisional governor and directed him to call for and convene a reconstruction convention.[23]

William L. Sharkey was admirably qualified to perform the difficult task of executing the moderate plan of reconstruction laid down by the President. As a prominent follower of Henry Clay, he secured the support of the Union Whigs, who were the most influential group in the state at this time. His past record in the public affairs of the state, including several terms as the chief justice of the High Court of Errors and Appeals and president of the Nashville Convention of 1850, gave relief and encouragement to many who had feared for the worst at the hands of a Northern military despot. Even former secessionists expressed delight at Sharkey's appointment, despite the fact that he had been jailed briefly by Confederate authorities during the war because of his Unionism.[24] For example, Henry T. Ellett, an influential secessionist and a justice on the state supreme court during the Confederate period, wrote Sharkey immediately after his selection as provisional governor and declared that he had "frequently expressed the wish that you might receive the appointment, [and] a more acceptable selection could not have been made." [25] As a conservative, Sharkey inspired confidence in the many who feared for their lives and property if crime and disorders continued.[26]

[22] *Convention Journal, 1865,* p. 146.

[23] Richardson (comp.), *Messages and Papers,* VI, 314–16.

[24] Orlando Davis to Sharkey, June 28, 1865, in Governors' Correspondence, E-69; Absalom M. West to Sharkey, July 3, 1865, and John J. McRae to Sharkey, July 13, 1865, *ibid.,* E-70. During the war Sharkey's refusal to sell goods to Confederate officers was seized upon as a pretext to arrest him. A friend of his later said that "Jefferson Davis not only hated him [Sharkey] because of his sentiments but feared his great influence, but for which Judge Sharkey's life would have become one more offering on the altar of the Union." Klingberg, *Southern Claims Commission,* 110–11.

[25] Henry T. Ellett to Sharkey, June 21, 1865, in Governors' Correspondence, E-69.

[26] See, for example, W. A. Champion to Sharkey, June 28, 1865, and petition of citizens of Itawamba County to Sharkey, undated, *ibid.*

Born in 1793 and reared in the predominately white Holston Valley of East Tennessee, Sharkey understood the character and aspirations of the yeoman class. He opposed, however, universal suffrage for whites; he preferred a property qualification for voting.[27] Yet the editor of the Carrollton *Conservative* believed that his selection "created a more unanimous rejoicing among the people of all classes than any other appointment that could have been made." [28]

After being notified of his appointment and formally introduced to the Cabinet by the President, Sharkey returned to Mississippi and made plans for the calling of a constitutional convention. On July 1, 1865, he issued a proclamation directing that an election be held on August 7 to select delegates to a convention, which was to meet one week later. Each county and town was to be represented in the convention by the same number of representatives it was entitled to in the lower house of the legislature before 1861.[29]

Even before Sharkey's call for an election, party politics and animosities had been revived in the state. After long years of frustration, persistent Whigs hailed Sharkey's ascension to the highest office in Mississippi with a great deal of delight and anticipation. Absalom M. West, a former Confederate brigadier general, unsuccessful candidate for governor in 1863, and president of the Mississippi Central Railroad, wrote Sharkey that Whigs "owe it to patriotism and the principles which were common to us all as Whigs (which principles were recognized in your appointment) to make yours a splendid success." Sharkey's administration could give Whig principles "a practical illustration by restoring liberty to the people and guarding and regulating the same by law, and stable government. The principles of which I speak are as important today . . . as they were in the days of Henry Clay, and quite as much our duty to maintain them now as then." [30]

[27] "Condition of Affairs in Mississippi," *House Miscellaneous Documents*, 40th Cong., 3rd Sess., No. 53, p. 32; *Dictionary of American Biography*, XVII, 21.

[28] As quoted in the Meridian *Clarion*, August 10, 1865.

[29] Morse (ed.), *Welles' Diary*, II, 524–25; Certificate of Election of Delegates to the Reconstruction Convention of 1865, in Legislative Records, File I-119, Mississippi Department of Archives and History, Jackson; New York *Times*, July 14, 1865.

[30] Absalom M. West to Sharkey, July 3, 1865, in Governors' Correspondence, E-70. The terms "former" or "old-line" will not be used in this study to describe antebellum Whigs, since such use would be repetitious and, furthermore, the term "Whig" was freely used in 1865 and long thereafter, although no organized party by that name existed.

William M. Pollan, who was a loyalist to the extent of serving in the Federal army during the war, asserted that the triumph of Whig principles in Mississippi was only the culmination of a movement that had already succeeded on the national level. "I have not forgotten the struggles we have had with rule or ruin Democracy from 1844 to the present time," he declared, "and at last we have a national Bank and all our favorite measures," namely, internal improvements, a protective tariff, and the repudiation of the secession doctrine.[31]

Some former Whigs thought that now, while the "hydra-headed" Democratic and secession party was beaten and demoralized, was an excellent time to work for the restoration of the Whig party organization in the South as well as in Mississippi. C. B. Nero reasoned that a revived and strong Whig party in the former Confederate states, sponsoring all of the nationalistic measures of Henry Clay, would keep the secession Democrats submerged politically and therefore the Republican party would not have an issue with which to profit from in the North. Thus it would lose its ascendancy in the national government.[32] William D. Holder, a former Confederate congressman, hoped that a national conservative party could be organized to counter the Democrats. Although suggesting that Whigs should form the nucleus of such a party in the South, he made no mention of the status of Northern conservatives or the Republican party if his dream came true.[33]

In proposing the reorganization of the Whig party in the state, Nero suggested to Sharkey a platform based on three principles: national sovereignty as opposed to state sovereignty, cooperation with Federal authorities in making the new labor system efficient, and opposition to "free negro suffrage."[34] Despite the efforts of Nero and others to rejuvenate the Whig party organization, no major attempt was made to do so, nor was there an effort made to organize a party of conservatives distinct from the two established parties. Such an attempt would have been impractical. After four years of civil strife, loyalties created as a result of varying interests during more rational days had become blurred by the passions and conflicts of war. Conservative politicians of the North would be reluctant to cooperate in a national organiza-

---

[31] William M. Pollan to Sharkey, July 18, 1865, *ibid.*

[32] C. B. Nero to Sharkey, July 1, 1865, *ibid.*

[33] William D. Holder to Governor Benjamin G. Humphreys, October 23, 1865, *ibid.*, E-71.

[34] Nero to Sharkey, July 1, 1865, *ibid.*, E-70.

tion with rebel-tainted Whigs of the South. Furthermore, North-easterners had secured federal legislation favorable to their interests by working through the Republican party, and they had no intention of abandoning the party which promoted their interests. Without national sustenance, a state or regional party could not expect to succeed. Within the state the breakdown of communications and transportation and the amorphous political, social, and economic conditions existing in 1865 made unlikely the formation of a regular statewide party organization.

In a more practical way, Whigs, especially those who were original Unionists, worked to obtain the selection of their men to office and to secure the election of their candidates as delegates to the reconstruction convention. Several urged Sharkey to appoint only Union Whigs to office.[35] Some were appalled when the governor permitted Democrats to continue in positions of public responsibility. "The only true Union element in this State is the Whig party," the dogmatic Nero reminded Sharkey. "You can not make the State loyal with democrats or secessionists in power. . . . By giving office to Democrats you lay the foundation for a disloyal party, which will have you and all true Union men from power, as soon as they can." Thomas S. Gathright, a Union Whig, perceived that "the original precipitators" of secession were already "rushing forward and receiving the 'lion's share' of the official distributions" of office.[36]

When complaints reached President Johnson that the Mississippi governor was retaining many Confederates in office, Sharkey was forced to defend his policy.[37] He explained to the President that it would be unwise and rash to remove from office all secessionists, since many were experienced officials and recognized leaders in their counties. If they proved disloyal, Sharkey assured Johnson that he

[35] Otto Frinke to Sharkey, June 22, 1865, ibid., E-69; Ira McDowell to Sharkey, July 19, 1865; Nero to Sharkey, July 1, 1865, all ibid., E-70.

[36] Nero to Sharkey, July 1, 1865, and Thomas S. Gathright to Sharkey, July 3, 1865, ibid., E-70.

[37] Carl Schurz, investigating conditions in Mississippi in August, wrote Johnson that Sharkey was surrounding himself with secessionists to the almost complete exclusion of Unionists. Schurz's idea of a "consistent Union man" was Judge L. S. Houghton of Vicksburg, a radical loyalist who urged the government to mete out severe punishment to those who supported the Confederacy. Schurz to Johnson, August 29, 1865, in Johnson Papers.

would remove them. For new appointments, he said that he was pursuing a policy of rejecting all who were tainted with secession.[38]

Sharkey's predilection for using moderate Whigs and other natural leaders of the communities caused him, however, to compromise his intention to choose only anti-secessionists for vacant offices. Two appointments to important state offices were granted to active Confederates, one of whom had urged the secession of the state in 1860–61.[39] Nevertheless, Sharkey generally selected Whigs who had opposed secession but supported the Confederacy during some part of the war.

For many Whigs the election of August 7, 1865, to choose delegates for the reconstruction convention was a golden opportunity to humiliate thoroughly their Democratic antagonists and to prove to the nation that the spirit of secession had been completely repudiated by the state. The campaign itself clearly indicated that secession Democrats were "thoroughly whipped" and demoralized. None of the antebellum state Democratic leaders came forward as candidates: William Barksdale was dead, Jefferson Davis was in prison, Jacob Thompson was in exile, John Pettus was living in obscurity in Arkansas, and John J. McRae, Albert G. Brown, Ethelbert Barksdale, William S. Barry, Lucius Q. C. Lamar, David C. Glenn, and Samuel J. Gholson were retired to their plantations or to their private law practices.[40]

Several reasons may be advanced for the political inaction of secession Democratic leaders after the war. Probably of a great deal of significance was a genuine feeling of responsibility for the state's misfortunes and the conviction that they were poorly qualified by their past records to participate in the negotiations with federal authorities which were necessary for the speedy restoration of the

[38] Sharkey to Johnson (telegram), August 25, 1865, in Johnson Papers; "Condition of Affairs in Mississippi," *House Miscellaneous Documents,* 40th Cong., 3rd Sess., No. 53, p. 43.

[39] Comment by Sharkey written on the petition of delegates to the reconstruction convention from the Columbus area to the governor, August 10, 1865, in Governors' Correspondence, E-71; Schurz to Johnson, August 29, 1865, in Johnson Papers.

[40] *Biographical and Historical Memoirs of Mississippi* (Chicago: Goodspeed Publishing Company, 1891), II, 410; *Biographical Directory of the American Congress, 1774–1961* (Washington: United States Government Printing Office, 1961), 521, 1708; Jackson *Clarion,* August 16, 1866; Vicksburg *Times,* February 2, 1868; James B. Ranck, *Albert Gallatin Brown: Radical Southern Nationalist* (New York: Appleton-Century Co., 1937), 252.

state to the Union.[41] Yet, as one recent student concludes, another factor merits attention as well. These antebellum leaders had suffered reverses in the 1863 Confederate and local elections; and there was no reason to expect that that trend would be changed by the materialization of the very consequences which their 1860–61 opponents had predicted. Thus, they had no desire to risk almost certain defeat at the polls.[42]

The methods of nominating candidates for seats in the reconstruction convention differed throughout the state. In some counties meetings were held to select candidates; in others, prominent men were prevailed upon by their friends to announce their candidacy.[43] In most areas where influential Democrats did not run for seats, little interest was aroused in the campaign, and "the office sought the incumbent and not the incumbent the office." [44] In Hinds County (Jackson), traditionally a strong Whig area, Democratic leaders did not participate in the election; however, a vigorous contest developed between the conservatives and the constitutional, or Potter, Whigs. The conservatives, led by William Yerger and Amos R. Johnston, believed that the convention should realistically accept the results of the war and recognize the fact that no compensation for the freed slaves would be granted by the federal government. The convention, according to their view, should explicitly placate the North on this matter and declare slavery unequivocally abolished.[45]

[41] Donald H. Breese, "Politics in the Lower South during Presidential Reconstruction, April to November, 1865" (Ph.D. dissertation, University of California at Los Angeles, 1963), 395; Edward Mayes, *Lucius Q. C. Lamar: His Life, Times, and Speeches, 1825–1893* (Nashville: Publishing House of the Methodist Episcopal Church, South, 1896), 120–21.

[42] Breese, "Politics in the Lower South during Presidential Reconstruction," 395–96.

[43] Drake, "The Mississippi Reconstruction Convention of 1865," 229; William M. Pollan to Sharkey, July 18, 1865, in Governors' Correspondence, E-70.

[44] Meridian *Clarion*, August 20, 1865, quoting the Mobile *Advertiser*.

[45] Drake, "The Mississippi Reconstruction Convention of 1865," 229–30. The small vote cast in counties where prominent Democrats did not run has led Drake to the conclusion that little interest was displayed in these counties. The election of 1860 for delegates to the convention of 1861 was used to determine the relative size of the electorate. Returns for forty-three of the sixty counties are included in Certificates of Election of Delegates to the Reconstruction Convention, 1865, in Legislative Records. Partial returns for two other counties may be found in the Meridian *Clarion*, August 9, 1865. For the returns of the 1860 convention election, see Percy L. Rainwater, *Mississippi, Storm Center of Secession, 1856–1861* (Baton Rouge: Otto Claitor, 1938), 198–99.

The constitutional Whig group declared that, if they secured control of the three seats in the convention allocated to Hinds County, they would vote against any proposal for the "unconditional abolition of slavery." George L. Potter, speaking for this party, argued that Mississippi had never been out of the Union, and that the state's citizens were entitled to their rights under the Constitution, which included the right to receive compensation for their slaves. Although the Potterites had no intention of reviving slavery, their purpose was to leave the door open for the courts to act. If abolition were declared unconstitutional, widows, orphans, and loyalists might be able to obtain compensation, they argued.[46]

In northeastern Mississippi a bitter struggle occurred during the campaign between loyalists and secessionists. In one county, Choctaw, William M. Pollan used his secret and militant "Union League" to suppress the disorganized Democrats of the area. Although he apparently succeeded in keeping the Democrats from running party candidates, the voters of the county rejected his selections. The electorate, evidently finding Pollan's radical loyalists too distasteful, selected three Whigs, or original Unionists, as delegates to the convention.[47]

Participation in the election was very light. In populous Adams (Natchez) and Warren (Vicksburg) counties where there was no Democratic opposition the total vote declined more than 00 per cent from that of 1860. In Hinds County voter participation was off 68 per cent from the 1860 election, in spite of the vigorous campaign by the two opposing Whig groups. Even in the traditionally strong Democratic counties of northeast Mississippi, the vote declined sharply, although the Democrats put forward candidates. Only in the central part of the state was there a pattern of voter participation similar to that of 1860.[48]

Some people, particularly demoralized secession Democrats, remained at home and did not vote because they were unconcerned about the selection of delegates to a convention that would only record the already obvious results of the war. Then, too, as the Meridian

[46] Drake, "The Mississippi Reconstruction Convention of 1865," 230, 238.

[47] William M. Pollan to Sharkey, July 18, 19, 20, 1865, in Governors' Correspondence, E-70. See also W. W. Foote to Sharkey, July 5, 1865, ibid., E-69, and H. E. Moore to Sharkey, September 23, 1865, ibid., E-72, for other illustrations of the loyalist-secessionist struggle at this time.

[48] Certificates of Election of Delegates to the Reconstruction Convention of 1865, in Legislative Records; Rainwater, Mississippi, 198–99.

Clarion pointed out, 25,000 potential voters did not return from the war.[49] Furthermore, many people were busy attempting to restore their economic means. But probably the main reason for nonparticipation in the election was that the people had had such a brief period in which to take the amnesty oath and thereby to qualify to vote. Confusion as to the proper administration of the oath, the tardiness of the arrival of forms in some interior counties, and the inconvenience of traveling considerable distances to take the oath were all factors contributing to the failure of many Mississippians to qualify in time to vote for delegates to the convention.[50] Union Whigs were more motivated than disillusioned Democrats to overcome the difficulties involved in taking the oath. Generally of the planter class and with extensive land holdings to be protected, many former Whigs thought that unless they secured amnesty papers their properties might be confiscated and they might be arrested by the federal government on the charge of treason. As original Unionists, Whigs, moreover, were more anxious than secession Democrats to demonstrate anew their allegiance to the Union.[51]

Whatever the reasons, members of the old party of Union and moderation won an extraordinary victory in the August election over the secession-tainted Democrats. Seventy-one Whigs won seats in the convention, while only eighteen Democrats were elected. The ten remaining successful candidates used a variety of designations to describe their political loyalties, such as "conservative" or "co-operationist."[52] The piney barrens, an area that the southern rights Democrats easily carried in 1860, almost completely repudiated the Democrats in the 1865 election. An anti-Confederate region during the latter part of the war, these counties sent all Whigs or "conservatives" to the convention except for one delegate. Even Democrats of

[49] Meridian *Clarion,* October 17, 1865.

[50] Robert A. Hill to Sharkey, July 17, 1865; R. G. W. Jewel to Sharkey, July 11, 1865; O. Osburn to Sharkey, July 11, 1865; Lock Houston to Sharkey, July 10, 1865, all in Governors' Correspondence, E-70.

[51] One Whig later recalled that many original Unionists rode to adjacent counties or districts to secure amnesty in order to avoid being administered the oath by local officers who were former secessionists but were now qualified to give the oath. Raymond *Hinds County Gazette,* May 5, 1869.

[52] A listing of the party preference of the delegates to the convention is given in the *Convention Journal, 1865,* pp. 278–83. One delegate who described his politics in this listing as "Opposed to Universal Suffrage" was actually a former Whig.

the piney barrens who had opposed secession in 1860–61 were defeated in the election. In Hinds County the conservative Whigs won two of the county's three seats in the convention, while Potter was selected for the other.[53]

The great majority of the delegates who assembled in Jackson on August 14, 1865, were known as men of ability and prestige.[54] Few of them, however, had served in high state offices, since the party of the majority of delegates had been the minority party in Mississippi before the war. Yet many of the men had participated in the campaigns and debates over the great issues of the preceding two decades. Seven of the members had served as delegates to the convention of 1861, and six of these had voted against secession. One delegate, William Yerger, was the only member to hold an important state office before the secession of the state. During the war John W. C. Watson and James T. Harrison served in the Confederate Congress. Thirty members had been in the state legislature, and several had had experience on the bench of the lower courts.[55]

On the first day of the convention J. Shall Yerger, an original Unionist and the brother of William, was elected president of the convention. He appointed the two committees which were to do the most important work of the convention. The Committee on the State Constitution, headed by Harrison, was to report the changes in the constitution necessary to restore the state to its proper relations with the federal government. The Committee on Ordinances and Laws, with Amos R. Johnston as chairman, was to study and to recommend what action should be taken on the ordinance of secession and the laws of the state passed since the state had left the Union.[56]

[53] Certificates of Election of Delegates to the Reconstruction Convention of 1865, in Legislative Records.

[54] Although President Johnson had directed that only those who had been pardoned or had been administered the amnesty oath could be members of the convention, thirteen delegates of the "exceptions" class served in the convention without having been pardoned.

[55] Drake, "The Mississippi Reconstruction Convention of 1865," 233–34. For the vote of the delegates on the secession ordinance, see *Journal of the State Convention and Ordinances and Resolutions Adopted in January, 1861* (Jackson: E. Barksdale, State Printer, 1861), 14.

[56] Drake, "The Mississippi Reconstruction Convention of 1865," 235. The best secondary accounts of the reconstruction convention of 1865 are Drake's work cited above and the last chapter in his "Constitutional Development in Mississippi, 1817–1865" (Ph.D. dissertation, University of North Carolina, 1954). The

Before the committees had had an opportunity to study and report to the convention, President Johnson wired Sharkey on August 16, indicating specifically what he thought the convention should do. Prior to this dispatch Sharkey had received no instructions from Johnson regarding the work of the convention except those contained in the proclamation appointing him governor.[57] The telegram read:

I am gratified to see that you have organized your convention without deficiency. I hope that without delay your convention will amend your State Constitution abolishing slavery and denying to all future Legislatures the power to legislate what ever is property in man, also that they will adopt the Amendments to the Constitution of the United States abolishing slavery. If you could extend the elective franchise to all persons of color who can read the Constitution of the United States in English and write their names and to all persons of color who own real estate valued at not less than two hundred and fifty dollars and pay taxes ther on [sic], you would completely disarm the adversary and give an example the other states will follow. This you can do with perfect safety and you thus place the Southern states in reference to free persons of color upon the same basis with the free states. I hope and trust your convention will do this and as a consequence the Radicals who are wild upon Negro franchise will be completely foiled in thier [sic] attempt to keep the Southern states from renewing thier [sic] relation to the Union by not accepting their Senators and Representatives.[58]

Because of the significance of the instructions included in this telegram, Sharkey probably showed the dispatch to members of the convention. However, no mention was made in the convention concerning Negro suffrage or, more specifically, Johnson's suggestion of limited suffrage for the freedmen. Sharkey replied on August 20 that the convention would leave the question of suffrage to the legislature.[59] Then a few days later he wrote the President that he saw little hope for any Negroes being given the privilege of voting by the legislature. "Indeed," he declared, "there is an inclination [in the state] to limit the right of suffrage with the white man." [60]

---

debates and actions of the convention are exceptionally well recorded in the above cited *Convention Journal, 1865*.

[57] Johnson to Sharkey, August 16, 1865 (telegram), in Governors' Correspondence, E-71; Drake, "The Mississippi Reconstruction Convention of 1865," 236.

[58] Johnson to Sharkey, August 16, 1865 (telegram), in Governors' Correspondence, E-71.

[59] Sharkey to Johnson, August 20, 1865, in Johnson Papers.

[60] Sharkey to Johnson, August 28, 1865, *ibid*.

The first and longest debate during the reconstruction convention occurred when the Committee on the State Constitution made its report concerning slavery. The committee recommended that the constitution be amended to read: "That neither slavery nor involuntary servitude, otherwise than in punishment of crimes, whereof the party shall have been duly convicted, shall hereafter exist in the State. . . ." [61] Hugh Barr of Lafayette County offered a substitute which was the same in substance as that reported by the committee, but it contained a preamble which declared that slavery had been abolished by the action of the federal government. Barr and his supporters claimed that it would be misleading to leave the impression that the abolition of slavery was the result of the voluntary action of the convention, when it was evident that it had been forced upon them by a conqueror. By a vote of fifty-four to forty-one Barr's substitute was laid on the table.[62] After several other substitutes were rejected, George L. Potter, an able Union Whig who had been trained in law at Yale University, arraigned the federal government for freeing the slaves of nonparticipants without compensation and, in effect, proposed that the convention do nothing regarding the institution of slavery. The federal courts, he said, were the proper ones to decide this question; and, if they decided in the affirmative, it would be the responsibility of the federal rather than the state government to take care of the freed slaves. Potter's argument evidently did not take into consideration the fact that the proposed Thirteenth Amendment would settle the question of the constitutionality of emancipation. His substitute was tabled by a vote of sixty-three to twenty-eight.[63]

The final, and according to many the ablest, speech on the report of the committee concerning slavery was made by William Yerger.[64] Yerger gave an account of his mission to Washington and declared that President Johnson had made it clear to him that Mississippi must pass an amendment freeing the slaves before the executive department would support the restoration of the state to its normal position in the Union. Unless the committee's report abolishing slavery were adopted, the state would not regain its privileges in the Union, and the Presi-

[61] Convention Journal, 1865, pp. 29–30.
[62] Ibid., 44; Garner, Reconstruction in Mississippi, 86–87; Drake, "The Mississippi Reconstruction Convention of 1865," 238–39.
[63] Drake, "The Mississippi Reconstruction Convention of 1865," 238–39.
[64] Niles Diary, August 15–19, 1865.

dent's moderate policy would be overwhelmed by the Radicals of the North, who were "clamoring, not for the abolition of slavery, but for universal suffrage and social equality of the negro." [65]

James T. Harrison, chairman of the committee that had brought in the proposal on slavery, now offered a compromise amendment to the report, so that it would read: "The institution of slavery having been destroyed in the State of Mississippi, neither slavery nor involuntary servitude . . . shall hereafter exist in this State." [66] Since the vote was eighty-seven to eleven in favor of the committee's report as reworded, Harrison's amendment apparently satisfied most of the Potterites and the delegates who wanted to place the responsibility for the freeing of the slaves specifically on the conquerors.[67]

The reconstruction convention avoided including in the constitution a precise statement concerning the new relationship of the Negro with the state. The delegates indicated that this was the responsibility of the legislature and that this body, when it assembled, "shall provide by law for the protection and security of the person and property of the freedmen of the State, and guard them and the State against any evils that may arise from their sudden emancipation." [68] A few delegates attempted to change the clause, so as to delete the word "property" and substitute "the regulation of labor and wages." The convention, however, voted down this change; and this action of the majority of the delegates provided a basis for later arguments that the convention fully intended that the freedman be protected in his property rights.[69]

The convention now authorized President Yerger to appoint a committee to prepare and to report to the next session of the legislature such laws and changes in existing laws as they might think expedient in view of the constitutional revisions made by the convention. Yerger selected for the commission Alexander H. Handy, chief justice of the high court and a secession Democrat; William Hemingway, a Douglas

[65] Drake, "The Mississippi Reconstruction Convention of 1865," 240–41; *Convention Journal, 1865*, p. 147.

[66] See the *Convention Journal, 1865*, p. 165, for the final wording of the abolition amendment to the constitution.

[67] Drake, "The Mississippi Reconstruction Convention of 1865," 241–42.

[68] *Constitution of the State of Mississippi As Amended, With the Ordinances and Resolutions Adopted by the Constitutional Convention, August, 1865* (Jackson: E. M. Yerger, State Printer, 1865), 44.

[69] See Sharkey's testimony before the Joint Committee on Reconstruction, "Report of the Joint Committee on Reconstruction," *House Reports*, 39th Cong., 1st Sess., No. 30, Pt. III, 133.

Democrat; and E. J. Goode, a "conservative." Handy refused the appointment, and Yerger appointed Robert S. Hudson, an impetuous Whig circuit judge from Yazoo County.[70]

After disposing of the slavery question, the reconstruction convention turned to the problem of the ordinance of secession. The Committee on Ordinances and Laws, to which the problem had been referred, brought in a report recommending that the convention declare the ordinance to be "null and void." [71] James F. Trotter, a secession Democrat, submitted a minority report urging that the convention simply proclaim the secession ordinance "repealed and abrogated." To declare it "null and void," Trotter and his supporters argued, would discredit the members of the convention of 1861 and would impute the charge of treason upon them and upon every person who obeyed the edict.[72]

In defending the majority report, Amos R. Johnston, the committee chairman, admitted that the report was intended to mean that the secession ordinance was null and void *ab initio*, and thus never had any binding force. Johnston's statement, as one scholar points out, clearly indicates that Mississippians were not holding onto the right of secession.[73] The report of the committee, declaring that the secession ordinance was "null and of no binding force," was finally adopted, but only after the Trotter proposal was tabled by a vote of forty-eight to forty-six.[74]

The convention also sought to clarify the nature of the state government after the passage of the secession ordinance. The most important action in this regard validated all laws enacted by the legislature since January 9, 1861, except those in conflict with the constitution of the United States or those in aid of the rebellion. The majority of the delegates evidently believed that the question of which laws had been unconstitutional or in aid of the Confederacy was a matter for the courts to decide.[75]

The reconstruction convention confined its actions almost exclusively

[70] *Mississippi Constitution As Amended, 1865*, p. 44; *Convention Journal, 1865*, p. 247.

[71] *Convention Journal, 1865*, pp. 33–34, 174.

[72] *Ibid.*, 174. See Trotter's speech in support of the minority report in *ibid.*, 174–76.

[73] Drake, "The Mississippi Reconstruction Convention of 1865," 244.

[74] *Convention Journal, 1865*, p. 220.

[75] Drake, "Constitutional Development in Mississippi," 301-302.

to those for which it had been called and resisted efforts by some of the delegates to incorporate various measures into the organic law of the state. Efforts were made by some convention members, nevertheless, in behalf of measures that were designed to settle some of the specific problems faced by the state. One proposal especially reflected the increasing concern of the planters about the reliability of Negro labor in view of the apparently widespread predilection of the freedmen to quit work as the arduous cotton-picking season approached. This proposed constitutional amendment would have given the boards of police in each county authority to make regulations governing the rights and duties of apprentices and to suppress vagrancy. The majority of the delegates, however, thought that policies of this nature should be left to the legislature.[76]

The convention did feel that the problem of the inundated Yazoo Basin or Delta counties could not await the action of the legislature. By a resolution the members directed President Yerger to appoint four commissioners to go to Washington and confer with federal officials regarding the rebuilding of the levees. The commissioners were granted the authority to negotiate loans and to secure laborers for the work of restoration; but the taxes necessary to finance this undertaking could be levied only by the legislature and solely on the counties or districts that would be protected by the levees. Reflecting strong antebellum party traditions and principles, the Whig-dominated convention specifically directed that the faith of the state could not be pledged for the payment of any money borrowed by the commissioners for the reconstruction of the levees.[77] Yerger appointed four men of the Delta counties, namely, James Lusk Alcorn, F. A. Owen, William Hunt, and William S. Langley, to the commission.[78]

Insistence on the repudiation of the war debt by the state conventions did not become a part of President Johnson's plan of reconstruction until after the Mississippi convention had met. The subject of debt repudiation was not an issue in the August convention, and the delegates evidently were not criticized at the time for its omis-

[76] Ibid., 305–307.

[77] Mississippi Constitution As Amended, 1865, p. 44. Before the war the Whig party had vigorously but unsuccessfully fought the repudiation of the bonds issued by the state for the purchase of stock in the Planters' and Union banks. Dallas C. Dickey, Seargent S. Prentiss, Whig Orator of the Old South (Baton Rouge: Louisiana State University Press, 1945), Chap. 3.

[78] Convention Journal, 1865, p. 274.

sion.[79] The convention, as was its disposition in other matters, probably felt that the question of wartime financial obligations was a matter for the courts. Even though they were vehement in their opposition to repudiation of antebellum debts, Whigs were confused and divided concerning the desirability of paying obligations contracted by the government of Mississippi as a Confederate state—a government that several of the Union delegates to the convention had consistently refused to recognize as a *de jure* government.

Finally, the convention took action to put into operation the machinery for the civil government of the state, believing that the state had met the requirements of the federal government for a speedy restoration of self-government. The convention provided that an election for state officers, congressmen, legislators, and local officers should be held on the first Monday in October; and all officers elected were to take office on the third Monday of that month.[80] Before adjourning on August 24 the delegates debated the question of submitting the work of the convention to the people for ratification at the October election. The members by a vote of fifty to forty-four decided that a referendum on the amendments and ordinances adopted by the convention was "not practical or expedient . . . under existing circumstances." Sharkey agreed that voter approval was not necessary. He later testified before the Joint Committee on Reconstruction: "I was so well satisfied with the temper, disposition, and wish of the people, that I did not think it necessary to submit the amended constitution to them at all. . . . The members of the convention were elected on the general proposition of reforming the constitution, and I have no doubt that they represented truly the sentiments of a large majority of the people of the State." [81]

[79] Drake, "Constitutional Development in Mississippi," 314–15. After debt repudiation became a part of Johnson's program, all of the other Confederate states except South Carolina repudiated their Confederate obligations.

[80] *Mississippi Constitution As Amended, 1865,* p. 42.

[81] "Report of the Joint Committee on Reconstruction," *House Reports,* 39th Cong., 1st Sess., No. 30, Pt. III, 134; New York *Times,* August 27, 1865. It should be pointed out that Sharkey in his appearances before the Joint Committee on Reconstruction was interested in presenting a favorable impression of conditions in Mississippi; and in so doing he naïvely believed that his report would be accepted and that the Radical pressure for Negro suffrage would be lessened in Congress. Carl Schurz, visiting in the state in late August, 1865, in contrast to Sharkey's opinion criticized the action of the convention in not submitting its work to the people for ratification. He claimed that some members of the convention

The work of the convention met with general approval among the conservatives of the North. The New York *Times* endorsed its actions and suggested that the other Southern states should follow Mississippi's example. The convention's work pleased President Johnson and encouraged him to pursue his program, with modifications, for the restoration of the remaining states. Since their convention had met all of the demands of the President, Sharkey felt that the people of his state were "entitled to the consideration of the Government and to be treated as though the Rebellion had ended"; specifically the government should remove Negro troops and restore the writ of habeas corpus and the full authority of the civil officers.[82]

There were some, however, who were not happy with the settlement made by the Mississippi reconstruction convention. Radical Republicans, who were already disposed to view with disfavor the Presidential plan, criticized the work of the convention, especially the failure of the body to grant the Negro any political privileges. They used this as a weapon against the entire Presidential plan of reconstruction. Schurz reported from Mississippi that the convention's action in abolishing slavery was very incomplete, and it left an opening by which the legislature might restore a form of Negro servitude.[83] A group of Vicksburg Negroes thought likewise. On September 18 they held a meeting to protest the work of the reconstruction convention. They denounced the system of "warranteeism" advocated by the official newspaper of the convention, believing that it reflected the view of the delegates that the activities of the freedmen should be strictly regulated. Before adjourning they passed a resolution declaring that "we view with alarm the efforts now being made to nullify the Proclamation of Emancipation. . . . It is our firm conviction . . . [that the legislature] will pass such proscriptive class laws against the freedmen as will result in their expatriation from the State or their practical reenslavement."[84]

"confessed openly that they knew they did not represent the people," and thus were reluctant to permit a popular vote on the changes to the constitution. On what questions the delegates allegedly did not represent the people, Schurz did not say. Schurz to Johnson, August 29, 1865, in Johnson Papers.

[82] New York *Times*, September 19, 1865; Sharkey to Johnson, August 28, 1865, in Johnson Papers.

[83] Meridian *Clarion*, October 17, 1865; Drake, "Constitutional Development in Mississippi," 312; Schurz to Johnson, August 29, 1865, in Johnson Papers.

[84] New York *Tribune*, October 10, 1865.

Nevertheless, the election of delegates to the reconstruction convention and the settlement that they arranged represented a conservative victory. It is true that some Whigs who were elected appeared reluctant in the convention to satisfy the conditions of the President regarding secession and slavery. The Potterites, who opposed action by the convention on the slavery question, did not deny that the institution was dead, but they approached its demise from a constitutional viewpoint in hopes of gaining some compensation for the loss of the freed Negroes. Some critics have pointed out that the weak wording of the convention's statement invalidating the secession ordinance represented a subtle effort to flank the President's requirement regarding the ordinance. Actually, the statement that the ordinance was "null and of no binding force" was designed to prevent the imputation of treason on those who drew up the ordinance and on those who obeyed it. The majority of the delegates believed that the secession ordinance was null and void from the beginning. And to Whigs who had developed an affinity for constitutional and legalistic processes, this was indeed an important distinction to be made, since most of them had recognized the validity of the Confederate government. If they were classified as traitors, they would be in danger of having their property confiscated by the United States government

With an opportunity to assail, if not proscribe, their secession antagonists, Sharkey and the Union-Whig-dominated convention evidently were content that their old foes had been humbled; thus they ignored loyalist pressure for the provisional government to expel secessionists from the political life of the state. Many Union Whigs had fought beside disunion Democrats during the war and had developed a feeling of comradeship for many of them. These Whigs were more sympathetic to the place of secessionists in the postwar society than they were to that of the embittered loyalists, who generally had remained at home and in some cases had attempted to obstruct the war effort.

The reconstruction convention refused to discuss President Johnson's suggestion that the franchise be extended to Negroes who could read and write and who owned $250 worth of property; otherwise, it met all of his requirements. To many conservative Whigs, Mississippi's unrestricted white male suffrage was distasteful, and Negro suffrage would be even more repugnant. Moreover, most Whigs in this assembly, despite their desire to please Johnson, certainly understood that their political ascendancy in the state would be brief if they became associated with a movement to extend the ballot to the freedmen. They easily dismissed the President's suggestion as a subject that was not within the scope of their meeting and one that should be referred to the legislature. Their refusal to act, or even to discuss the proposal, indicates the basic conservatism of the delegates rather than any inclination on their part to be recalcitrant in implementing the President's policies.

The vagueness of the work of the convention in regard to the position of the freedman was probably dictated by the fact that labor and political conditions in the state were still uncertain and confusing. By the time of the October election and the subsequent meeting of the legislature, however, planters were to face labor problems in the harvesting of their crops and at the same time to be gravely concerned about the need for a stable supply of workers for the cultivation of the 1866 crop. The crucial nature of these problems was not so clear when the reconstruction convention met in August, 1865; thus the delegates conveniently confined their work almost exclusively to the task for which they had been assembled by the provisional government.

4

Attempts to Restore Order and Security

THE VAGUENESS of the authority of Governor Sharkey and the civil officials created confusion and conflict from the beginning of the provisional government of the state. Mississippi during this period, and even after the election and installation of the new officers, was occupied by Federal troops who were, like the civil officials, uncertain of their functions and responsibilities. In his proclamation of June 13 appointing Sharkey, President Johnson asserted that the military was in the state to aid but not to interfere with the provisional government. Neither Johnson nor the War Department apparently issued any explicit instructions to the military commanders regarding their functions in the reconstruction process.[1] On the other hand, the act creating the Freedmen's Bureau, with a military organization, and placing it under the control of the War Department suggested to many officers that the purpose of the military in Mississippi was to aid the Negro in his adjustment to freedom.[2] Sharkey and his civil officers thought the Negro needed no such aid.

[1] Richardson (comp.), *Messages and Papers*, VI, 316. A telegram, dated August 30, 1865, from Johnson to Schurz, who was visiting in Mississippi as the President's special commissioner, suggests that no explicit instructions had been given to the military commander in the state regarding the army's relationship to the civil authorities. Johnson did indicate in referring to Sharkey's organization of the militia, which the military opposed, that one purpose for the army's being in the state was "to detect, and suppress, on the first appearance, any move insurrectionary in its character." A copy of this telegram (August 30, 1865) is found in Governors' Correspondence, E-71.

[2] For example, see Major General Thomas J. Wood to Governor Benjamin G. Humphreys, December 3, 1865, a copy in Military Records, Mississippi District, Office of the Adjutant General, Miscellaneous Branch, 1861–70, Records Group 94, National Archives.

Furthermore, the purpose of the Civil War for many Federal officers had ceased during the last two years of the struggle to be one of merely restoring the Union and had become a crusade to remove the incubus of chattel slavery from the United States. Since they had won the war and occupied the land of the enemy, it was inevitable that these officers, particularly the commanders and the officers of the Freedmen's Bureau, would be anxious to retain the fruits of their victory and to interpret their responsibilities in this light. Very few would admit of a desire to secure political rights for the freedmen, but most of them were insistent on protecting the basic freedom of the Negroes.[3] To Federal officers, therefore, the question was a practical one of protecting the results of the war. On the other hand, the question of the place of the Negro in Mississippi society was to Sharkey and his supporters primarily a legal and a constitutional one to be settled by the reconstruction convention and the legislature. Sharkey believed almost from the beginning that there was no need for martial law or military interference to aid the Negro in his adjustment to freedom. Army officers thought otherwise. That these two groups would clash, despite genuine manifestations of good will toward one another, was almost inevitable.

After the war the state was made a military department and was divided into five districts, to be occupied by army units. Troops were not garrisoned in all of the counties but were placed in significant towns with the expectation that they would be able to move to any part of their particular district if trouble developed. Garrisons were not established in some of the designated towns until the last part of June 1865.[4] In the river towns quasi-martial law of a mild nature had existed since the occupation of the Mississippi Valley in 1862 and 1863. In fact, in Natchez Federal military rule had been enlightened and had been "a model of financial economy," the Natchez *Courier* claimed.[5] Street lighting and sanitary conditions had been improved, outstanding public debts paid, and still the treasury had been able to show a balance of $8,501 at the end of May, 1865. The *Courier* editor

---

[3] As an indicator of this sentiment, see Major General Peter J. Osterhaus' General Order number 57 in the Meridian *Clarion*, June 21, 1865.

[4] Meridian *Clarion*, June 22, 1865.

[5] Natchez *Tri-Weekly Courier*, June 22, 1865. The *Courier* had long been edited by Giles Hillyer, a former Whig. The liberal treatment that the people of Natchez received at the hands of the conqueror was probably due to their strong and consistent Union sentiments.

hoped that the civil authorities would be able to do as well when they assumed control of Natchez. By the first of June the military authorities apparently had relinquished to appointees of Governor Sharkey their civil responsibilities in the river communities.[6] In the interior of the state, where garrisons had not been established until the end of the war, Federal officers did not have an opportunity to assume control of civil functions before the provisional government was established. In communities where they exercised civil control their primary purpose during the summer of 1865 became one of maintaining law and order until local governments were restored.[7]

Immediately after the war a confusion of authority developed in the state when United States Treasury agents entered Mississippi to confiscate cotton. This confusion contributed greatly to the mismanagement of the Treasury's program and to a veritable mania for cotton stealing and surreptitious operations in the state in 1865. Mississippians became involved, as well as Treasury agents from the North and military troops, in these illicit activities.[8] In addition to their economic effects, these cotton operations accentuated the difficulties faced by the provisional government in restoring order and security immediately after the war.

By legislation passed in 1863, Congress had authorized the Secretary of the Treasury to appoint agents whose duty it would be to go into the insurrectionary states and confiscate all abandoned property for the government. With the coming of peace, the main objective of these agents was to appropriate cotton owned by the former Confederate government.[9] Laws and regulations allowed them as compensation from 25 to 50 per cent of the proceeds of their seizures. Actually, the special agents who came south did not expect in most

[6] *Ibid.*, A. K. Smedes to Sharkey, September 16, 1865, in Governors' Correspondence, E-72.

[7] Schurz to Johnson, August 29, 1865, in Johnson Papers. No record has been found of the number of Federal troops serving in garrison during the summer of 1865; however, in January, 1866, General Wood reported that he had 10,193 troops in the state, of whom 8,784 were Negroes. "Message of the President of the United States and Accompanying Documents to the Two Houses of Congress, at the Commencement of the Second Session of the 39th Congress," *House Executive Documents*, 39th Cong., 2nd Sess., No. 1, pp. 50–51.

[8] Memphis *Appeal*, December 31, 1865; New Orleans *Picayune*, May 21, 1865; Meridian *Clarion*, October 11, 1865.

[9] "Captured and Forfeited Cotton," *House Executive Documents*, 39th Cong., 2nd Sess., No. 97, p. 2.

cases to collect the cotton themselves, for they were permitted to contract with individuals and groups in their districts for the delivery of the staple to convenient shipping points. Supervising agents at Memphis, New Orleans, and other large commercial centers received the cotton from the special agents in the districts and consigned it to a general agent in the North.[10] If the local agent requested assistance, military forces in the states were instructed to aid in collecting and forwarding the cotton. In cases of doubtful title, the agents were still to forward the staple, and the Treasury Department in Washington would determine its ownership.[11] This system for appropriating Confederate cotton, with the attendant disorganized state of affairs in Mississippi and the high price of cotton, offered tremendous opportunity for peculation and outright thievery.[12]

Confederate officials had estimated as of October, 1864, that their government held 127,341 bales of cotton in Mississippi, with an estimated market value of $7,947,455. Most of this cotton was supposed to have been stored in safe places on the plantations to await shipment to Europe as soon as the blockade was lifted; however, by the end of the war much of it had been stolen, burned, or seized by Federal or Confederate troops. When Mississippians in the interior received information that Treasury agents would arrive soon in their communities to confiscate all Confederate cotton, many hastened to secure possession of as much of it as possible and to ship it to market immediately. Although some of the staple appropriated in this manner was stolen, much of it was taken by planters and others in compensation for worthless Confederate bonds and apparently valueless state cotton notes held by them. With money from the sale of this cotton, cotton growers hoped to purchase provisions and to procure labor for a beginning toward recovery.[13]

[10] *Ibid.;* "Seizure of Cotton," *Senate Executive Documents,* 43rd Cong., 2nd Sess., No. 23, p. 2.

[11] General Wood to Governor Humphreys, February 9, 1866, in Governors' Correspondence, E-78; Secretary of Treasury Hugh McCulloch to Sharkey (telegram), August 5, 1865, *ibid.,* E-71.

[12] Cotton was selling for approximately forty cents a pound on the New Orleans market—which was almost thirty cents higher than the price of the staple in 1860. James E. Boyle, *Cotton and the New Orleans Cotton Exchange: A Century of Commercial Evolution* (Garden City, New York: Country Life Press, 1934), 179–80.

[13] "Statements, Letters, and Testimony Relative to Captured and Abandoned Property, before the Committee on Expenditures of the Treasury Department,"

When Treasury agents moved into the interior of the state to commence their work, establishing themselves along lines of communications and transportation, they found it extremely difficult, if not impossible, to distinguish Confederate from private cotton and to trace that which had been sold. Confederate officials in charge of cotton procurement had failed to keep adequate records; and Treasury agents, according to the admission of one in northeast Mississippi, "are compelled to rely upon such information as may be given by honest and good men who desire the General Government protected." [14] William W. Orme, supervising agent at Memphis, admonished his subordinates in Mississippi to beware of people who would use every means at their disposal "to defraud the government of this property," and he called upon them "to use rigid systems in order to protect the interest of the government." [15] Obviously such instructions might give opportunity for profit to unscrupulous agents, particularly since disputed property seized by them could not be adjudicated by the civil courts.

The greatest irregularities in the confiscation of Confederate cotton probably occurred where Treasury agents contracted with local individuals to collect the staple from the planters and merchants and to deliver it at designated places for shipment. Supervising agent Orme instructed his district agents to select as many men as necessary for this purpose and to arrange in writing with them "to give such reasonable compensation on the sale of the cotton, as may be for the best interests of the Government." [16]

With the authority of the federal government and troops behind them, many formerly responsible citizens, now impoverished and disillusioned, could not resist the opportunity for profit, even at the ex-

House Miscellaneous Documents, 44th Cong., 1st Sess., No. 190, pp. 37–39; New Orleans *Picayune*, May 21, 1865; Thomas A. Watkins to Sharkey, July 20, 1865, in Governors' Correspondence, E-70.

[14] M. S. Jay to Sharkey, August 5, 1865, in Governors' Correspondence, E-71.

[15] Instructions from William W. Orme, supervising agent at Memphis, to M. S. Jay, enclosed in *ibid*. Orme did point out to his agents that "we have no intention of interfering with any cotton clearly private property and will render every assistance to facilitate the interest of every individual."

[16] "Captured and Forfeited Cotton," *House Executive Documents*, 39th Cong., 2nd Sess., No. 97, p. 3; Orme to Jay, June 7, 1865, in Governors' Correspondence, E-71. See also Circular, Second Agency, Treasury Department, Okolona, Mississippi, June 15, 1865, in Governors' Correspondence, E-71.

pense of their neighbors who held cotton. Contractors and opportunists representing themselves as agents went about the country seizing cotton indiscriminately and in many cases appropriating it for their own use.[17] When individuals proved recalcitrant about producing the cotton demanded, one contractor simply jailed them, and, when the cotton was finally delivered, he appropriated most of it for himself.[18]

In the large cotton producing region near Columbus, a Memphis visitor reported that "cotton is the absorbing topic here. No one talks politics or thinks of politics. But the point which interests all ears is, . . . where is there any government cotton that I can steal, or rather appropriate?" [19] Federal troops became involved in what the Memphis *Appeal* termed "a general grab game." The Federal brigadier in east Mississippi was accused of seizing cotton along the Mobile and Ohio Railroad and shipping it to England as private property. The arsenal at Columbus, which supposedly contained 3,600 bales at the time, was burned, and the Federal officers there reported that only sixty bales were saved. Many concluded that the fire represented a plan for placing stolen cotton on the army loss report.[20]

Although some Treasury agents were honest and forwarded the cotton that they and their contractors collected, others were unscrupulous and engaged in schemes to appropriate for themselves private as well as Confederate cotton. The agent for the west Mississippi district established a post on the Yazoo River and stopped all cotton going down the river, seizing that which the owners could not prove was theirs. Planters who filed claims for property forwarded in this manner never heard of their cases coming before Treasury officials in Washington. Another agent was alleged to have been in collusion with the commander of the garrison in his district to appropriate private cotton. Some agents exceeded their instructions and charged a fee

[17] See Secretary of Treasury Hugh McCulloch's report of November 8, 1866, in "Captured and Forfeited Cotton," *House Executive Documents*, 39th Cong., 2nd Sess., No. 97, pp. 3–4.

[18] James T. Harrison, *et al.*, to Governor Humphreys, May 8, 1866, enclosed in a letter from Humphreys to President Johnson, May 19, 1866, in Johnson Papers.

[19] As quoted in the Friar's Point *Coahomian*, December 8, 1865.

[20] *Ibid.*; Memphis *Appeal*, December 31, 1865.

for issuing permits to planters for the unobstructed shipment of their cotton.[21]

Governor Sharkey's office was flooded with complaints concerning the manner in which Treasury agents were operating. Early in his administration Sharkey attempted to secure civil jurisdiction over disputed cases, but he failed.[22] He then appealed to the military commanders in the state to take action to prevent troops from participating in cotton ventures and from aiding contractors and agents in collecting cotton that had not clearly belonged to the Confederacy. Major General Peter J. Osterhaus, commander of the southern region of the state, agreed that the activities of his troops should be limited, and he directed his officers not to interfere with any cotton "which is not positively declared to be Government property." He admonished his officers that "our policy must naturally be, to have all the cotton brought to market, in order to re-introduce money among the impoverished people, and you will therefore render such assistance as you consistently can, to attain that object."[23]

In spite of these instructions, illegal dabblings in cotton matters on the part of garrison troops continued. Finally, in late 1865, Major General Thomas J. Wood, the new commander of the department of Mississippi, effectively curtailed the improper conduct of military persons in this traffic. Wood also brought the authority of the army to the assistance of the civil officers in ferreting out persons who were representing themselves as Treasury agents or contractors and seizing cotton illegally.[24] Reform, however, in the collection of Confederate

[21] C. M. Vaiden to Sharkey, July 25, 1865, and James H. Maury to Sharkey, July 3, 1865, in Governors' Correspondence, E-70; Major General M. F. Force to Governor Humphreys, November, 1865, ibid., E-77; Robert Bowman, "Reconstruction in Yazoo County," Publications of the Mississippi Historical Society, VII (1903), 117.

[22] Copy of a letter from Sharkey to Secretary McCulloch, August 2, 1865, and McCulloch to Sharkey, August 5, 1865, in Governors' Correspondence, E-71.

[23] Instruction of General Osterhaus to his officers, July 27, 1865, ibid., E-70.

[24] Wood reported to his superiors that when he assumed command in Mississippi he found that "a fruitful source of corruption among the officers and of complaints from citizens was the improper and illegal dabbling of officers in the collection and disposition of cotton alleged to have belonged to the so-called Confederate States." "Message of the President of the United States and Accompanying Documents to the Two Houses of Congress, at the Commencement of the Second Session of the 39th Congress," House Executive Documents, 39th Cong., 2nd Sess., No. 1, p. 52. See also General Wood to Humphreys, February 12, 1866, in Governors' Correspondence, E-78.

cotton occurred late, since most of the cotton stored during the war had been appropriated or marketed by the winter of 1865–66. Of the estimated 127,341 bales of Confederate cotton held in Mississippi in late 1864, only 20,240 were collected and sold through the proper Treasury channels after June 1, 1865.[25] Thus it is evident that most of the Confederate cotton of the state, even after taking into consideration losses by destruction during the last months of the war, was appropriated and sold illegally by government agents and their collaborators, or by local citizens, some of whom may well have been the original owners of the staple.

Denied jurisdiction over alleged government cotton, Governor Sharkey established special courts of equity to try all cases of disputed private property, especially cotton. The decisions of these "cotton courts" were to be final. The reconstruction convention gave constitutional sanction to these tribunals but provided that they should be dissolved when the regular courts were established.[26] A few members of the new government who took office in October, 1865, felt that the cotton courts should be continued, since they were proving successful in settling vexatious claims. Their opponents, however, thought that the judges were too energetic in sustaining the claims of creditors. After considerable debate the legislature passed a bill declaring the special courts of equity dissolved and transferring their business to the regular courts. Governor Benjamin G. Humphreys, a Whig of strong property-right principles, rejected the measure, but the legislature mustered the two-thirds vote necessary to override his veto.[27]

Civil disturbance was the greatest problem confronting the provisional government during the summer of 1865. A drift toward

[25] "Seizure of Cotton," *Senate Executive Documents,* 43rd Cong., 2nd Sess., No. 23, pp. 58, 64–69.

[26] Meridian *Clarion,* October 13, 1865; New Orleans *Picayune,* November 2, 8, 1865.

[27] New Orleans *Picayune,* November 8, 1865. The legislature also sought to halt the continuing fraudulent transactions in cotton. The southwestern part of the state, near the Mississippi River and near the marketing centers of Natchez and New Orleans, by late 1865 was the center of the trade in stolen and disputed cotton. The legislature enacted a measure declaring that "to send cotton to market otherwise than in bales put up in the usual loose bags, sacks or bundles . . . shall be *prima facie* evidence of the same having been stolen or fraudulently acquired." *Laws of the State of Mississippi, Passed at a Regular Session of the Mississippi Legislature, Held in the City of Jackson, October, November, and December 1865* (Jackson: J. J. Shannon and Co., State Printers, 1866), 168, hereinafter cited as *Laws of Mississippi, 1865.*

anarchy had developed during the last months of the war, and it did not abate with the coming of peace and the establishment of the Sharkey regime. After a form of civil government was established in the counties, the military became reluctant to take the initiative in suppressing disorders, except occasionally to maintain justice for Negroes and to aid Treasury agents.[28] Local governments, however, were extremely weak and were incapable of restoring law and order without military assistance. From all areas of the interior people wrote Sharkey of the operations of lawless white groups in their communities and pleaded with him to do something to protect life and property.[29] One newspaper correspondent reported that from the descriptions that the delegates to the reconstruction convention had given, "it is certain that a most frightful amount of crime and lawlessness exists in all parts of the State."[30]

The activities of lawbreakers and desperadoes were not primarily directed against the freedmen, nor were they politically motivated. Frontier conditions existed in Mississippi in 1865, and felonious crimes were common. Benjamin G. Truman, an observer for the President, reported that "Mississippians have been shooting and cutting each other all over the State, to a greater extent than in all the other States of the Union put together. . . . I read of cutting and shooting in every little paper I take up, while I have seen more of it in the last few days than I saw in New York in six years." [31] Judge Jason Niles recorded in his diary that violence resulting in death was a usual occurrence in central Mississippi.[32]

The prevalence of disorders of all types throughout the state, and the inability of local officials to cope with them without substantial aid from the military, convinced Governor Sharkey that vigorous mea-

[28] Copy of a letter from Sharkey to General Osterhaus, August 22, 1865; W. J. Taylor to Sharkey, July 22, 1865, in Governors' Correspondence, E-71; Sharkey to President Johnson, August 25, 1865, in Johnson Papers. For a description of these disturbances at the end of the war, see above, pp. 35–36.

[29] For example, see the petition of members of the bar and civil officers of Pontotoc County to Sharkey, July 17, 1865, in Governors' Correspondence, E-70; Milton Bacon and J. J. Davenport to Sharkey, September 20, 1865; J. Evans to Sharkey, September 3, 1865; ibid., E-72; Resolutions of a meeting of citizens of Itawamba County, undated, ibid., E-69; Carl Schurz to Johnson, August 29, 1865; Mayor W. T. Epperson of Yazoo City to Sharkey, undated, in Johnson Papers.

[30] Mobile Advertiser and Register, August 27, 1865.

[31] New York Times, February 4, 1866.

[32] Niles Diary, August 25, October 5, 1865.

sures were necessary to restore peace. He appealed to the officers in command of the occupation troops to render active assistance to civil authorities in apprehending law violators and placing them in the military stockade at Jackson, if necessary, for safekeeping while awaiting civil trial. The army commander in west Mississippi promised to aid the governor, and some Federal provost marshals in this section took action in support of the civil officials' war on desperadoes.[33] In some of the river counties, which had been under Federal control since 1863, the provost marshals were permitted to enroll militia units consisting of local persons for the maintenance of law and order.[34]

The dispersal and strength of the troops, however, was not sufficient to sustain the efforts of the civil authorities in the interior of the state. Furthermore, the mass substitution of Negro troops for whites, who were being mustered from the army, confounded the cooperative endeavors of army and local officials to stamp out lawlessness and produced tension and conflict between the races. With the stationing of the first Negro soldiers in rural garrisons, local whites began vociferously complaining ot a deterioration in relations between them and the occupation forces. County officials ceased to call upon Federal officers, who now commanded Negro military units, for assistance.[35]

As white hostility toward black troops increased, many Negro soldiers found excuses to use their authority and their assumed immunity from punishment to show their resentment toward the old master class. Mainly they resorted to committing small offenses and using intemperate and abusive language in the presence of whites.[36] At times, however, depredations were perpetrated on whites and weaker "country" blacks.[37] Twice during 1865 Negro troops and white

[33] *Convention Journal, 1865,* p. 5.

[34] Colonel William E. Bayley to Sharkey, July 10, 1865, and J. M. Patridge to Sharkey, July 25, 1865, in Governors' Correspondence, E-70.

[35] Copy of a letter from Sharkey to General Osterhaus, August 22, 1865, *ibid.,* E-71; petition of citizens of Chickasaw County to Sharkey, undated, *ibid.,* E-72; Sharkey to President Johnson, August 28, 1865, in Johnson Papers.

[36] Memphis *Appeal,* November 10, 1865; Natchez *Democrat,* November 23, 1865; John W. C. Watson to Governor Humphreys, November 29, 1865, in Governors' Correspondence, E-77.

[37] J. M. Wade to Sharkey, August 23, 1865, in Johnson Papers; Friar's Point *Coahomian,* November 24, 1865. Oftentimes when depredations were alleged to have been committed against whites, accounts of these incidents were exaggerated. For example, compare the petition of citizens of Chickasaw County to Sharkey, undated, in Governors' Correspondence, E-72, reporting such "outrages," with the report of the officer who was dispatched by General Osterhaus to make

militiamen met and engaged in minor skirmishes. Individual clashes resulting in violence between whites and Negro soldiers were not uncommon and resulted on several occasions in military intervention to secure justice, or possibly favoritism, for the Negroes.[38]

In most cases of conflict, Negro soldiers probably committed no overt acts against the native whites.[39] Nevertheless, even when the troops maintained proper military discipline, planters claimed that their presence had the effect of demoralizing the "country" Negroes, who in most cases, they said, were settling down and working faithfully at the time of the arrival of the Negro soldiers. Thereafter, contracts were frequently broken and an increase in irregular acts by freedmen was reported.[40] Sharkey complained to President Johnson that "the negroes congregate around the negro garrisons in great numbers, and are idle and guilty of many petty crimes." The governor admitted that a few of the garrison commanders had dispersed the "country" blacks, but he feared that a majority of them had not taken action against vagrant freedmen around their camps. Sharkey likewise accused the officers of the Freedmen's Bureau of encouraging Negro idleness. The New Orleans *Picayune* also claimed that the presence of Negro troops had disrupted the labor system. It asserted that the development of the new railroad town of Hazlehurst was being retarded because it was impossible to secure labor for construction work with Negro troops in town.[41]

With widespread white lawlessness and with threats of Negro disorders and defiance reported, Sharkey sought to re-establish state

a "thorough investigation of the depredations." Lieutenant Colonel John J. Bishop to Osterhaus, October 5, 1865, *ibid.*

[38] J. L. Milton to Governor Humphreys, December 4, 1865; James T. Semmes to Humphreys, October 31, 1865; Major General M. F. Force to Humphreys, December 22, 31, 1865, all in Governors' Correspondence, E-77; Natchez *Democrat*, December 5, 1865; Friar's Point *Coahomian*, December 8, 1865; Raymond *Hinds County Gazette*, December 23, 30, 1865, January 20, 1866.

[39] See, for example, the New Orleans *Picayune*, November 17, 1865, the Jackson *Clarion*, April 19, 1866, and Hattie Magee, "Reconstruction in Lawrence and Jefferson Counties," *Publications of the Mississippi Historical Society*, XI (1910), 178.

[40] A. Gillespie to Sharkey, July 29, 1865, in Governors' Correspondence, E-70; H. H. Montgomery to Sharkey, August 16, 1865, *ibid.*, E-71; citizens of Noxubee County to Humphreys, October 31, 1865, *ibid.*, E-77; Memphis *Appeal*, November 10, 1865.

[41] Sharkey to President Johnson, August 28, 1865, in Johnson Papers; New Orleans *Picayune*, November 17, 1865.

militia units in counties where Federal troops were not providing adequate protection for the people. At first he suggested to local officials that they re-institute the county patrol system, but this plan failed, probably because of the inchoate state of the provisional government at the time and because of the failure of Sharkey to give continuing encouragement to the scheme.[42] Sharkey next attempted to use militia forces which had already been enrolled by Federal officers and had been sanctioned by the department commander. But most of these units were found in the fairly stable and orderly river counties; the real need for militia forces existed in the interior regions of the state.[43]

Reacting to pressure from citizens and probably from members of the reconstruction convention then in session, Sharkey on August 17, 1865, issued a proclamation calling upon the people to organize two militia companies in each county for the suppression of crime and disorders. He particularly urged those who were familiar with military discipline, namely former Confederate soldiers, to come forward and serve as the nucleus of these organizations.[44] Three days later, as if to stifle anticipated opposition to his proclamation, Sharkey wired the President explaining the reasons for his action and asking that the state's arms be returned for use by the militia. The Freedmen's Bureau, Sharkey declared, "is badly mismanaged here" and doing much harm. "The negroes are bold in their threats, and the people are afraid. I have called for volunteer companies of militia in each county to suppress crime, which is becoming alarming. . . . I may think it necessary to organize the whole of the militia." [45]

Events now moved rapidly toward a clash between the provisional governor and suspicious military authorities. Upon receiving information of proposed meetings of young men in the Jackson area to form militia companies, General Osterhaus immediately, and probably

[42] Petition of citizens of Madison County, undated, in Petitions to Reconstruction Convention, 1865, Legislative Records, File I–119, Mississippi Department of Archives and History, Jackson; *Convention Journal, 1865*, p. 5. The attitude of the military commanders toward the re-establishment of the antebellum system for patrolling the counties is unknown.

[43] James Allen to Sharkey, July 11, 1865; Colonel William E. Bayley to Sharkey, July 10, 1865; Milton Bacon and J. J. Davenport to Sharkey, September 20, 1865, all in Governors' Correspondence, E-70.

[44] Meridian *Clarion*, August 25, 1865.

[45] Sharkey to Johnson, August 20, 1865, in Johnson Papers.

without consulting his superiors, reminded Sharkey that Mississippi was still under military occupation and that martial law was still in force. Therefore, the general declared, no military organizations would be tolerated except those under the control of United States officers. Osterhaus, who evidently was sincerely alarmed at the prospects of Confederates in arms again, assured the governor that the number of Federal troops in the Jackson area was sufficient to give civil authorities all the assistance that they might need to prevent crime.[46]

Sharkey replied that he regretted the general's position or view of the proclamation, and "I beg to remind you that for twelve of fifteen consecutive nights, passengers traveling in the stages between here and Vicksburg have been robbed, and these things have occurred within twelve or fifteen miles of your own headquarters." Notwithstanding the number of these depredations committed in communities garrisoned by army troops, the greatest number of outrages were being perpetrated in remote parts of the state where there was no military force, Sharkey said. It was to give these areas relief that he called for the organization of militia companies. If authority were needed for his action, Sharkey informed Osterhaus "that in the last interview I had with the President, in speaking of anticipated trouble, he distinctly stated to me that I could organize the militia if it should become necessary." In conclusion, the governor assured Osterhaus that "this is not in any sense a hostile demonstration" against the military or the United States, and he felt quite sure "that no evil can result from it."[47]

The militia imbroglio was now referred to Major General Henry W. Slocum, commander of the department of Mississippi and Osterhaus' superior, with headquarters at Vicksburg. Slocum had earlier made it clear that the power to organize the militia rested solely with Sharkey.[48] Now, however, probably desirous of sustaining his subordinate, Slocum urged his superiors in Washington to revoke Sharkey's proclamation. Johnson immediately ordered Sharkey to cease the organization of militia companies and instructed him that, if he needed military force to preserve order and enforce the law, he should request it of the department commander. Slocum now issued a general order denouncing Sharkey's proclamation as unauthorized and

[46] Osterhaus to Sharkey, August 21, 1865, in Governors' Correspondence, E-71.
[47] Copy of a letter from Sharkey to Osterhaus, August 22, 1865, *ibid.*
[48] Colonel L. M. Hall to Sharkey, August 1, 1865, *ibid.*

at the same time ordered his district officers to prevent the formation of militia units.[49]

To this, Governor Sharkey replied in a letter to the President, elaborating on his reasons for forming the militia and including a reason that he had not mentioned in his proclamation or in his letter to Osterhaus. Beyond the need for protection from disorderly whites, he declared, "there is also a wide spread opinion among the people, and it is justified by threats, that about Christmas [Negroes] intend a general uprising for the purpose of taking property, as they say that they have not yet got all their rights. It was to satisfy the people, and begin preparation for such an emergency, and to suppress crime, that I ordered the organization of the militia." [50] Sharkey, reinforced by William Yerger's recollection of the interview with the President at Washington, reminded Johnson that he had distinctly said during the conference that the militia could be called out to maintain law and order. In explanation of General Slocum's opposition, Sharkey derisively declared: "His chief reason seems to be because I did not consult him. Here is a collision that must be settled, and it exists with you to do it. I wish to be able to vindicate myself when trouble comes, as we apprehend it will." [51]

In a remarkable reversal, President Johnson now withdrew his earlier instructions concerning the militia proclamation, in spite of Carl Schurz's observation from Mississippi that the general's course "is the only one by which public order and security can be maintained." [52] The President telegraphed Schurz at Vicksburg that "I presume Genl. Slocum will issue no order interfering with Gov. Sharkey in restoring the function of the State Govt. without first consulting the Government, giving the reason for such proposed interference." Johnson declared that the provisional governor should be able to organize in each county militia units to suppress crime and prevent disorders.[53]

[49] Johnson to Sharkey, August 24, 1865, *ibid.;* "Condition of the South," *Senate Executive Documents,* 39th Cong., 1st Sess., No. 2, pp. 62–63.

[50] Sharkey to Johnson, August 28, 1865, in Johnson Papers.

[51] Sharkey to Johnson, August 31, 1865, *ibid.;* William Yerger to Sharkey, August 29, 1865, in Governors' Correspondence, E-71.

[52] Schurz, *Reminiscences,* III, 191.

[53] Copy of a telegram from President Johnson to Schurz, September 1, 1865, in Governors' Correspondence, E-71. Johnson had sent Sharkey a copy of this telegram. In the message Johnson rebuked Schurz for his interference in the militia controversy. "The main object of Major General Carl Schurz's mission to the

Clearly Sharkey was elated over his triumph, and he asked Johnson if he could publish the President's dispatch to Schurz, "since it would sooth a troubled public mind [and] . . . give implicit confidence in you."[54]   Johnson granted the desired permission, and the militia controversy was reported in detail in newspapers throughout the North and South.[55] The President's action in permitting this publicizing of the conflict undoubtedly was unwise, since it could not but further demoralize his military commanders in Mississippi. Then, too, it was his contradictory policies that had created much of the confusion that had let to the humiliation of his officers. Furthermore, the mismanagement of the affair by Johnson gave the Radicals another reason to attack his administration. Even Northern moderates thought that he was "traveling a little too fast" in permitting the organization of the Mississippi militia, which would consist predominantly of former Confederate soldiers.[56]

Schurz continued to take issue with the President on the militia question and argued that militia patrols "indulged in the gratification of private vengeance, persecuted helpless Union people and freedmen, and endeavored to keep the plantation negroes in a state of virtual slavery."[57] These charges appear not to have been without foundation. As rumors and threats of a Negro insurrection multiplied during the fall of 1865, race tensions increased and whites in some areas found it convenient to terrorize helpless blacks. Oscar J. E. Stuart,

---

south was to aid as far as practical in carrying out the policy adopted by the government for restoring the States to their former relation with the federal government. It is hoped such aid has been given."

[54] Sharkey to Johnson, September 2, 1865, in Johnson Papers.

[55] Professor Eric L. McKitrick in his *Andrew Johnson and Reconstruction* (Chicago: University of Chicago Press, 1960), 183, 192–95, severely indicts the President for humiliating "publicly and deliberately two Union major generals [Slocum and Schurz] for doing what they had assumed to be their duty." In spite of this "humiliation," Slocum supported Johnson's program for reconstruction, subsequently resigning his commission to run for secretary of state of New York on the Democratic ticket. New York *Tribune,* October 9, 1865; Meridian *Clarion,* October 4, 1865. Slocum later served several terms in Congress as a Democrat from New York. *Dictionary of American Biography,* XVII, 217.

[56] See, for example, the New York *Times,* September 5, 1865. Actually, the organization of the militia was not pushed by Sharkey, apparently because he recognized the political necessity for mollifying the North on the matter. Furthermore, lack of arms delayed the formation of companies in the counties. Schurz to Johnson, September 26, 1865, in Johnson Papers; John Pickford to Sharkey, October 4, 1865, in Governors' Correspondence, E-72.

[57] Schurz to Johnson, September 4, 1865, in Johnson Papers.

militia commander for southwest Mississippi, after an inspection tour of his counties, reported that "there has been some irregularity in the action of the Militia, which might be attended with mischievous consequences, and I have issued a general order for their better action."[58] Governor Humphreys, who had assumed control and improved upon Sharkey's militia, ordered the disbanding of several militia companies upon receiving information that they were committing depredations on the freedmen. But still bands of armed whites posing as militiamen were reported to be attacking and robbing Negroes. Unauthorized groups of men were found by Stuart to be "rambling through the country, generally at night, blacked or masked, shooting at, and otherwise maltreating the negroes." Because of the earlier rebuke by the President on the militia question, Federal officers did not intervene to suppress these groups but worked through Governor Humphreys to prevent attacks on Negroes.[59] In essence, the organization of the militia probably aided in the restoration of law and order in the state, but it is evident that in some localities companies of white men, whether authorized or not, added to the difficulties confronting responsible officials there.

Even after the elected state officers were installed in October, 1865, Federal troops, in addition to Freedmen's Bureau officials, remained in the state and occasionally intervened to insure what they considered to be justice for the freedmen. But after General Wood assumed command of the department in November, military interference became rare, and military occupation became more palatable for the whites.[60]

[58] Oscar J. E. Stuart to Governor Humphreys, December 8, 1865, in Governors' Correspondence, E-77; General Wood to Humphreys, January 8, 1866, ibid., E-78.

[59] Port Gibson Standard, January 27, 1866; Trowbridge, The Desolate South, 197; Stuart to Humphreys, December 8, 1865; Wood to Humphreys, November 27, 1865, in Governors' Correspondence, E-77. Humphreys in his first general order, November 3, 1865, admonished his militia officers to do their duty and "to aid the civil authorities in the suppression of crime and the prevention of lawlessness of all kinds." Militiamen "are not authorized to take the law into their own hands and be judge and jury—such conduct would rather add to, than decrease the evils that surround us. . . . It should [also] be borne in mind that any oppression of any class of the population of the State is not only contrary to law and will bring sure and speedy punishment upon the offenders, but it is also contrary to good policy."

[60] Wood also was appointed in February, 1866, assistant commissioner of the Freedmen's Bureau for Mississippi, after acting for two months as head of the bureau in the state.

Wood, a native of Kentucky, from the beginning was sympathetic with conservative groups in the state, preferring a policy of "cordial cooperation" with civil authorities in matters pertaining to Negroes rather than direct intervention to secure redress for wrongs. Even when forced to act strongly in preventing the enforcement of the more discriminatory measures passed by the legislature of 1865, commonly referred to as the Black Code, Wood reminded the civil officers that "the military authorities have very delicate duties to perform; that under the orders of their superior—not of their own seeking, they are specially charged with the interests and protection of a helpless and ignorant race." [61] By the fall of 1866 General Wood had ceased to intervene in civil affairs, believing that no cases involving freedmen had arisen which proved "the impracticability of securing justice to them through the civil tribunals of the State." [62]

General Wood, furthermore, sought to remove the most disagreeable feature of Federal occupation—Negro troops. Upon his recommendation, the War Department ordered in January, 1866, the mustering out of seven Negro regiments. In April Wood's superiors directed that the remaining black regiments be disbanded, and by June all Negro troops in Mississippi had been removed. Only a small battalion of regular infantry remained, along with officers of the Freedmen's Bureau.[63]

Wood's policy of conciliation and sympathy made desirable and politically possible cooperation on the part of state officers with the military and the Freedmen's Bureau in undoing or mitigating subsequently passed obnoxious laws pertaining to the freedmen.[64] A

[61] Wood to Humphreys, November 27, 1865, in Governors' Correspondence, E-77; Wood to Humphreys, March 14, 1866; Wood to Humphreys, February 14, 1866, *ibid.*, E-78. For a discussion of the labor provisions of the Black Code, see Chap. 5; and for an account of the proceedings in the legislature which led to the formulation of these measures and other acts which attempted to define the place of the Negro in Mississippi, see Chap. 7.

[62] "Freedmen's Affairs," *Senate Executive Documents,* 39th Cong., 2nd Sess., No. 6, p. 96.

[63] Garner, *Reconstruction in Mississippi,* 106–107.

[64] Governor Humphreys evinced the highest praise for General Wood's relations with the civil authorities. Humphreys declared in his October 16, 1866, address to the legislature that since Wood had been commander of the department "no violent collison has yet occurred between the State and Federal authorities, and I fear none so long as the military District of Mississippi is under the administration of the present distinguished military commander, who has, in the settlement of the many delicate questions that have arisen, shown so just a sentiment toward

similar spirit of cooperation and understanding between military and civil officials during the summer and fall of 1865 might have lessened or moderated the forces at work in Mississippi which demanded a settlement of the Negro problem based on tradition rather than on the sober realities of postwar adjustment.

our State and people." Humphreys' address is printed in *Appleton's Annual Cyclopaedia and Register of Important Events* (New York: Appleton, 1861–75), VI, 520–21.

5

The Travail of Freedom

THE CIVIL WAR had dislocated the economy of Missisippi, and it had shattered a labor and social system which was based on fixed attitudes and behavior and conditioned by experience and tradition. The fertile, fresh lands had not been destroyed, however, and these still represented the greatest potential resource of the state.[1] With upland cotton selling for as much as forty-five cents a pound on the Memphis and New Orleans markets in May, 1865, and for more than fifty cents in October and November of the same year, it was apparent that the great hope for rapid recovery was based on the restoration of the production of this staple.[2] To secure the greatest possible benefit from this resource, planters would have to plant, harvest, and market their cotton before the price declined to the levels of the 1850's.

Newspaper editors, political leaders, planters, and merchants were well aware that economic recovery for both individuals and the state depended upon revenue derived from cotton.[3] Cotton was king in 1865—a position that it had never been able to attain during the war, although there were many who had sought to make it king at that

[1] In 1880 a special Bureau of the Census report on the cultivation and production of cotton affirmed the desirability of the soils of the state. The report concluded that "few of the cotton states can compare with Mississippi as to the extent of the area occupied by first class soils, such as those of the Yazoo bottom, tablelands, and prairies, the like of which cannot be found, save in small bodies, in the Atlantic states." U.S. Bureau of the Census, *Tenth Census of the United States: 1880, Cotton Production,* 79.

[2] Boyle, *Cotton and the New Orleans Cotton Exchange,* 180; New Orleans *Price Current,* December 9, 1865; Raymond *Hinds County Gazette,* December 2, 1865; Friar's Point *Coahomian,* October 20, 1865.

[3] For example, see the Raymond *Hinds County Gazette,* February 2, 1866, and the Jackson *Clarion,* December 19, 1865.

time. But in spite of the inducements that the cultivation and marketing of this staple offered to Mississippians, there were several barriers to be surmounted before cotton production could be resumed on a large scale. Of these, probably the greatest, and certainly the most perplexing, was that of labor. Potentially an adequate labor force was available in the state after the war, although, according to an estimate made in late 1865, one fourth of the white men had died in the war and thousands of soldiers who returned were maimed or sick and unable to perform heavy manual labor.[4] Former slaves, who had provided the major source of labor during the antebellum era, remained in the state in 1865 and, notwithstanding a general belief that they would not work without compulsion, held the most important key to the labor problem and to the restoration of the cotton economy of Mississippi. Planters were skeptical of the reliability and efficiency of the Negro as a free worker, and the all-absorbing questions for them during the first few months after the war were, "Will the Negro work," and "Can cotton be produced profitably with free labor?"[5] The answers to these questions depended upon the extent and rapidity of adjustment by the former slaves to freedom and its responsibilities and upon the acceptance by planters of the changed status of the Negro and of the need to deal justly with him.

The irresponsible practices and behavior of the Negroes at the first flush of freedom suggested that their adjustment to postwar conditions would be indeed difficult and would be attended with severe sufferings for many. Months before the end of the war, river towns and Delta villages were overrun with Negroes; and after the war many of the newly freed slaves of the interior moved to Columbus, Meridian, Jackson, and other towns to celebrate the "day of jubilee." In these towns the freedmen lived in wretched poverty and died by the hundreds when the Negro ghettoes were swept by epidemics of cholera and smallpox.[6] A doctor in Aberdeen reported almost one year after the end of the war that in his town with a Negro population of 2,000 two thirds were "absolutely indigent" and 10 per cent were continually sick.[7]

[4] See Chap. 2, p. 27.

[5] Moore, "Social and Economic Conditions in Mississippi during Reconstruction," 30.

[6] Wharton, The Negro in Mississippi, 51–53; Reid, After the War, 456.

[7] J. M. Greene to Governor Humphreys, March 12, 1866, in Governors' Correspondence, E-78.

The majority of the freedmen remained at home, and many of the others returned to the plantations after one disillusioning trip to town. Those who lived on large, well-managed plantations especially tended to be faithful to their old masters.[8] Yet most of these Negroes were dependent upon their former owners and, to a limited extent, the Freedmen's Bureau to provide subsistence and clothing for them. At the same time, almost wholly inexperienced in matters of property ownership, they continued the antebellum practice of appropriating the property of their old masters. That pilfering was not a habit peculiar to freedom for the blacks was attested to by one planter when he admitted that the Negroes had pilfered more when in slavery than they did in freedom. After visiting the state, Whitelaw Reid reported that to the freedmen "petty pilfering seemed as natural to three fourths of them as eating."[9]

Without a clear conception of the responsibilities of freedom, many who stayed at home refused to work when given the least excuse to go to town or to visit their neighbors. Judge Robert S. Hudson, a leader in the reconstruction convention, wrote President Johnson that the "country" Negroes were living in "idleness and utter demoralization. The freedmen generally refused to work in the fields on any terms. . . . If not allowed to do as they pleased in every respect, [they ran] to town to make complaint" to the Freedmen's Bureau or to the provost marshal. Although the Federal officers instructed them to return to the plantation, several days were lost, and Hudson claimed that the "constant repetition and recurrence of this thing" rendered their labor valueless, even if they labor well when at home. He declared that he was merely "boarding" his old slaves.[10] Still others reported the general inefficiency of those who remained at home. A correspondent to the New Orleans *Picayune* wrote that, although most of the slaves in the interior of Mississippi stayed with their masters, "not in a single

[8] See, for example, Thomas E. B. Pegues to Secretary of State William H. Seward, September 4, 1865, in Amnesty Papers, Mississippi; Robert S. Hudson to President Johnson, November 2, 1865, in Johnson Papers; Henry W. Warren, *Reminiscences of a Mississippi Carpetbagger* (Worcester, Massachusetts: The Davis Press, 1914), 18; Smedes, *A Southern Planter*, 228; and Reid, *After the War*, 478.

[9] Meridian *Clarion*, June 22, 1865; New York *Times*, July 2, 1866; E. H. Saunders to Sharkey, July 15, 1865, in Governors' Correspondence, E-70; Reid, *After the War*, 303.

[10] Hudson to Johnson, November 2, 1865, in Johnson Papers.

instance have we heard that they prove of one half of their ordinary value as laborers," working only when constantly supervised.[11]

Because of the difficulties involved in the transfer of the inexperienced and ignorant Negroes from slavery to freedom, it was evident that some agency was necessary to aid them in adjusting to their new position in society. On March 2, 1865, a bill had been passed by Congress and signed by President Lincoln on the same day, creating the Bureau of Refugees, Freedmen, and Abandoned Lands in the War Department, with the purpose of assisting the Negroes in their adjustment. President Johnson, following Lincoln's decision, appointed the able General Oliver O. Howard commissioner of the bureau. Not until May 30, 1865, did Howard order the establishment of the Freedmen's Bureau in Mississippi, with Colonel Samuel Thomas as assistant commissioner.[12] Simultaneously, General Howard directed that the new agency was to strive to make the Negroes self-supporting and to discontinue as soon as possible relief measures that had been initiated during the war. Officers of the bureau were instructed to settle all difficulties arising between freedmen and whites, or between freedmen, except in cases involving men in the army. Negroes were to be free to choose their own employers, and they were to be paid for their labor. Family ties were to be solemnized by marriage, and plans for education were to be made.[13] A few days after issuing these instructions, Howard reminded Thomas that his officers should show a spirit of moderation toward the whites in the performance of their duties, since "the constraints and exactions of military law are neither normal or congenial to the American spirit. . . . It is absolutely necessary to have officers above corruption and prejudice, who propose to do simple justice." [14]

The organization and strength of the bureau in Mississippi varied

[11] New Orleans *Picayune,* December 2, 1865. See also the Raymond *Hinds County Gazette,* March 30, 1866.

[12] "Report of General Oliver O. Howard, December 1865," *House Executive Documents,* 39th Cong., 1st Sess., No. 11, p. 45. For a detailed account of the Freedmen's Bureau in Mississippi, largely gleaned from the reports and circulars of bureau officers, see Clifton L. Ganus, Jr., "The Freedmen's Bureau in Mississippi" (Ph.D. dissertation, Tulane University, 1953).

[13] General Howard's instructions may be found in the Friar's Point *Coahomian,* September 29, 1865.

[14] Letter of advice from Howard to assistant commissioners, June 14, 1865, in Governors' Correspondence, E-69.

from time to time, but at first Colonel Thomas divided the state into three districts, each of which had a senior officer in charge of the bureau agents in the counties. At first, these officers were mainly, if not exclusively, former officers in Negro regiments. In December, 1865, there were fifty-eight local officers and sixty-seven teachers, plus numerous medical officers and attendants, in the service of the bureau.[15] Apparently no agents were sent to several of the predominantly white counties, and in several other localities bureau officers were withdrawn in early 1866. In at least two communities native whites were eventually appointed as agents, one of whom was a former Confederate officer.[16]

There is little doubt that some bureau representatives in Mississippi were guilty of misconduct in office. This, however, was limited to minor officials and only rarely did it take the form of outright corruption.[17] Apparently the most common act of malfeasance was that of charging planters more than the authorized fifty cents for registering labor contracts. A major conflict between civil and military authorities occurred as a result of this practice when an offending bureau agent was arrested and jailed at Hazlehurst by local authorities. General Osterhaus, commanding the southern district of the state, demanded his release; and when it was refused he dispatched an armed force consisting of Negro troops to free the officer. The officer in charge of the detail not only released the bureau agent but also jailed the civil official who had arrested him. Governor Humphreys immediately wrote the President that civil authority had been blatantly defied and asked Johnson to intervene against the military. The President replied, sustaining the civil officers and ordering that there be no further military interference of this type.[18]

[15] Garner, *Reconstruction in Mississippi*, 254; John S. McNeily, "From Organization to Overthrow of Mississippi's Provisional Government," *Publications of the Mississippi Historical Society, Centenary Series*, I (1916), 213–14.

[16] Jackson *Clarion*, April 10, May 3, 1866; Jackson *Clarion and Standard*, May 30, 1866; William D. Lyles to Governor Humphreys, December 31, 1865, in Governors' Correspondence, E-77; [George C. Benham], *A Year of Wreck: A True Story by a Victim* (New York: Harper and Brothers, 1880), 222–23.

[17] Natchez *Democrat*, November 25, 1865; Jackson *Clarion and Standard*, May 24, 1866; Major General Alvan C. Gillem to M. A. Lathrop, December, 1865, in Freedmen's Bureau Records, Mississippi; Reid, *After the War*, 577.

[18] General Osterhaus to Humphreys, October 25, 1865, in Governors' Correspondence, E-77. Johnson also ordered that the offending officer be removed

One of the major tasks of Colonel Thomas and his officers was to provide for the physical needs of the destitute and sick freedmen. In 1865, 182,889 rations were issued to Negroes and the following year 170,018, of which 16,129 were furnished to "refugees," apparently whites, and 154,889 to freedmen. General Howard, however, ordered on August 22, 1866, that the issuance of provisions be discontinued, except to freedmen in bureau hospitals and asylums.[19] Although the dispensing of rations was one of the greatest causes of complaint by the whites against the bureau, it is evident from the above figures that only a small portion of the Negroes, for a limited period of time, could have received these government doles regularly. For example, at the rate at which the bureau issued rations in 1865 only 2,975 blacks could have been entirely sustained for the year on these provisions.

Bureau hospitals were established in ten towns to care for mentally and physically sick freedmen. These hospitals were little more than dispensaries and were unsuited for their intended purpose. Most of these hospitals were closed by July, 1866.[20] Of broader significance were the efforts of the bureau to encourage the Negro to follow better health and sanitary practices. Local medical doctors under contract to the bureau were directed to inspect their particular districts and to take action to secure obedience to rules of sanitation on the part of the Negroes. Their task of improving the health habits of the freedman was quite formidable, if not impossible at the time.

Education of Negroes was given a great deal of attention by the Freedmen's Bureau from the beginning of the organization in the state. Officials of the bureau hoped that through schooling the freedmen would be better prepared to improve their position in society. Dr. Joseph Warren, the bureau's superintendent of education in Mississippi, refused to hire teachers directly, preferring to work through Northern benevolent and missionary societies. However, he often

---

from his command. Humphreys to Johnson, November 1, 1865, in Johnson Papers; New York *Tribune*, November 24, 1865; New Orleans *Picayune*, November 8, 1865.

[19] "Reports of the Assistant Commissioners of the Freedmen's Bureau Made since December 1, 1865," *Senate Executive Documents*, 39th Cong., 1st Sess., No. 27, p. 30. A ration was designed to sustain an individual for a few days, but not to exceed one week. "Report of General Oliver O. Howard, December 1865," *House Executive Documents*, 39th Cong., 1st Sess., No. 11, p. 47.

[20] Information concerning bureau health and educational activities in the state comes primarily from Ganus, "The Freedmen's Bureau in Mississippi," 148, 169, 173, 307–308, 312, 322.

provided the facilities for the schooling. The professional abilities of the Northern teachers varied. Some were college graduates, while others were self-taught and could barely write an intelligible letter. Almost all who came believed that the basic need of the Negroes was for moral and religious instruction. Warren admonished these teachers to avoid politics and to win the respect of Mississippians by a pleasing personality and faithful performance of duties. In general, whites refused to accept the Northern teachers, and many of them were ostracized and even persecuted.[21] Conservative whites of the state gradually came to the conclusion that in order to stifle the training of Negroes by Northern teachers, the work should be undertaken by Mississippians. Interest in native-directed education for the freedmen reached its height in 1866 and 1867, and was encouraged by General Wood. But the movement was almost completely without results because of the hostility of large numbers of whites and a lack of funds.[22]

Although the great bulk of the Negro population, even if interested, could not be served by the bureau schools, the efforts in terms of numbers were impressive during the first year of the existence of these schools. By January, 1866, there were sixty-eight such institutions in Mississippi, with 5,271 pupils enrolled.[23] At this time Whitelaw Reid found a "feverish anxiety" for education on the part of Negroes in the towns and along the lines of communication and transportation. In the interior, where the planters retained a great deal of control, the freedmen were indifferent. After the middle of 1866 the number of students enrolled declined, but at the same time the quality of instruc-

[21] General Wood to Governor Humphreys, September 22, 1866, in Governors' Correspondence, E-80; Lieutenant H. R. Williams to Lieutenant Stuart Eldridge, May 16, 1866, ibid., E-79; Meridian Chronicle, March 13, 1868; Jackson Clarion, April 29, 1866.

[22] Meridian Semi-Weekly Gazette, April 24, 1867; Raymond Hinds County Gazette, July 13, 1866; Friar's Point Coahomian, April 20, 1866; Captain William Shields to Lieutenant Merritt Barber, January 31, 1868, in Freedmen's Bureau Records, Mississippi, 1865–68, Bureau of Refugees, Freedmen, and Abandoned Lands, National Archives. The purpose of the conservative-directed education also was to inculcate moral and religious values in the Negroes, but their objective in so doing was to instill industrious and obedient virtues in them. See a statement by Doctor C. K. Marshall, an influential Vicksburg minister, in the Jackson Clarion, December 16, 1866.

[23] "Reports of the Assistant Commissioners of the Freedmen's Bureau Made since December 1, 1865," Senate Executive Documents, 39th Cong., 1st Sess., No. 27, p. 31; Reid, After the War, 511.

tion improved.[24] Nevertheless, the accomplishments of the Freedmen's Bureau and the benevolent societies toward improving the condition of the Negro through education obviously fell far short of their visionary plans of the summer of 1865.

With disorders common and local governments ineffective during the summer of 1865, the Freedmen's Bureau acted to protect the virtually defenseless Negroes against whites who committed mean, and sometimes brutal, acts against the freedmen and to protect them against those who would deny justice to them. In a circular issued to his officers and to the freedmen on July 29, 1865, and in pursuance of earlier instructions from General Howard, Colonel Samuel Thomas directed that whenever civil officers and courts "do not do justice to the colored man, by refusing the testimony of colored witnesses, or in any other way, the freed people must apply to the nearest officer of the Bureau," who would adjudicate all such cases. Bureau officers were instructed by Thomas to open courts of record to try all petty cases and to punish those who violated the personal freedom of the Negroes. Complaints of abused freedmen, if substantiated, were to be followed by the prompt arrest and military trial of the offenders.[25]

The purpose of the bureau, as expressed by Federal officers in the state, was not to give the freedmen immunity from the law or to oppress the whites, but rather to insure them equality before the law.[26] Yet such an arbitrary system of administering justice could easily result in injustice to whites and, on occasion, to freedmen, particularly when the "Freedmen Courts" were presided over by unqualified young officers. The most serious cause for white complaints occurred where civil courts were open but bureau officials denied them jurisdiction over whites accused of offenses against Negroes. In cases in which whites were charged with serious crimes, Colonel Thomas bound them over to the regular army authorities for trial by a military commission.[27] A serious conflict between civil and military officials occurred on one occasion when General Henry W. Slocum arrested

[24] Ganus, "The Freedmen's Bureau in Mississippi," 334, 359.

[25] Fleming (ed.), *Documentary History of Reconstruction,* I, 337–38; Meridian *Clarion,* August 15, 1865.

[26] See General Wood to Governor Humphreys, March 1, 1866, in Governors' Correspondence, E-78. See also a statement by General Henry W. Slocum in the Natchez *Courier,* October 5, 1865.

[27] Thomas A. Marshall and Walker Brooke to Provisional Governor Sharkey, July 15, 1865, in Governors' Correspondence, E-70; Dan R. Russell to Governor Humphreys, January 12, 1866, *ibid.,* E-78.

Judge D. O. Merwin of Vicksburg for issuing a writ of habeas corpus to secure the release of a planter held by the military for trial. Governor Sharkey denounced Slocum's action and even threatened to resign his office if the civil officers were not sustained by the federal government. Evidently Judge Merwin was released, but the military retained jurisdiction in the case of the planter.[28]

It became apparent to Slocum that the anomaly of the dual military and civil courts would continue to create confusion and conflict if they were allowed to continue. In his general order of August 3, 1865, he directed that the regular military forces were not to interfere in the future in any cases involving freedmen where the civil courts were willing to give them the same privileges as were granted to whites.[29] Although independent of Slocum's command, Colonel Thomas approved this order and worked to secure an arrangement with Sharkey in which the Freedmen's Bureau courts could be discontinued. Thomas offered to turn over to the civil courts all jurisdiction in cases concerning freedmen, if the courts would recognize Negro testimony in litigation where their own interests were involved. Believing that the reconstruction convention had already implicitly bestowed upon the freedmen this legal privilege, Sharkey readily accepted Thomas' proposition. On September 25 the governor issued a proclamation directing that civil courts admit Negro testimony.[30] In spite of assertions by some radical state newspaper editors that Sharkey's proclamation would be nullified by the legislature and the subsequent failure of some courts to obey the edict, Colonel Thomas announced on October 31, 1865, that the proclamation had been carried out in such good faith that all Freedmen's Bureau courts would be abolished immediately. Officers of the bureau, however, were to continue to assist the Negroes in presenting their cases in court and in instructing them regarding their rights and responsibilities.[31] Meanwhile, the question of Negro

[28] D. O. Merwin to Sharkey, July 20, 1865, copy of a letter from Sharkey to Slocum, July 22, 1865; Slocum to Sharkey, July 25, 1865, all *ibid.*, E-70; C. A. Seward to Sharkey, August 3, 1865, *ibid.*, E-71.

[29] Wharton, *The Negro in Mississippi*, 76.

[30] Thomas to Sharkey, September 24, 1865; Lieutenant Stuart Eldridge to Lieutenant Colonel R. S. Donaldson, September 21, 1865, in Governors' Correspondence, E-72; New York *Tribune*, October 2, 1865; Meridian *Clarion*, October 4, 1865.

[31] New Orleans *Picayune*, November 4, 1865; "Report of the Commissioner of the Freedmen's Bureau," *House Executive Documents*, 39th Cong., 1st Sess., No. 70, p. 173; Friar's Point *Coahomian*, December 1, 1865.

testimony had become an important issue in the campaign for the election of state officers for the restoration government.

The difficulty of satisfying the Negroes' desire for land proved to be the most formidable and perplexing problem that the Freedmen's Bureau faced. Many, if not most, freedmen wanted to become land-owners, and they looked to the bureau to obtain their fabled "forty acres and a mule." Acts by Congress and the President during the war regarding captured and abandoned property tended to arouse in blacks the hope of future land divisions. Under the last of these measures, the Freedmen's Bureau Act, land which had been abandoned or acquired by confiscation or sale could be set aside for the use of freedmen.[32] As a result of this measure and other wartime acts, the bureau held in Mississippi by the summer of 1865 about 80,000 acres of farm land and 142 town lots.[33] These holdings, however, were entirely insufficient to provide a small farm for each Mississippi Negro family which desired one. Furthermore, the Freedmen's Bureau lost these properties soon after peace was restored.

On July 1, 1865, President Johnson directed the Freedmen's Bureau to restore to the owners all abandoned property in its possession, provided that the proprietors had been pardoned or had secured amnesty. Colonel Thomas interpreted these orders literally and, in fact, went beyond his instructions in ordering his officers not only to retain abandoned properties of unpardoned Confederates but also to seize the houses and lands of those whose pardons were not received immediately.[34] The President's intention was to pardon eventually all former Confederates who applied to him; however, he issued no clear directives amplifying his policy. Accordingly, Colonel Thomas and his officers misunderstood the President's intention; and, believing that these lands should be retained for the use of the freedmen, they executed Johnson's general instructions in a manner that resulted in confusion and conflict with civil authorities concerning the government's land policy.[35] When complaints reached General Howard during the late summer of the confiscation activities of his officers in

[32] Oscar Zeichner, "The Transition from Slave to Free Agricultural Labor in the Southern States," *Agricultural History*, XIII (1939), 23–24.

[33] Wharton, *The Negro in Mississippi*, 58.

[34] Extract of a letter from Thomas to Lieutenant Colonel R. S. Donaldson, July 19, 1865, in Governors' Correspondence, E-72.

[35] Lieutenant Stuart Eldridge, Thomas' adjutant, to Donaldson, July 19, 1865, *ibid.*

Mississippi, he ordered such practices stopped and steps taken to restore abandoned property to its owners. By the end of the year most of this property had been returned to the owners.[36]

Many Negroes were bitterly disappointed when it became evident during the fall of 1865 that they would not receive their forty acres. No doubt inspired by Negro troops and by the misdirected efforts of bureau agents on their behalf, some freedmen refused to believe that there would be no division of lands. Rumors were circulated among them that the federal government would provide for a general distribution of land during the Christmas season. Only a small portion of the blacks of the state, and these mainly in the interior and in communities removed from the arteries of commerce and communications, believed such stories, according to the Natchez *Democrat*.[37] Nonetheless, as these rumors multiplied freedmen in all areas of Mississippi were affected, and many refused to make contracts for the new year in anticipation of something occurring at Christmas that would prevent their having to work for the whites.[38] With labor conditions already disturbed and uncertain for 1866, planters became increasingly excited and apprehensive as to the intentions of the freedmen. Rumors soon began to circulate among the whites that the Negroes planned to rise in rebellion and seize land by force if the government did not give it to them.[39] Although white fears of a Negro insurrection had no real basis in fact, the actions of some freedmen to secure arms, probably to

[36] Natchez *Democrat*, October 17, 1865; New Orleans *Picayune*, November 7, 1865; "Reports of the Assistant Commissioners of the Freedmen's Bureau Made since December 1, 1865," *Senate Executive Documents*, 39th Cong., 1st Sess., No. 27, p. 30. During the war Federal officers had established from confiscated lands several experimental colonies for Negroes, the most notable being the one at Davis Bend. By 1866 all of these lands had been restored to their owners, except the Davis Bend colony which remained under the control of the Freedmen's Bureau. Ganus, "The Freedmen's Bureau in Mississippi," 134.

[37] Natchez *Democrat*, November 18, 1865. The editor of the Jackson *Clarion*, also thought that no considerable number of Negroes anticipated a division of land.

[38] Copy of a letter from William T. Martin to Major George D. Reynolds, November 18, 1865, in Governors' Correspondence, E-77; Governor Humphreys to Senators-elect Sharkey and Alcorn, December 8, 1865, in Johnson Papers; "Report of the Commissioner of the Freedmen's Bureau," *House Executive Documents*, 39th Cong., 1st Sess., No. 70, p. 174.

[39] Raymond *Hinds County Gazette*, December 23, 1865; Canton *American Citizen*, October 1, 1865; Reid, *After the War*, 422; John Lamkin to Governor Humphreys, December 6, 1865; Citizens of Noxubee County to Humphreys, October 31, 1865, in Governors' Correspondence, E-77.

defend themselves against disorderly whites, suggested to many that the former slaves were plotting against their old masters. The Jackson *Mississippian* asserted that the reasons for white apprehensions "arise from the insolence, threats and general bearing of the negroes toward the whites." [40] A report was made to Governor Humphreys that Negroes were holding meetings in east Mississippi "in which they gravely discuss the ways and means by which they could acquire and hold possession of the states of Alabama, Mississippi, Louisiana and Texas. These meetings are largely attended and the negroes are well armed."[41] Oscar J. E. Stuart, militia commander for southwest Mississippi, wrote Humphreys that after an inspection of his district, an area of traditional rumors of race disorders, he was of the opinion that an insurrection was contemplated and that the blacks expected to receive aid from Negro troops in Natchez. William T. Martin, an influential leader in Natchez and a former major general in the Confederate army, believed at first that no insurrection was planned by the freedmen of southwest Mississippi; but as tensions mounted during the late fall he changed his mind and predicted that sooner or later "a war of races" would occur unless the Negroes were disarmed.[42] Reports of Negro threats in the Livingston and Vernon area of Madison County prompted the Canton *American Citizen* to refer the whites of the county to the tradition of a major slave plot that had horrified the people of those communities in 1835, and it suggested that "history repeats itself." [43] So strong was the belief that Negro-inspired disorders, if not insurrection, would occur during the Christmas season that whites in southwest Madison County and in adjoining Yazoo County hastened to the towns for protection.[44]

[40] As quoted in the Vicksburg *Journal,* November 15, 1865.

[41] Citizens of Noxubee County to Humphreys, October 31, 1865, in Governors' Correspondence, E-77.

[42] Oscar J. E. Stuart to Humphreys, December 8, 1865; William T. Martin to Major George D. Reynolds, November 18, 1865; Martin to Humphreys, December 5, 1865, all *ibid.*

[43] Canton *American Citizen,* October 1, 1865. During the 1835 scare a virtual mob hysteria swept Madison County and the northern portion of Hinds County after a few slaves were allegedly overheard plotting an uprising. Before the excitement had subsided, twelve white men, who were implicated by slaves under torture, and a much larger, but undetermined, number of Negroes were hanged without trial. Edwin A. Miles, "The Mississippi Slave Insurrection Scare of 1835," *Journal of Negro History,* XLII (1957), 50–55.

[44] Raymond *Hinds County Gazette,* December 23, 1865.

As the Christmas season approached and the probability of rash action on the part of intemperate whites became increasingly evident, moderate leaders rejected the idea that the freedmen were plotting against the whites and denounced those who were inciting the masses. The Vicksburg *Journal* advised that if people would quit discussing the subject of Negro insurrection the danger of race conflict would subside. Even the Canton *American Citizen* editor in tense Madison County came to denounce the rumors of revolt as preposterous.[45]

Notwithstanding a growing spirit of moderation and rationality on the part of many whites, great injustice was perpetrated on some blacks who were suspected of harboring hostile intentions toward whites. Most of these outrages were committed by the militia or persons acting in the name of the militia. Provisional Governor Sharkey had organized militia units in August, giving as one reason for his action the necessity for countering Negro threats. Humphreys inherited these units, as well as Sharkey's fear of Negro disorders. He re-organized and strengthened the militia, but at the same time he warned the officers that their purpose was to suppress crime and prevent lawlessness of all types and not to oppress the freedmen.[46] Nevertheless, when Humphreys directed militia companies in tense counties to disarm Negroes, many militiamen and persons claiming to be agents of the state seized arms in a harsh manner and in some cases plundered helpless freedmen. Efforts of General Wood and his officers to halt these attacks, short of intervention, produced no fruit until after the insurrection scare had subsided.[47]

Although provoked by intemperate whites and incited by irresponsible Negro troops, the freedmen made no gestures of hostility or defiance at Christmastide.[48] Furthermore, planter fears, seemingly realistic during the fall, that Negroes would not come forward to make

[45] Vicksburg *Journal*, December 20, 1865; Canton *American Citizen*, December 7, 1865. See also the Jackson *Clarion*, December 20, 1865.
[46] Proclamation of Governor Humphreys, November 3, 1865; Humphreys' general order number one to militia officers, November 3, 1865, both in Governors' Correspondence, E-77.
[47] Wood to Humphreys, December 3, 1865, and Lieutenant Colonel R. S. Donaldson to Humphreys, November 2, 1865, *ibid.*; Port Gibson *Standard*, January 27, 1866; Humphreys to Donaldson, November 2, 1865, in Executive Journal of Governor Benjamin G. Humphreys, 1865–68, Mississippi Department of Archives and History, Jackson.
[48] Raymond *Hinds County Gazette*, January 22, 1866; Trowbridge, *The Desolate South*, 190.

labor arrangements for 1866 proved foolish. Blacks, in many cases experiencing destitution and sickness, were generally coming to recognize their economic responsibilities in freedom. They were encouraged toward this awareness by the Freedmen's Bureau and army officers in the state.

When the insurrection scare was at its height, the Freedmen's Bureau played a significant roll in disabusing Negroes of the notion that they had been promised land and should receive a portion of their former owners' lands. Colonel Thomas directed his officers to tell the freedmen that "what they gain in property or advancement of any kind will come after patient labor, by which they may merit such reward." [49]	Then, too, Commissioner Howard, visiting Jackson in November, 1865, issued a special circular to bureau officers in the state ordering them to exert every effort to remove the erroneous impression among the Negroes that the government would provide them with land.[50]

The nearest that the federal government came to answering the freedman's desire for land was an act of June 21, 1866, which modified the Homestead Law. This act threw open over three million acres of public lands in Mississippi to settlement by Negroes and whites alike, although former Confederates were excluded for a year. The most desirable tracts, however, had already been claimed, and what was left was practically all located in the sandy, short-leaf pine region and generally was not suitable for agricultural purposes. By the fall of 1866 General Wood, who was now both military commander and head of the bureau in the state, reported that little had been done to implement this act, since he had been unable to secure maps or other records that would show where the lands were located.[51] Very few freedmen claimed these public lands, and then only if they had a white benefactor like John F. H. Claiborne. This historian and former congressman aided almost two hundred blacks, many of whom were

[49] "Report of the Commissioner of the Freedmen's Bureau," *House Executive Documents*, 39th Cong., 1st Sess., No. 70, p. 174.

[50] Natchez *Democrat*, November 16, 1865; Memphis *Appeal*, December 1, 1865. Apparently bureau agents energetically carried out Howard's instructions. See the Natchez *Democrat*, November 25, 1865.

[51] E. Merton Coulter, *The South during Reconstruction, 1865–1877* (Baton Rouge: Louisiana State University Press, 1947), 108; Wharton, *The Negro in Mississippi*, 60. Without credit to secure provisions or contacts in the piney barrens, Negroes found it virtually impossible to move; furthermore, many were reluctant to leave communities and lands with which they were familiar.

his former slaves, to become independent farmers under the provisions of the Homestead Act.[52]

The Freedmen's Bureau and the military authorities in the state gave far more practical assistance to the freedmen than through the homestead program by attempting to disabuse them of the idea that personal freedom meant freedom from toil. Both, furthermore, rendered an important service to the planters of the state during the period of confused labor conditions in insisting that the freedmen honor their contractual obligations and become responsible workers. Planters in the beginning applauded the labor policies of the army in the state.[53] But when the Freedmen's Bureau became the guardian of the Negroes and interfered with the planters' management of their workers, whites became hostile to the government's efforts. Furthermore, bureau interference in judicial matters as the protector of Negro rights convinced most planters that its officers were hindering rather than encouraging the stability of the Negro workers. Only in a very few cases, however, did this opposition take the form of violence against representatives of the bureau, and these attacks were not usually perpetrated by employers of Negroes.[54]

The Freedmen's Bureau played no part in the initial arrangements made during the spring of 1865 between landowners and former slaves. On plantations in the Delta that were not inundated, Negroes agreed in general to work for a share of the crop or for a monthly wage. Planters, or wives of planters in the absence of their husbands who had not returned home from the war, consented to supply them with provisions for the year.[55] Throughout the state similar arrangements were made at this time between planters and freedmen. These arrangements, however, proved quite imperfect since many of

[52] "Freedmen's Affairs," Senate Executive Documents, 39th Cong., 2nd Sess., No. 6, p. 96, Jackson Clarion, May 17, 1867.

[53] Reid, After the War, 577; Trowbridge, The Desolate South, 196; Lieutenant A. Probst to Major T. L. Free, August, 1865, in Freedmen's Bureau Records, Mississippi.

[54] William L. Gibson to Sharkey, July 10, 1865, in Governors' Correspondence, E-69; Natchez Democrat, November 22, 1865; Ethan A. Allen to President Johnson, May 17, 1867, in Johnson Papers. One bureau officer was killed during the four-year period in which the organization was active in the state. This murder occurred in the turbulent railroad town of Grenada and was committed by a band of desperadoes who had been terrorizing the county. General Wood to Humphreys, August 17, 1866, in Governors' Correspondence, E-79.

[55] Meridian Clarion, August 9, 1865; Montgomery, Reminiscences, 260.

the blacks, experiencing the first flush of freedom, could not understand why, if they were free, they should have to bind themselves to work for the whites.[56]

When the army assumed control of the state in late May, 1865, Major General Peter J. Osterhaus, commander of the Department of Mississippi, immediately exhorted the freed slaves to remain with their former masters and to labor faithfully as long as they were treated kindly and were given reasonable wages. Idleness on the part of the freedmen would not be tolerated by the army. The general informed planters that they were to treat the Negroes as free laborers and that any injustice to their workers would result in punitive measures being taken by the government. Osterhaus dispatched provost marshals to the counties to enforce these instructions.[57] Unlike their later counterparts in the Freedmen's Bureau, these provost marshals generally sympathized with the landowners in their energetic efforts to secure and maintain a stable labor force for the planting season.

Colonel William E. Bayley, provost marshal for Bolivar County in the Delta, indicated that he would enforce a strict compliance with contracts on the part of both planters and laborers, and "for misdemeanors and offences of the servant class the punishment used in the United States will be promptly administered." Furthermore, he enrolled a citizen militia company to aid in carrying out his directives.[58] Within a month of Colonel Bayley's arrival labor conditions had stabilized in the county, and the planters were loud in their praise of him.[59] Evidently other provost marshals in the Mississippi bottoms also worked vigorously to aid the landowners in securing a permanent labor supply for the year. One newspaper reported in August, 1865, that the system of free labor was entirely satisfactory for most planters in the alluvial counties.[60]

[56] Meridian *Clarion*, August 9, 1865.

[57] Osterhaus' instructions were included in his General Order number 57, May 27, 1865. This order may be found in the Meridian *Clarion*, June 21, 1865. When Henry W. Slocum became commander of the department on June 23, 1865, Osterhaus continued in the state as commander of the southern district.

[58] Order number one of Colonel William E. Bayley, June 22, 1865, in Governors' Correspondence, E-69.

[59] William L. Gibson to Sharkey, July 10, 1865, *ibid.;* G. G. Lorrey to Sharkey, July 21, 1865, *ibid.,* E-70.

[60] Meridian *Clarion*, August 9, 1865. On occasion, military authorities apprehended and returned laborers who had broken their contracts. Cincinnati *Enquirer*, October 7, 1865. A probable reason for the strong insistence by military

In areas where the army's labor program was not enforced, planters continued to complain of the difficulty of keeping the freedmen in the fields. One planter near Vicksburg wrote Governor Sharkey that the provost marshal had advised the Negroes of his community to honor their contracts and to go to work, "but they don't believe a word he said to them and they are now in a worse condition than before he came. I would propose that you send bodies of soldiers with discreet commanders to read the law to the negroes and to show them an officer (in Blue) that would be left to carry it out by the aid of the citizens if he had to use force." He said that his proposal was endorsed by all the planters of the area.[61]

The Freedmen's Bureau generally took over the labor policies instituted by the army, except that it insisted on the equality of the Negroes in labor arrangements. Colonel Samuel Thomas issued several circulars during the summer of 1865 which, in effect, indicated that the bureau had no intention of pampering the freedmen. In most of these instructions to his officers and to the freedmen, Thomas avowed that the Negroes must work and, in a circular issued on July 29, declared to the blacks that "it must be clearly understood that belonging to a place and lying about without work does not entitle any one to wages, nor even to food."[62] Planters were instructed by Thomas to draw up written contracts with their workers and to secure approval from the local bureau officer of these arrangements. Although the bureau did not attempt to regulate wages, at least one supervising officer directed that planters in his district must also provide food, housing, clothing, and medical care for their Negro laborers. These compensations could be forfeited, of course, when freedmen broke their contracts.[63]

Colonel Thomas also directed his officers to instill into the minds of the freedmen "respect for civil law and the sacredness of all contracts and obligations."[64] Some of Thomas' officers diligently carried out his

officers that Negroes perform labor faithfully was that many former comrades-in-arms were investing in lands and planting in the Delta with Negro labor.

[61] J. Pearce to Sharkey, July 15, 1865, in Governors' Correspondence, E-70.

[62] "Report of the Commissioner of the Freedmen's Bureau," *House Executive Documents*, 39th Cong., 1st Sess., No. 70, p. 149; Wharton, *The Negro in Mississippi*, 75; Meridian *Clarion*, July 19, 29, 1865.

[63] Meridian *Clarion*, June 21, 1865; "Report of the Commissioner of the Freedmen's Bureau," *House Executive Documents*, 39th Cong., 1st Sess., No. 70, pp. 150, 157.

[64] Meridian *Clarion*, July 19, 1865.

instructions, and with a great deal of impartiality. Especially was this true of Major George D. Reynolds, supervising officer for the southern district of the state. Not only did Reynolds admonish the Negroes to remain in their old communities, but he reminded them that a planter would not hire a freedman who was "impudent, lazy, and fails to do as he says." If a Negro laborer were mistreated, Reynolds recommended that he quit when his contract lapsed and go to work for someone else.[65] When General Howard visited the state, he also encouraged the blacks to go to work and pointed out that "indolence is not freedom. True freedom is the result of honest industry." [66]

As well as reproving the irresponsible freedmen, Colonel Thomas at times lectured in like manner the planters on their duties and responsibilities toward their laborers. For example, in a circular issued on August 4, 1865, he pedantically pointed out that "the interest of the Freedmen and planter lie parallel to each other. They cannot become hostile unless prejudice makes them so. Land is valueless without labor, and the labor of the great majority of the Freedmen is vain without land. These interests must be combined, or each is comparatively valueless. For the planters then to abuse or even alienate the class on whom they must depend for the labor that makes their plantation valuable is foolish as well as wicked. Conciliation and kindness is the true policy, and is self remunerative." [67] Planters, who were experienced managers of Negroes, albeit in slavery, resented these lessons in agricultural economics; and, coming so soon after the sympathetic labor policies of the army provost marshals, the counsel and assistance of bureau officers were not appreciated and were denounced by planters as meddling in affairs with which they had no practical knowledge.[68]

Actually the bureau had very little effect upon the structure of the labor system of the state in 1865. Labor arrangements had been made by the time the bureau was organized in the counties, and its officers evidently did not interfere with these contracts, many of which had the sanction of the provost marshals of the districts. With only a

[65] Natchez *Democrat*, November 25, 1865.

[66] Friar's Point *Coahomian*, November 17, 1865; Memphis *Appeal*, December 1, 1865.

[67] Meridian *Clarion*, August 23, 1865.

[68] See Sharkey's view of the Freedmen's Bureau in "Report of the Joint Committee on Reconstruction," *House Reports*, 39th Cong., 1st Sess., No. 30, Pt. III, 134.

skeleton organization with which to work, Colonel Thomas devoted most of his attention during the summer of 1865 to printing and distributing circulars urging the Negroes to work and insisting that planters treat their laborers kindly.[69] The effect of these publications was not very great at first. One army officer reported to his superiors: "The whites hear nothing of his announcements, much less the blacks." [70] It was speculated in the Columbus *Sentinel* that the publication of circulars and orders, especially in Mississippi newspapers, "was labor lost." The *Sentinel* explained that the freedmen, the great majority of whom were illiterate, were dependent upon the whites to read and explain the bureau instructions to them. They, however, "do not believe anything that we can tell them or which we may read from papers that is at variance with their ideas of freedom." [71] But by the new year bureau pronouncements, now sterner and more direct than during the summer, were having the desired effect on the impoverished and disillusioned Negroes of the state.[72]

Labor conditions in Mississippi were at no time more unsettled than from October, 1865, to January, 1866. Many freedmen were expecting to receive land as a present from the government at Christmas and were told by malcontents that if they contracted for 1866 they would lose their claims to this land.[73] Some whites were reportedly advising Negroes that if they agreed to work for their old masters it was prima facie evidence that they preferred servitude to freedom. Editor George W. Harper of the *Hinds County Gazette* suspected that the whites who were counseling the freedmen in this manner "are of the class of persons . . . who owned no negroes, but are now anxious to hire, regardless of the means necessary to be employed to effect that object. "[74] Yet many reluctant Negroes might have been willing to hire for the year, had they not been demoralized by the crop failure of

[69] Wharton, *The Negro in Mississippi*, 75–76.

[70] John S. McNeily, "War and Reconstruction in Mississippi, 1863–1890," *Publications of the Mississippi Historical Society, Centenary Series*, II (1918), 243–44.

[71] As reported in the New Orleans *Picayune*, November 22, 1865.

[72] For an example of this new hard policy of the bureau, see Colonel Thomas' order of December 31, 1865, in the Jackson *Clarion*, January 9, 1866, directing the Negroes to make contracts for the new year.

[73] "Report of the Commissioner of the Freedmen's Bureau," *House Executive Documents*, 39th Cong., 1st Sess., No. 70, p. 174; Jackson *Clarion*, December 17, 1865.

[74] Raymond *Hinds County Gazette*, December 16, 1865.

1865 and the inability of their old masters to compensate them for their work. These and other freedmen preferred to contract by the month or the week instead of making the longer arrangement desired by the planters.[75]

As the new year approached, planters appeared almost desperate in their efforts to secure dependable laborers. On November 19 the Jackson *Clarion* claimed that approximately one half of the improved land of the state would not be cultivated because of the chaotic labor situation. Even in the alluvial bottoms planting conditions had deteriorated from those of the summer months. Landowners hurriedly met and formed associations to devise means to procure laborers, white as well as black. Elaborate proposals were offered to secure white immigrants, but such schemes could not possibly materialize in time for planting the crop of 1866.[76] The *Clarion* editor warned planters that Negro labor offered the only prospect in the immediate future for the large-scale production of cotton. So anxious were cotton growers from the river counties to secure laborers that they were willing to compensate Union war veterans quite lucratively simply to come and live on their plantations, since Negroes tended to be attracted to Northerners.[77] Planters of the alluvial bottoms, or their agents, were offering to pay as high as twenty-five dollars a month for prime field hands —a wage which greatly exceeded the rate in the other cotton states.[78]

[75] The editor of the Jackson *Clarion*, December 21, 1865, claimed that many Negroes remained unpaid because they ran away before their contracts expired. For a different view, see Trowbridge, *The Desolate South*, 176.

[76] Natchez *Democrat*, December 21, 1865. Pessimistically, Editor H. P. Reid of the Friar's Point *Coahomian*, November 3, 1865, reported that in the Delta all planters "agree that labor is now in too disorganized a state to attempt to raise cotton." Many Negroes on alluvial lands that had been cultivated in 1865 refused to contract for the new year because they were not willing to take the risk that the crops would be free of destructive floodings. *Convention Journal, 1865*, p. 268. See also Henry M. Crydenwise to Charles Crydenwise, March 21, 1866, in Henry M. Crydenwise Papers, Duke University Library.

[77] Jackson *Clarion*, December 19, 1865, January 2, 1866; New York *Times*, February 4, 1866; Henry M. Crydenwise to his parents, April 3, 1866, in Crydenwise Papers. Crydenwise, a Northerner who was hired to attract Negro laborers, took his duties as "supervisor" seriously and worked in the fields with the freedmen.

[78] Reid, *After the War*, 561; New York *Times*, February 4, 1866; Friar's Point *Coahomian*, November 3, 1865. Planters of the river counties found an unexpected source of labor in Vicksburg where several Negro regiments were being mustered out and many of these Negroes were seeking jobs. [Benham], *Year of Wreck*, 164.

The state legislature, meeting at this time, acted to regulate Negro labor. Encouraged by Governor Humphreys, the legislature first passed a vagrancy law which was designed to insure that idle freedmen made contracts for the new year and to provide a permanent labor force for the planters.[79] This act provided that all freedmen over eighteen years of age "found on the second Monday in January, 1866, or thereafter, with no lawful employment or business, shall be deemed vagrants," and on conviction were to be fined, but not more than fifty dollars, or imprisoned. Those who could not pay the fine were to be hired out to planters who would pay the levy and who would be reimbursed by the labor of the offender. The last clause of the act stipulated that failure by the freedmen to pay the one dollar annual poll tax levied on members of their race to support indigent Negroes was prima facie evidence of vagrancy.[80] The legislature next incorporated in a general "civil rights bill" a measure requiring that labor contracts be written and witnessed by a civil official and two disinterested white persons. The legislature also provided that a freedman who quit before his term of service expired might be arrested and returned to his employer. Any person could apprehend a fleeing Negro and would receive five dollars, plus ten cents for each mile of travel involved.[81]

These measures, with the exception of the provision providing for the return of contract violators, generally met the approval of the Freedmen's Bureau and the army. Bureau officials insisted that they be applied equally to both whites and blacks, but General Wood was reluctant to intervene to secure compliance.[82] He preferred to work through the state officers "to correct individual cases of abuse."[83] With the enactment of the federal civil rights bill in April, 1866, Wood

[79] Humphreys' message of November 20, 1865, to the legislature may be found in the Natchez *Democrat*, November 25, 1865.

[80] *Laws of Mississippi*, 1865, pp. 90–93.

[81] *Ibid.*, 83–84. Any person enticing a Negro to break his contract could be fined or imprisoned for two months in the county jail. See below, Chap. 7, for an account of these labor regulations in context with the measures enacted by the legislature of 1865 that were designed to define the place of the Negro in Mississippi society.

[82] Friar's Point *Coahomian*, December 1, 1865; New York *Times*, July 7, 1866; Colonel Thomas to General Wood, March 12, 1866, in Governors' Correspondence, E-78.

[83] Wood to Humphreys, March 12, 1866, in Governors' Correspondence, E-78. Wood at this time was serving both as military commander of the department and as acting assistant commissioner of the bureau in Mississippi.

thought that the state provision directing the summary arrest and return of fugitive workers was invalid. When apprehensive planters, including Northerners, asked him what action could be taken to make the freedmen fulfill their contracts, he invariably suggested that they seek civil redress, yet admitted that little could be accomplished without force.[84] General Howard further recommended that if the legislature would repeal all provisions of the controversial Black Code of 1865 which discriminated against the Negro and enact new labor measures that would apply to all, state officials would be able to require "specific performance of contracts." Otherwise, laborers would continue to desert their employers with impunity and the crop of 1866 would fall far short of its potential.[85]

Other acts of the legislature to regulate labor were sanctioned by the Freedmen's Bureau, since they were substantially the same as Colonel Thomas had required. Soon after the passage of the vagrancy law, Thomas indicated his approval, except where its execution would discriminate, and declared that as far as his office was concerned bona-fide vagrants could be put to work on roads, levees, and other public works.[86] Thomas lectured the freedmen regarding the justice of the vagrant act: "The State cannot and ought not to let any man lie about idle, without property, doing mischief. A vagrant law is right in principle. I cannot ask the civil officers to leave you idle, to beg or steal. If they find any of you without business and means of living, they will do right if they treat you as bad persons and take away your misused liberty." [87] Yet Thomas directed his officers to serve as "next friends" of the Negroes in their relations with the planters and to watch the civil authorities to see that no injustices were perpetrated on the freedmen. The bureau, however, under the direction of General Wood and his successor, Major General Alvan C. Gillem, an East Tennessean, apparently did not intervene forcibly in any case to require equal treatment for Negroes in labor arrangements.[88]

The extent of enforcement of the vagrancy law varied throughout

[84] Wood to General Howard, June 30, 1866, ibid., E-79.

[85] Order of General Howard to his officers in Mississippi, June 30, 1866, ibid.

[86] Jackson Clarion, January 9, 1866; Friar's Point Coahomian, December 1, 1865; New York Times, July 7, 1866.

[87] "Report of the Commissioner of the Freedmen's Bureau," House Executive Documents, 39th Cong., 1st Sess., No. 70, p. 263.

[88] Ibid., 176; Jackson Clarion, January 9, 1866; Ganus, "The Freedmen's Bureau in Mississippi," 203.

the state. In the black belt of east Mississippi, the mayor of Aberdeen rigidly enforced the act and reportedly resorted to harsh means to send "hundreds of idle laborers to the plow." [89] But in Vicksburg and Jackson influential citizens attempted to prevent the execution of the law because of the injurious effect politically it might have upon the state at a time when the acts of the "Black Code" legislature were being sharply assailed in the North.[90] Although the discriminatory wording of the act was later repealed by the legislature, the vagrancy law remained in effect after the restoration government under the Presidential plan had been overturned.

Because of the forces at work, including economic enticements, to return the Negroes to the cotton fields, most freedmen came forward after the first of January and made labor contracts for 1866. From all parts of the state came reports during the first months of the year that Negroes were laboring diligently. Coming after the racial tension of late 1865, planters were pleasantly surprised at this development, although they only partially understood the reasons for the actions of blacks in accepting contract terms. For the first time since the end of the war, planters felt optimistic toward free labor and their chances for economic recovery.[91] A survey by a central Mississippi cotton growers' association of five leading cotton producing counties in the area indicates, however, that the labor force available in 1866 was decidedly smaller than that of 1860. Three hundred and twenty-three planters reported to the association that in 1860 they had 7,624 workers, while in 1866 they had been able to employ only 3,499.[92] Furthermore, when the long, hot summer days came, some Negroes working on a monthly wage found it convenient to break their contracts and leave the planters in the lurch.[93]

[89] From the Aberdeen *Sunny South*, as reported in the Jackson *Clarion*, April 13, 1866.

[90] New York *Times*, July 7, 1866; report of bureau agent J. H. Chapman to Major Greene, May 1, 1866, in Freedmen's Bureau Records, Mississippi; Vicksburg *Weekly Republican*, March 3, 10, 1866.

[91] Jackson *Clarion*, April 20, 1866; Raymond *Hinds County Gazette*, January 6, 1866; Friar's Point *Coahomian*, January 19, 1866; Trowbridge, *The Desolate South*, 196; L. T. McKenzie to President Johnson, April 1, 1866, in Johnson Papers.

[92] Their crop acreage was reduced from 84,311 acres in 1860 to 32,222 in 1866. Raymond *Hinds County Gazette*, August 31, 1866.

[93] Copy of a letter from General Wood to General Howard, June 21, 1866, in Governors' Correspondence, E-79; *Report of the Commissioner of Agriculture for the Year 1866* (Washington: Government Printing Office, 1867), 190.

But freedmen were not the only parties to labor contracts who violated their agreements. Reports reached General Wood during the late summer of 1866 that small planters, faced with a depreciated cotton yield, were discharging Negroes, whom they had hired for the year, without settling fully with them for their previous labor. These discharges were made, according to the general in his report to his superiors, "upon the miserable subterfuge that the employee has failed to comply with the terms of his agreement, and the most frivolous mistakes of the freedmen have been alleged as such failures." He indicated, however, that "only a comparatively small portion of the [white] community can be guilty of practicing such an enormity." [94] The usually mild-mannered Wood published instructions to employers of Negroes that white violation of contracts would not be permitted, even if it were necessary to dispatch troops to a locality to prevent it.[95]

The editor of the Jackson *Clarion* immediately denounced Wood's proclamation as "calculated to create an erroneous impression and do great injustice to the large majority of our planters. . . . It will encourage the freedmen, upon every real or imaginary wrong, to invoke military protection and military interference." [96] Sensitive to white criticism and desirous to show impartiality in the matter, General Wood a few days later announced that no portion of his proclamation was intended to refer to Negroes who had not complied with their contracts. On the contrary, he believed that in cases in which they refused to work they should be forced to leave; and military assistance would be granted to insure that freedmen honored their contracts.[97]

After their experience of 1865 and 1866 planters became more reconciled to the vicissitudes involved in using free labor and Negroes to the fact that freedom did not mean freedom from work. Difficulties

[94] Jackson *Clarion*, August 25, 1866; McNeily, "Mississippi's Provisional Government," 222–23; "Freedmen's Affairs," *Senate Executive Documents*, 39th Cong., 2nd Sess., No. 6, p. 97. A woman planter in Jefferson County calculated at the end of 1866 that one of her Negro laborers owed her $161, after she had deducted $305 from his $144 annual wages for "lost time." Among these deductions she charged the freedman $200 for "damages, charges, and abuses." Other miscellaneous deductions included $50 for neglect and killing an ox and $10 for refusing to feed the horses. A page from the accounting records of Mary Shaw for 1866, in Mary Shaw Papers, in the possession of Ann Bowman, Fayette, Mississippi.

[95] McNeily, "Mississippi's Provisional Government," 222–23.

[96] Jackson *Clarion*, August 25, 1866.

[97] McNeily, "Mississippi's Provisional Government," 223.

in getting blacks to contract for each new year still varied largely in proportion to the size and market value of the preceding crop. When the crops fell short of expectations and they did not receive the compensations that they anticipated, freedmen often believed that they had been cheated by the planters, and thus they became extremely reluctant to make labor contracts for the new year.[98] But usually these difficulties were settled in time for the "spring breaking" of the land and for the subsequent planting of the cotton.

[98] Hiram Cassedy to William Whitehurst, December 16, 1866, in William Whitehurst Papers, Mississippi Department of Archives and History, Jackson; Raymond *Hinds County Gazette,* November 30, 1866; Jackson *Weekly Clarion,* October 9, 1867; Meridian *Weekly Gazette,* November 5, 1867; Vicksburg *Herald and Mississippian,* June 7, 1867.

6

The Election of the Restoration Government

THE GOVERNMENT elected on October 2, 1865, had the formidable task of completing the work of restoration, of continuing the process of readjustment, and of inaugurating policies that would lead to the restoration of effective government and the economic development of the state. The task of the reconstruction convention was relatively simple as compared to that of the restoration government. The convention's purpose was largely to acknowledge a *fait accompli,* whereas the problems facing the new government were more comprehensive, more complex, and far more difficult. When the reconstruction convention met in August, political and economic conditions were quite amorphous; but by the time elections were held in October and the new government was established, planters were facing acute labor problems, rumors of a Negro insurrection were sweeping the state, and prospects for the forthcoming crop year were becoming critical. Furthermore, the prolongation of military occupation, especially by Negro troops, and the irksome Freedmen's Bureau complicated and emotionalized the questions confronting state leaders by the fall of 1865. Less emotion-charged problems, which included the acquisition of capital and money, levee repairs, possible redemption of state cotton notes, debtor relief, and state aid for transportation, received less attention than that of the place of the Negro in Mississippi society. The people of Mississippi looked to the officers who were to be elected in October to find solutions for all of these problems.

Even before the reconstruction convention adjourned, candidates began to announce for office in the restoration government.[1] Probably to insure that able conservatives and original Unionists would be can-

[1] Meridian *Clarion,* August 20, 1865.

didates for the more important state positions, most of the delegates to the convention met as a caucus on August 23, 1865, to nominate a gubernatorial candidate and congressional candidates.[2] Since more than 75 per cent of the delegates were Whigs, their selections for office obviously reflected their political persuasion and especially their identification with Unionism during the antebellum period. The analytical correspondent for the Mobile *Advertiser and Register* at the convention thought that party ties were weaker than before the war, "yet it is very clear that they are not entirely broken up. . . . This may be exhibited in the nominations" made by the caucus.[3] The caucus chose Ephraim S. Fisher, a Union Whig, for governor, and three Whigs and one Union or Douglas Democrat for four of the five seats in Congress. Although one of these four nominees had served as a brigadier general in the Southern forces, one as a colonel, and one in Congress, all had opposed secession.[4] Apparently the delegates made no nomination for Congress from the Fifth District. To avoid all reasons for awakening prejudices against caucuses, delegates were advised to go home and place the nominees before the people, not as selections of the convention, but as conservative candidates and as the personal preferences of the local delegate.[5]

Ephraim S. Fisher, the convention caucus' candidate for governor, had served during the 1850's on the High Court of Errors and Appeals and had not participated in the war until late 1864, when he accepted a commission as colonel of the home guard.[6] Fisher was one of the most influential Whigs in the state at the end of the war. Both Sharkey and Yerger recommended that President Johnson appoint him judge of

[2] *Ibid.*, October 1, 1865; Cincinnati *Enquirer*, August 25, 1865; Mobile *Advertiser and Register*, August 26, 1865.

[3] Mobile *Advertiser and Register*, August 26, 1865.

[4] *Ibid.*, August 27, 1865; *Biographical and Historical Memoirs*, I, 739–40, 959–60; Meridian *Clarion*, August 29, 1865; James T. Harrison to President Johnson, undated; Abram Murdock, *et al.*, to President Johnson, September 15, 1865, both in Amnesty Papers, Mississippi. Lock Houston, the Douglas Democratic candidate and speaker of the state house of representatives during the last two years of the Confederate period, later declined to become a candidate for Congress.

[5] Mobile *Advertiser and Register*, August 27, 1865. This subtle method of advancing nominees of the caucus did not completely prevent criticism. Sylvanus Evans, a candidate for Congress opposing Absalom M. West, denounced his opponent's nomination by the caucus as undemocratic. "Condition of the South," *Senate Executive Documents*, 39th Cong., 1st Sess., No. 2, p. 64.

[6] C. T. Purnell to Governor Humphreys, October 29, 1865, in Governors' Correspondence, E-77; *Biographical and Historical Memoirs*, I, 729–40.

the federal district in the state, an appointment that he did not receive. His candidacy for governor had the tacit support of both the President and Provisional Governor Sharkey.[7]

Fisher's opponents in the governor's race were Benjamin G. Humphreys and William S. Patton, both Union men during the sectional controversy of the antebellum period. Humphreys of Claiborne County was an unsuccessful Union candidate for delegate to the convention of 1861. Sharkey in his testimony before the Joint Committee on Reconstruction explained Humphreys' position on secession: "There was no man in the State of Mississippi more opposed to secession than he was; and I will tell you more: he did not believe [that] the confederates could establish a government, even if they were free and independent. . . . He ultimately got into the rebellion by accident, you might say; he went out with a company as its captain, and was promoted to be a general."[8] A planter by profession, Humphreys wrote President Johnson after the surrender that he had lost everything except his land as a result of the war and was still heavily in debt.[9] Patton, a Union Democrat from east Mississippi, had served as speaker of the state house of representatives from 1852 to 1854 but otherwise was little known outside of the piney woods.[10]

The campaign for governor was quite confusing, since communications were still disrupted and many believed that the unpardoned Humphreys would not be eligible to serve if elected. In fact, in several areas of the state reports were circulated a few days before the election that Humphreys had withdrawn from the race because of his presumed ineligibility for the office. In at least one piney woods county, and possibly two, his candidacy was not known until after the election.[11]

None of the candidates for governor campaigned actively, and the issues distinguishing the two leading contenders, Fisher and Hum-

[7] Sharkey and William Yerger to President Johnson, June 13, 1865, in Johnson Papers; "Report of the Joint Committee on Reconstruction," *House Reports,* 39th Cong., 1st Sess., No. 30, Pt. III, 137.

[8] Meridian *Clarion,* October 8, 1865; Jackson *Clarion and Standard,* July 6, 1866; "Report of the Joint Committee on Reconstruction," *House Reports,* 39th Cong., 1st Sess., No. 30, Pt. III, 137.

[9] Humphreys to Johnson, August 1, 1865, in Amnesty Papers, Mississippi.

[10] Dunbar Rowland (ed.), *The Official and Statistical Register of the State of Mississippi, 1908* (Nashville: Brandon Printing Co., 1908), 44.

[11] Raymond *Hinds County Gazette,* December 9, 23, 1865; George L. Donald to Humphreys, March 1, 1866, in Governors' Correspondence, E-78.

phreys, were quite vague. Since both were conservative Whigs and
original Unionists, the only significant political difference discernible
between the two was the matter of the degree of support each had
rendered the Confederacy.[12] Probably only a few Mississippians
thought that the election of Humphreys, a Confederate brigadier,
would give the Radicals of the North another reason to attack Johnson's home rule program.[13] The campaign for governor was thus primarily a popularity contest with no other issues being raised by the
candidates or by their supporters.

On the other hand, pertinent and debatable issues were advanced
by aspirants for other state offices. The problem of the freedmen attracted by far the greatest attention, yet most candidates could agree
that the state should at least regulate the labor of the blacks, if not all
of their economic and many of their social activities. Where the
whites differed sharply was on the question of admitting Negro testimony in court. This, however, did not become an issue until after
Sharkey published his proclamation of September 25, 1865, directing
the state courts to accept Negro testimony. The few days remaining
before the October 2 election actually did not allow sufficient time for
political lines to be formed on this question, except in trade centers
and along lines of communication.[14]

In those areas where the issue of Negro evidence in court was
raised, the question became entangled in the broader argument of
Negro equality. The anti-testimony party, led by George L. Potter
and Edward M. Yerger, Whigs of Jackson, sought to convince the
people that to grant the freedmen the privilege of testifying in court
would open Pandora's box for political rights for Negroes, especially
the privilege of suffrage. This group argued that the blacks should be

[12] C. T. Purnell to Humphreys, October 29, 1865, in Governors' Correspondence, E-77; Natchez Democrat, October 26, 1865; H. M. Watterson to President
Johnson, October 7, 1865, in Johnson Papers. Fisher was in Washington at the
time, reportedly interceding for former Confederates. He did not return to the
state until eight days before the election. Vicksburg Herald, October 11, 1865.

[13] Edward M. Yerger, the usually fiery editor of the Jackson News, however,
opposed Humphreys' election for fear it would disturb public sentiment in the
North. Meridian Clarion, October 10, 1865.

[14] In commenting on the issues of the campaign, the Friar's Point Coahomian,
September 29, 1865, made no mention of the Negro testimony question, thus sug-
gesting that, only four days before the election, it had not become an issue in the
Delta. See also the Jackson Clarion, November 23, 1865.

given no rights or privileges other than those held by free Negroes before the war.[15]

Those who supported the freedmen's right to testify asserted that the issue was "a settled question." The August convention, they said, had provided that Negroes be protected in their rights of person and property; and in order that they be assured of this protection, it was implicit in the work of the convention that they be permitted to testify in court. Moreover, Sharkey's proclamation of September 25 had already made Negro testimony a fixed policy of the state.[16] The Natchez *Courier* carried editorial denunciations of those who associated freedmen's testimony with black suffrage, declaring that "the hue and cry on this subject is another of those unmitigated humbugs which has survived the death of agitation, secession and fanaticism." [17] The Meridian *Clarion* editor joined in arraigning the anti-testimony party but reassured his readers that the privilege of testifying in court in no way suggested that Negroes be permitted to serve on juries, much less imply suffrage for them. "We hold it to be essential," this editor declared, "for the legislature to shape the laws of the State to harmonize with the amended [state] constitution. If they fail in this, the work of reconstruction will stop, and our delegation to Congress will be refused admission." [18] The *Courier* proclaimed that the person who refused this privilege to freedmen did "more for strengthening the radical party of the North, and to ensure negro equality at the ballot-box, than the vilest ranter of the school of Beecher and Phillips," and that, furthermore, instead of Negro troops being withdrawn, more would be sent to the state.[19]

In sections of the state where the admission of Negro evidence in court was not a campaign issue, other questions were debated. Besides the problem of the freedmen, the main issue was the question

[15] New York *Tribune*, September 30, 1865; New York *Times*, October 10, 1865; Natchez *Courier*, October 5, 1865; Meridian *Clarion*, October 1, 1865. Both Humphreys and Fisher, the leading gubernatorial candidates, supported Negro testimony in court. Dunbar Rowland (ed.), *Mississippi: Comprising Sketches of Counties, Towns, Events, Institutions, and Persons, Arranged in Cyclopedic Form* (Atlanta: Southern Historical Publishing Association, 1907), I, 893.

[16] For example, see the Meridian *Clarion*, October 1, 1865.

[17] Natchez *Courier*, October 5, 1865.

[18] The Meridian *Clarion*, October 1, 1865, in the same editorial further declared that "we hold this to be a white man's government," but Negroes "should be treated with humanity and justice."

[19] Natchez *Courier*, October 5, 1865.

of relief for debtors in view of the impoverished condition of the people. The status of financial obligations made during the war by the state, especially the unredeemed cotton money issue, was also discussed during the canvass. In the inundated Delta, the question of levee repair was of critical concern to the planters and brought forth demands that, contrary to antebellum policy, the whole state share in financing a program to control the river.[20]

The position of candidates during the sectional crisis of 1860–65 was again an important political issue. Provisional Governor Sharkey, among others, admonished the people to support and elect men who were not tainted with the act of secession.[21] L. J. Dupree, congressional candidate against former Confederate Congressman James T. Harrison went further. He criticized his opponent for being too closely associated with the Confederacy, even though Harrison was a former Union Whig. President Johnson's reconstruction policy must be sustained and Northern hostilities placated, Dupree frankly told the people of his district. Harrison's election to Congress, he asserted, would give an erroneous impression in the North of the attitude of Mississippians toward the Union and would play into the hands of those who were demanding a radical settlement for the South.[22] A writer to the Meridian *Clarion* believed that Franklin Smith, a Douglas Democrat who supported the Confederacy, "would be more acceptable to our friends in Washington" than his two Whig opponents for Congress in the Meridian district.[23]

Most leaders in the state encouraged the people to support neither secessionists or "dirt-eating submissionists," who in the popular mind were associated with persistent Unionism during the war. Whigs generally had occupied the broad and somewhat ambiguous ground between these two extremes, and, as during the summer of 1865, many of them now believed that the time was ripe to revive their party in the state.[24] But again Whig efforts to organize as a party were abortive, and for the same reasons as before.

The results of the October 2 election, nevertheless, appear to have

[20] Friar's Point *Coahomian*, September 22, 1865.
[21] *Ibid.*; "Report of the Joint Committee on Reconstruction," *House Reports*, 39th Cong., 1st Sess., No. 30, Pt. III, 136; Meridian *Clarion*, October 1, 1865.
[22] Macon *Beacon*, September 20, 1865.
[23] Meridian *Clarion*, October 1, 1865.
[24] New Orleans *Picayune*, October 6, 1865; Friar's Point *Coahomian*, September 22, 1865.

been another triumph for conservatism and Whiggery.[25] A conservative Whig, Humphreys, was elected governor; Whigs won all of the seats in Congress; conservative Democrats were chosen for the traditionally nonpartisan high court; and Whigs won a majority of the seats in the legislature.

The selection of the restoration governor clearly attracted more attention than the other contests for office. Yet voter participation in this election declined 42 per cent from that of the presidential election of 1860.[26] As in the case of the election for delegates to the reconstruction convention, voting was quite light in the more populous counties. From an examination of the beat returns (available for ten counties) it is evident that voters of many communities, especially in interior counties, were either unaware of Humphreys' candidacy or believed that he was ineligible to serve as governor. Many rural precincts of the back country from which returns are available recorded no votes for Humphreys. On the other hand, several communities in west and central Mississippi showed no support for William S. Patton. Apparently information regarding Fisher's candidacy was received in all of the communities of the state, although several gave him little support.[27]

In spite of the confusion concerning the candidacy of Humphreys, he received 19,036 votes and was thus elected governor. Fisher secured 15,551 votes and Patton 10,329. Humphreys' support was strongest in the river counties, both in the Delta and below Vicksburg, and weakest in the piney woods of southeast Mississippi where Confederate military forces had clashed with deserters during the war. John Bell, the Constitutional Union party's candidate for President in

[25] See Sharkey's opinion of the results of the election in "Report of the Joint Committee on Reconstruction," *House Reports*, 39th Cong., 1st Sess., No. 30, Pt. III, 137.

[26] In any correlation of the votes of the 1860 and the 1865 elections, it should be remembered that one fourth of the white males aged fifteen and above in 1860 did not return after the war.

[27] Official Returns of the Election for Governor and Other State Officers, 1865, State Totals, in Records of the Secretary of State for the State of Mississippi, File E-89, Mississippi Department of Archives and History, Jackson, hereinafter cited as Official Election Returns, 1865, State Totals; Official Returns of the Election for Governor and Other State Officers, 1865, Precinct Returns, in Records of the Secretary of State for the State of Mississippi, File F-89, Mississippi Department of Archives and History, Jackson, hereinafter cited as Official Election Returns, 1865, Precinct Returns.

1860, likewise had been strongest in the river counties and weakest in the piney woods. This tends to suggest that there may be a close correlation between Humphreys' and Bell's votes. But this is not necessarily true, for the candidacy of Fisher, also a Whig, complicated the picture in the alluvial counties. Of the nine counties in the Delta (including Warren) carried by Bell in 1860, Fisher won four. But in the other Bell counties, Fisher was quite weak and Humphreys was strong in winning.[28]

In the piney woods, it is obvious from the combined vote of Fisher and Humphreys that the support for Whigs was less in 1865 than it had been in 1860. Both sectionalism and old party loyalties appear in this vote, in which Patton, a Democrat of the piney woods trade center of Meridian, carried all but three of these southeastern counties. On the other hand, he won only two counties outside of the piney barrens, including Fisher's home county. All of the piney woods counties carried by Patton had voted for the Southern Democratic candidate, John C. Breckinridge, in 1860. This close correlation between Patton and Breckinridge votes represents a persistence of party loyalties, although within the framework of Unionism in 1865. Despite a tradition of strong Unionism during the latter part of the war, Unionists were not willing to transcend old party lines. Otherwise, Fisher, a Union Whig who did not participate very actively in the Confederate war effort, would have received more support in the area. The failure of Humphreys and Fisher to secure a large following in the piney barrens suggests that the yeoman whites of the area, as during antebellum days, decidedly opposed the selection of a broadcloth, planter-lawyer of the fertile counties of the west for governor when an acceptable Democrat was a candidate.

Patton, however, received few votes in predominantly Democratic northeast Mississippi. Fisher carried five of the six counties in the

[28] Election Returns, 1865, State Totals. For the vote in the Presidential Election of 1860, see Official Returns of the Presidential Election of 1860, State Totals, in Records of the Secretary of State for the State of Mississippi, File F-89, Mississippi Department of Archives and History, Jackson. Of the four Bell counties that Fisher won, in only two, De Soto and Panola, did he win an overwhelming victory over Humphreys. These two counties were near Memphis and were strong in their support of the Union in 1860. From an examination of the beat returns in Panola County, where Douglas, the National (Union) Democratic candidate was strong in 1860, it is evident that there is a high degree of correlation between Douglas' and Patton's votes. See *ibid.*, and Official Election Returns, 1865, Precinct Returns for Panola County.

northeast corner, an area that had endured periodic military raids during the war and that had become disenchanted with the Confederate cause as early as 1862. Apparently the electorate of the area preferred for governor a noncombatant, Fisher, to a Confederate general, Humphreys, notwithstanding the fact that two residents of the section, Arthur E. Reynolds and John M. Simonton, both original Unionists like Humphreys, had served in the Confederate army and yet had retained their political popularity. However, in several precincts of one county Humphreys received no ballots, thus suggesting that the voters of the area were not generally aware of his candidacy.[29]

Humphreys secured a great deal of support throughout the state from former Confederate soldiers. He had been quite popular with Mississippi troops in Virginia, and the image of his "thrice perforated coat" played an important part in his victory at the polls.[30] Somewhat ironically, Federal officers and soldiers in Vicksburg, who had acquired citizenship in the state, campaigned and voted almost unanimously for their former enemy, Humphreys, who was a resident of nearby Claiborne County. The effectiveness of their support is indicated by the vote in Warren County (Vicksburg), in which Humphreys received 843 of the 868 votes cast, or over 95 per cent of the total ballots of the county.[31]

A few days after the election Humphreys wrote President Johnson giving him a somewhat simple explanation for his victory. "A majority of my fellow citizens, believing [that] clemency would be extended to me, and in view of my political antecedents, elected me to the office of Governor." [32] But probably a more accurate analysis of the election results would conclude that of the two conservative Whig candidates

[29] Official Election Returns, 1865, State Totals.

[30] William D. Holder to Humphreys, October 23, 1865, in Governors' Correspondence, E-77; H. M. Watterson to President Johnson, October 7, 1865, in Johnson Papers. Except in the case of the popular Humphreys, voters apparently showed little preference for military heroes, even maimed ones. For example, see J. B. Hughes to Humphreys, December 30, 1865, in Governors' Correspondence, E-77. See also a statement of the war record of J. L. McCullum, candidate for state treasurer, in the Meridian Clarion, October 1, 1865. McCullum deprecated the fact that his opponents had not served in the army and asked former Confederate soldiers to vote for him. He lost the election.

[31] New Orleans Picayune, October 11, 1865; Meridian Clarion, October 8, 1865; Official Election Returns, 1865, State Totals.

[32] Humphreys to Johnson, October 26, 1865, in Johnson Papers.

the voters of the state preferred the one with the war record—Humphreys.

In the election of a legislature Whigs won a distinct majority of the seats in both houses, although not as overwhelmingly as in August. Of the thirty-one successful candidates for the senate, seventeen identified themselves as Whigs, thirteen as Democrats (including four Union Democrats and one Douglas Democrat), and one as a "Secessionist." Whigs won fifty-two house seats and the Democrats captured thirty-nine (three Douglas Democrats and two Union Democrats included) of the ninety-eight seats in that body. The other seven members used a variety of designations to identify themselves, such as "Southern," "Opposed to Secession," and "Co-operation."

Only four members of the new legislature had served in the secession convention, and three of them had worked for the preservation of the Union.[33] The secession party had thus been bypassed. Sixteen of the thirty-one senators had served previously in the legislature; however, only twenty-five in the populous house of representatives had had experience in the lawmaking branch. Only Samuel J. Gholson and James Lusk Alcorn had held a prominent state or federal position before 1865. Gholson had served briefly in Congress and had been a federal district judge for twenty years.[34] Alcorn, representative from Coahoma County, had headed the levee commission before the war.

Although only four of the new senators and ten of the representatives had sat in the reconstruction convention, the October election does not necessarily represent a repudiation of that body's actions. Many of the conservative delegates of the convention evidently thought that the changes they had made to the constitution in August established a conservative pattern which the legislature was obligated to follow. Therefore they saw no necessity for their leadership in the new legislative body. Then, too, some convention delegates were simply too busy attempting to make a living to campaign and to leave

[33] *Tabular View of the Legislature of 1865*, in Broadsides Collection, 1831–70, Mississippi Department of Archives and History, Jackson. Roderick Seal, the "Secessionist," was a Democrat.

[34] See Rowland (ed.), *Statistical Register of Mississippi*, 25–46, 216–28 *passim*, for a listing of persons who had served in state and federal offices. Only four members of this legislature held prominent state offices after 1867—Robert Lowry, governor; Horatio F. Simrall and James M. Arnold, state supreme court justices; and J. Prentiss Carter, lieutenant governor.

their businesses or plantations to go to Jackson during the most active period of the cotton season.[35]

Leaders in the August convention generally preferred to run for higher office, or for circuit judgeships which would keep them near their homes, than to be selected for the legislature. Ephraim G. Peyton, Arthur E. Reynolds, and James T. Harrison, conservative leaders in the reconstruction convention, ran successfully for Congress; J. Shall Yerger, James F. Trotter, and James F. Hamm preferred circuit judgeships to seats in the legislature. George L. Potter, who campaigned on an anti-testimony platform in September, lost by 114 votes to Alexander H. Handy in the election for a seat on the High Court of Errors and Appeals.[36] William Yerger, the most influential conservative in the convention, had always preferred his quiet and highly remunerative private law practice to public office with its low pay and political factionalism. On the other hand, John W. C. Watson, leader of the conservative Whigs of north Mississippi, apparently hoped to run for the legislature but did not seek a seat because he had not received a pardon.[37]

The five men elected to Congress obviously reflected the conservative spirit of the electorate and their desire to send no one to Washington who had been tainted with secession. All had opposed secession, and all were of the Whig persuasion. Four of the Congressmen-elect, however, had participated actively in the Confederate experiment. James T. Harrison, who won an overwhelming victory in the Columbus district, had served as a delegate to the convention at Montgomery which formed the Confederate States and had also served in Congress throughout the entire war.[38] Absalom M. West had risen to the rank of brigadier general in the Southern armed forces, while Richard A. Pinson and Arthur E. Reynolds had served as colonels.[39] Even the

[35] Jason Niles Scrapbook, Vol. XLI; Meridian *Clarion,* October 1, 1865.

[36] Official Election Returns, 1865, State Totals.

[37] Sharkey thought that, in contrast to its policy regarding the eligibility of delegates to the reconstruction convention, the federal government would insist that no unpardoned candidates take office in the restoration government. New York *Tribune,* October 4, 1865; Meridian *Clarion,* October 6, 12, 1865.

[38] "Report of the Joint Committee on Reconstruction," *House Reports,* 39th Cong., 1st Sess., No. 30, Pt. III, 136; James T. Harrison to President Johnson, undated, in Amnesty Papers, Mississippi; *Biographical and Historical Memoirs of Mississippi,* I, 884–85.

[39] J. G. Deupree, "Colonel R. A. Pinson," *Publications of the Mississippi His-*

men who ran unsuccessfully for Congress were generally either Union Whigs or Union Democrats in 1860–61. Of the five unsuccessful candidates whose position on secession has been identified, only one, John D. Freeman of Holly Springs, was a secessionist in 1861; he ran in 1865 on a conservative platform endorsing Sharkey's Negro testimony proclamation.[40]

Of the prominent state officers, only to the High Court of Errors and Appeals were secessionists elected, and two of them had served on the court during the war. In probably the only election in which old party lines were clearly drawn, Chief Justice Alexander H. Handy, a Democrat, defeated George L. Potter for central Mississippi's representative on the court. Handy won the overwhelming support of the electorate of the traditionally Democratic counties of east Mississippi, but received only 116 of the 1,178 votes in Hinds County, a strong Whig area.[41] The fact that Potter's home county was Hinds and the fact that he raised the Negro testimony issue might have influenced the voters in that county. But more likely his overwhelming victory in Hinds could be attributed to the strong Whig sentiments of the county in 1865, evidenced earlier by the complete lack of Democratic opposition to Whig candidates for delegates to the August convention. Probably not entirely by coincidence, Potter received almost the same total vote that John Bell had secured in 1860 in Hinds County; and, furthermore, he received approximately the same support as the combined votes for Fisher and Humphreys, the two Whig candidates for governor. The Breckinridge (or Southern Democratic vote in 1860 was 1,015, whereas Handy in 1865 received only 116 votes, and Patton, the Democratic (Union) candidate for governor, received 123.[42] These figures suggest that in the 1865 election almost all of the Democrats of Hinds County remained at home, and the few who participated supported the Democratic candidates for governor and the court. The

torical Society, Centenary Series, II (1918), 10; Biographical and Historical Memoirs of Mississippi, II, 1013; Arthur E. Reynolds to President-elect Rutherford B. Hayes, February 25, 1877, in Rutherford B. Hayes Papers, Hayes Memorial Library, Fremont, Ohio.

[40] Official Election Returns, 1865, State Totals; New Orleans Picayune, October 11, 1865.

[41] See Official Election Returns, 1865, State Totals.

[42] Ibid.; Official Returns of the Presidential Election of 1860, State Totals. Handy's home county, Madison, was fairly evenly divided between the two candidates, as it was in the John Bell–John C. Breckinridge election of 1860.

other two successful candidates for the bench, William L. Harris and Henry T. Ellett, won virtually without opposition.

Chief Justice Handy had been one of the leading secessionists in the state, and in 1862 he had written and published an influential pamphlet entitled *Seccession Considered as a Right in the States Composing the Late American Union of States.* Harris had served on the court since 1858, and President James Buchanan had offered him a place on the United States Supreme Court in 1860.[43] Ellett had served briefly in Congress during the 1840's and had been a member of the committee which drafted Mississippi's ordinance of secession.[44] In spite of their early radicalism, all three of the new justices were tending toward conservatism at the time of their election in 1865, according to Sharkey who had earlier counseled against their election because of the effect in the North the selection of secessionists to the court would have.[45]

Three days after the election President Johnson approved Governor-elect Humphreys' request for pardon.[46] On October 16 the former Confederate brigadier was inaugurated as governor, and the legislature convened at Jackson; yet the President was reluctant to approve such a speedy restoration of home rule in Mississippi, especially with a former Confederate general as governor. Johnson instructed Sharkey that he should continue to function as provisional governor, exercising

[43] Dunbar Rowland, *Courts, Judges, and Lawyers of Mississippi, 1798–1935* (Jackson: Hederman Brothers, 1935), 94–95; *Biographical and Historical Memoirs of Mississippi,* I, 884. Harris declined the position on the Supreme Court reportedly because of the approaching disruption of the Union and his desire to remain in his home state.

[44] *Biographical Directory of Congress,* 354.

[45] Sharkey's testimony before the Joint Committee on Reconstruction on the political ideas of the judges of the high court is, according to Sharkey, erroneously reported in "Report of the Joint Committee on Reconstruction," *House Reports,* 39th Cong., 1st Sess., No. 30, Pt. III, 136–37. In this report he is quoted as saying that "the judiciary department has fallen into bad hands. . . . The election of these judges to the highest tribunal in the State was a very sore thing to many of us." His corrections to the published reports of this testimony may be found in the Jackson *Clarion and Standard,* May 17, 1866. In his corrected statement Sharkey declared that he had not expressed the regret regarding the election attributed to him in the congressional report, although he had advised Mississippi voters not to select secessionists. Actually, Sharkey said, these men were loyal and conservative men by the fall of 1865. Only one other secessionist, Attorney General Charles E. Hooker, was elected to a high state office.

[46] Johnson to the Attorney General of the United States, October 5, 1865, in Amnesty Papers, Mississippi.

apparently a sort of vague guardianship over the restoration officials.[47] Although this dual arrangement for governing the state, plus the continuance of military jurisdiction in Negro matters, could have proved confusing and disconcerting, difficulties did not arise between Humphreys and Sharkey. This rapport between the two governors was due mainly to Sharkey's deep commitment to constitutional process and his belief that there was no longer any justification for a provisional government. Sharkey did not use his authority at any time to intervene in state affairs. In fact, when Major General George H. Thomas visited Jackson in November on orders from Washington to inquire into the intentions of the legislature concerning the freedmen, Sharkey refused to discuss the matter with him and suggested that he talk to the *de jure* governor, Humphreys.[48] By December, 1865, Johnson had come to realize the anomaly of the situation, and on December 25 he authorized Humphreys to assume full direction of the government.[49]

Sharkey's deference to civil and constitutional procedures and his publicized victory over General Slocum on the militia issue, made him the leading candidate for a seat in the United States Senate.[50] When the Whig-controlled legislature met in October, it immediately began balloting to determine who would represent the state in the Senate. In a futile effort to block the selection of Sharkey, and possibly that of James Lusk Alcorn as well, a resolution was offered in the state senate proposing that it support no one for Senator "who is or shall be in favor of giving to the slaves thus manumitted, any rights, civil, political, or social, further than was [*sic*] vouchsafed unto the same

[47] Currier, *Reconstruction in Mississippi*, 96. By this time Radical Republicans were bent upon the defeat of the Presidential plan of reconstruction. Coulter, *The South during Reconstruction*, 41. These Radicals denounced Humphreys as "a rebel general who was heralding the restoration of the old slavocracy to power." C. T. Purnell to Humphreys, October 29, 1865, in Governors' Correspondence, E-77. At least one historian, John Hope Franklin, believes erroneously that the 1865 elections in Mississippi and other Southern states ushered in "reconstruction, Confederate style. . . . The spirit of the South and the principles underlying it were very much alive. More than that, those who had fought against the Union were in control, pursuing most of their prewar policies as though there had never been a war," Franklin asserts. *Reconstruction: After the Civil War* (Chicago: University of Chicago Press, 1961), 53.

[48] Percy L. Rainwater (ed.), "The Autobiography of Benjamin Grubb Humphreys, August 26, 1808-December 20, 1882," *Mississippi Valley Historical Review*, XXI (1934), 248.

[49] William H. Seward to Humphreys, December 25, 1865, in Governors' Correspondence, E-77.

[50] James T. Harrison to Sharkey, September 22, 1865, *ibid.*, E-72.

person and property of the domiciliated free negro, by the statutes of the State prior to the late revolution." [51] Several of the legislators who advanced this resolution had won election on a platform opposing Sharkey's Negro testimony proclamation and advocating strict laws to regulate the freedmen.[52] Some who supported the resolution may have already been aware of Alcorn's liberal views toward the place of the Negro in Mississippi's postbellum society. From Washington in August, 1865, Alcorn had written his wife that the Republicans would prevent the admission of Southerners to Congress in December unless the former Confederate States enfranchised the Negroes, at least to a limited extent. "I think it would be politic for the Southern States to meet this issue with an acceptance at once," Alcorn declared. "We must make the negro our friend, and we can do this if we will. Should we make him our enemy under the promptings of the Yankee, whose aim is to force us to recognize an equality, then our path lies through a way red with blood, and damp with tears. To let the negro approach the witness stand and the ballot box by no means implies his social equality." [53] Largely by a party vote, with the Whigs opposing the resolution, the senate voted twenty-one to eight to table the motion aimed at prospective candidates for the United States Senate who held liberal views on Negro rights.[54]

On the first ballot of the legislature, meeting in joint session, Sharkey was elected to the Senate by a vote of 100 to 26 over Fulton Anderson, a former Confederate congressman and an influential Whig lawyer of Jackson. The selection for the second seat in the Senate proved more difficult and required four ballots before a choice was made. Democrats were determined to elect one of their members, specifically Samuel J. Gholson, a secessionist after Lincoln's election and a wounded Confederate brigadier.[55] When the legislature was organized

[51] Jackson *News*, October 22, 1865; Meridian *Clarion*, October 22, 1865.

[52] Meridian *Clarion*, October 6, 7, 1865; New York *Tribune*, October 9, 1865.

[53] Alcorn to Amelia Alcorn, August 26, 1865, in Alcorn Papers.

[54] Meridian *Clarion*, October 22, 1865.

[55] Friar's Point *Coahomian*, October 27, 1865. Some Democrats desired the election of William S. Featherston to the Senate. His friends in the legislature believed, however, that, since he had not been pardoned by the President, he was not eligible for the office. Furthermore, even if he were pardoned and selected for the Senate, they feared that because he was a former secessionist and a Confederate brigadier general he would not be permitted to take his seat in Congress. Therefore they made little effort to secure his selection. Jackson *Clarion*, December 7, 1865.

on October 16, the popular Gholson was chosen speaker of the house, probably to preclude his candidacy for United States Senator. As far as the Whig majority was concerned, to select a man with the disunion record of Gholson for the Senate would be extremely impolitic and would make it more likely that Mississippi's representatives would be rejected by the Republican majority in Congress.[56]

Yet the Whigs in the legislature could not agree on a party candidate for the second Senate seat. Whigs of the river counties and Hinds County (Jackson) preferred William Yerger, but those of the interior were divided in their support of Alcorn of Coahoma County in the Delta and John W. C. Watson of Marshall County for the position.[57] Watson was more influential in populous northeast Mississippi, but he had served in the last Confederate Senate and therefore was unacceptable to many legislators who were anxious to placate the North on this matter. Alcorn, a large slaveholder, had served as a Union Whig delegate to the secession convention of 1861, but after the state withdrew from the United States he entered the army for a brief period as a brigadier general of Mississippi troops.[58] On the fourth ballot in the legislature, Watson Whigs, along with a few Democrats, gave their support to Alcorn and he was elected to the Senate.[59] Whigs thus won the governorship and all seven of the seats in Congress. Their success in the election of 1865 appears in sharp contrast to their frustrating efforts to win prominent political offices during the latter part of the antebellum period. Only two Whigs, Walker Brooke and William A. Lake, had been selected for Congress during the 1850's. None had been elected governor.

The press of the state in 1865 applauded the choices of the legislature for the United States Senate. It was predicted in the Friar's Point *Coahomian* that Sharkey and Alcorn, because of their original Union-

[56] Although a secessionist, Gholson's tenure as a federal judge generally kept him removed from the bitter party politics of the 1850's; thus Whigs did not find it too difficult to support him for speaker of the house of representatives in 1865. For his background, see Samuel J. Gholson to President Johnson, undated, in Amnesty Papers, Mississippi.

[57] *Journal of the Senate of the State of Mississippi, October, November, and December Session of 1865* (Jackson: J. J. Shannon and Co., State Printer, 1866), 36–37, hereinafter cited as *Senate Journal, 1865.*

[58] Lillian A. Pereyra, *James Lusk Alcorn: Persistent Whig* (Louisiana State University Press, 1966), 40–42, 50.

[59] *Senate Journal, 1865,* pp. 36, 39.

ism and their conservatism, would be immediately permitted to take their seats in the Senate when Congress met in December.[60]

In the election of the legislators also, newspaper editors believed that conservatism had triumphed, despite the selection of several opponents of Negro testimony and some debt repudiators.[61] The editor of the Meridian *Clarion* expressed this hopeful sentiment and proclaimed that "we feel no hesitation in pronouncing the present General Assembly of Mississippi one of the ablest ever convened." Their abilities would be fully tested, for they would be faced with the most momentous questions in Mississippi history, he declared. "It is for them to preserve intact the leading features of our new constitution and qualify the State for immediate representation in the national council." [62]

[60] Friar's Point *Coahomian*, October 27, 1865. See also the Meridian *Clarion*, October 8, 1865.

[61] Raymond *Hinds County Gazette*, October 28, 1865; Meridian *Clarion*, October 8, 1865. See also the remarks of the editor of the Brandon *Republican* concerning the character of the new legislature, as reported in the Meridian *Clarion*, October 7, 1865.

[62] Meridian *Clarion*, October 17, 1865.

7

Formulation of the Black Code

THE LEGISLATURE that convened on October 16, 1865, immediately took steps to act on the problem of the freedmen. The problem involved not only the restoration of a stable labor system, but also the broader question of the place of the Negro in Mississippi society, legally, socially, and economically. The new legislature was divided on this problem along radical and conservative or moderate lines, with radicals favoring a settlement that would place the freedmen in a position similar, if not identical, to that of the free Negro before 1865, and with little reference to public sentiment in the North or to the wishes of President Johnson.[1] One writer to the Jackson *Clarion* observed that the radicals were generally "young men, whose eyes yet beam with the light and fire of youth." They were anxious to settle the "nigger question, as they termed it."[2]

In urging that laws be enacted to place the blacks in a position like that of the free Negro of the slavery period, radicals were indeed suggesting a rigidly restrictive settlement. For example, prior to 1865 the laws of the state provided that if a free Negro went outside of his

---

[1] The terms "radical" and "conservative" were not consistently applied at the time to distinguish these two groups in the legislature; in fact, most people, especially in the North, were probably not aware of any division of opinion on the Negro question in the Mississippi assembly. The state press often referred to the radicals in the legislature as members of the "anti-testimony" group. The editor of the Canton *American Citizen*, however, thought that legislators who were resolved not "to elevate the negro one iota above his present status" were "able and conservative men." Canton *American Citizen*, October 15, 1865. For the best statements of the position of the radicals, see comments by James H. R. Taylor and William D. Lyles before the senate soon after the session began, as reported in the Jackson *News*, October 22, 1865.

[2] Jackson *Clarion*, November 11, 1865.

county, he had to show evidence that he had some honest employment. Furthermore, he could only sell goods in an incorporated town, and he was required to have a license to keep arms or weapons. The Negro could own property if he had been legally freed in the state, that is, freed with the approval of the legislature. In judicial proceedings, a free Negro could not be a witness in a case in which a white person was a party, much less could he serve on a jury.[3]

Conservatives, on the other hand, desired the legislature to pass measures that would reflect the spirit, if not the letter, of the reconstruction convention and that would meet the approbation of the national administration. A settlement of this nature would clearly guarantee the civil rights of the freedmen and would protect their property rights. Such a moderate program, it was hoped, in keeping with the forces at work in the state at the time, would be welcomed by the Negroes, and they would therefore be motivated to work and to improve their condition. Nevertheless, the conservatives agreed with the radicals that the Negroes should be forced to labor and that they should receive no political privileges. Thus not even the conservatives were willing to grant to freedmen all of the privileges usually associated with male adult citizenship in the United States. They desired actually to place the freedmen in a position somewhere between that of the free Negro of slavery days and that of a citizen, and they believed that such an arrangement would satisfy the President and would promote his policies in the North. Furthermore, they predicted that a moderate program would result in the acceptance of Mississippi's representatives in Congress and the complete restoration of the state to the Union.[4] Party lines were drawn somewhat on the Negro issue, as Whigs, in a majority in the legislature, tended to support the conservative position and Democrats favored a radical approach. Clearly the leadership in the legislature for those seeking a moderate settlement came from the Whigs, and especially Horatio F.

[3] Charles S. Sydnor, "The Free Negro in Mississippi before the Civil War," *American Historical Review*, XXXII (1927), 770–73.

[4] For the best statement of the conservative approach, see Horatio F. Simrall's speech before the house during the debate on the civil rights bill, as reported in the Jackson *Clarion*, November 18, 1865. See also an editorial in the *Clarion*, November 12, 1865, and the remarks of Sylvanus Evans, a Whig candidate for Congress in 1865, in "Condition of the South," *Senate Executive Documents*, 39th Cong., 1st Sess., No. 2, p. 64.

Simrall, while the radicals generally looked to two Democrats, Samuel J. Gholson and James H. R. Taylor, for guidance.[5]

The organization of the legislature reflected more of a conservative spirit toward the Negro than a radical one. John M. Simonton, a young Union Whig of northeast Mississippi, was chosen with little opposition as president of the senate.[6] In the house, however, Gholson, who disapproved of civil privileges for Negroes, was selected speaker as some Whigs and moderates joined the radicals in voting for him.[7] As previously noted, conservatives may have supported the popular and experienced Gholson for this position in order to preclude his candidacy for a seat in the United States Senate, where as a former secessionist he would not have been welcomed. Despite his radicalism on the Negro question, Gholson after his selection as speaker apparently made no effort to block the conservatives, since he appointed more moderates than radicals to the important Joint Committee on Freedmen. This special committee was instructed to prepare and report to the legislature any laws and changes in laws that the committee "may deem expedient and proper for the protection and security of the person and property of the Freedmen of this State, including their social relations toward each other, that of husband and wife, and parent and child; and what laws are necessary to make their labor available to the agricultural interests of the State, and to protect the State from the support of minors, vagrants and paupers." [8] Simrall, a Whig lawyer-planter of Wilkinson County and the ablest man in the house, according to the Jackson *Clarion* editor, was selected to head this important committee.[9]

[5] The conclusion that the conservative-radical division followed political party lines is based on an examination of roll-call votes in the senate and the house on the civil rights bill and proposed amendments to it. *Senate Journal, 1865,* pp. 223, 226–28; *Journal of the House of Representatives of the State of Mississippi, October, November, and December Session of 1865* (Jackson: J. J. Shannon and Co., State Printers, 1866), 212–13, 284, hereinafter cited as *House Journal, 1865.*

[6] *Senate Journal,* 1865, p. 4; Canton *American Citizen,* October 19, 1865.

[7] *House Journal, 1865,* p. 5; Gholson to President Johnson, undated, in Amnesty Papers, Misissippi.

[8] *House Journal, 1865,* pp. 32–33.

[9] Jackson *Clarion,* November 22, 1865. Simrall served in the Kentucky legislature during the antebellum period and occupied a chair of law at the University of Louisville. He moved from his native state to Mississippi in 1861 and participated in the Confederate "council" for Kentucky. Simrall to President Johnson, undated, in Amnesty Papers, Mississippi. After the failure of Presidential Reconstruction, and the inauguration of Congressional Reconstruction, Simrall was ap-

The demands for legislation to regulate Negroes increased as the Joint Committee on Freedmen began its work during late October, 1865. Reflecting the anxieties and tensions created by the hesitation of Negroes to contract for the new year and by the insurrection scare, most of these demands and proposals were not tempered by moderation. Former Governor William McWillie called upon the legislature to deal harshly with the freedmen in order to return them to the fields and to punish severely law offenders of both races.[10] The Quitman *Messenger* agreed with McWillie's proposal that rigorous measures should be initiated to restore the tranquility of the state and added that, instead of placing criminals in the penitentiary, "cheaper and quicker engines of punishment, the gallows, whipping post and pillory" shoud be instituted to punish them.[11]

Editors of the Jackson *News* and the Canton *American Citizen* urged the legislature to grant no privileges to the freedmen that the free Negro did not possess earlier. They continually reminded the assembly that its duty was to pass laws that would require the Negro to contract and also protect him against fraud and injustice, yet such protection should "avoid equalizing him with the white man as a competent witness in our courts. If we admit the negro to full equality with white men in the courts, we had as well bestow upon him the right of suffrage at once," the *American Citizen* declared.[12] In its masthead the *News* stated, "This is a white man's country—President Johnson." Its editor, Edward M. Yerger, exclaimed, "The freedman and the free Negro must stand on the same footing." The legislature must insure that the Negro "be kept in the position which God almighty intended him to occupy; *a position inferior to the white man.*" [13]

Of the many proposals and suggestions before the Joint Committee on Freedmen, the most significant was the report of the special com-

---

pointed to the state supreme court by Governor Alcorn and served in this capacity for nine years. During the 1880's he actively supported Republican presidential candidates and was elected to the state constitutional convention of 1890, the only regular Republican in that body. *Biographical and Historical Memoirs of Mississippi*, II, 773–74.

[10] As reported in the New Orleans *Picayune,* November 1, 1865.

[11] *Ibid.* See also A. D. McLean to Sharkey, August 1, 1865, in Governors' Correspondence, E-71.

[12] Canton *American Citizen,* October 15, 22, 29, 1865.

[13] The italics are those of the editor. Jackson *News,* November 14, 1865.

mittee appointed and instructed by the reconstruction convention to recommend to the legislature any changes in the laws, or the incorporation of new laws, needed for adjustment to the constitutional revisions made by the convention. The committee, headed by Judge Robert S. Hudson, an impetuous Whig of Yazoo County, made no proposal concerning specific laws to regulate the freedmen, but, rather, limited its recommendations to suggesting general principles or policies for the legislature to follow. The committee "thought it best to deny to the freedmen some unbridled privileges for the present, not from any apprehension or sense of danger to the white population, but from the clear conviction that such denial and restrictions will be for their present and ultimate good in the suppression of vice, idleness, vagrancy, impositions and poverty, the promotion of industry, and the diminution of crime and its long train of baneful consequences and monstrous evils. . . ." [14] The legislature, the report continued, should place upon both blacks and whites "the harness of obedience and subordination to duty [and to] the laws of the State."

While some of the proposed legislation may seem rigid and stringent to the sickly modern humanitarians, they can never disturb, retard or embarrass the good and true, useful and faithful of either race, but . . . [are] absolutely necessary to secure their repose, usefulness and happiness, while the wayward and vicious, idle and dishonest, the lawless and reckless, the wicked and improvident, the vagabond and meddler must be smarted, governed, reformed and guided by higher instincts, minds and morals higher and holier than theirs, and by laws stronger and more potent than those of mere public opinion and sentiment, and if they rudely thrust their hands and feet in the flames of the law, it will be a wilful and deliberate act of self punishment and trouble that can excite no sympathy from the good and pure in heart, of any clime or age, that should induce them to unloose the workers of evil and the instruments of fearful destruction.

If either whites or blacks felt that the policies instituted by the restoration government were too stringent, the special committee suggested that they leave the state.[15] In essence, the Hudson committee pro-

[14] The report of the Hudson committee is given in the appendix of the *House Journal, 1865*, pp. 13–17.

[15] The Hudson committee said that its proposed harsh policy, if enacted by the legislature, should be only temporary. "By timely and thorough legislation now, such healthy improvements in the habits, practices, industry and pursuits of both races will soon result, as to enable the State to modify her laws and proclaim to all her people the generous plaudit of 'well done good and faithful servants.'" *Ibid.*, 15–16.

posed a rigorous and harsh program of regulation by the state that, although designed primarily for Negroes, actually on paper was to be applied to both blacks and improvident whites.

In his inaugural address on October 16 Governor Humphreys reminded the legislature of the need for immediate action on the freedman problem. The new governor at first took a middle and somewhat vague position on the issue, even though his resolute remarks in his inaugural speeech evidently gave encouragement to those legislators who desired to give the Negroes few privileges. Humphreys advised that the blacks of the state must be permitted to rise as high in the scale of civilization as they could, with rights of person and property protected, but they should not be admitted to political or social equality with whites. "The purity and progress of both races require that caste must be maintained," he declared. Although the state and the planters must deal justly with them, Negroes must be required to labor, since "to work is the law of God," and, furthermore, the planters needed continuous labor from January to January to restore the productivity of the soil.[16]

Several conservative or moderate newspapers plainly cautioned the new legislature against any intemperate measures designed to curb the freedom of the Negroes or to restrict their testimony in the courts. The editor of the influential Jackson *Clarion* expressed this sentiment when he counseled that "there is no way by which we can be restored to Congress, military domination superseded by civil authority, order and industry established, [and] the resources of the country developed" except by showing a moderate spirit toward the freedmen. The *Clarion* urged the legislature to give the Negroes civil liberties, including the right to own property and the privilege of testifying in court. Although a stringent vagrancy law was felt to be necessary and desirable, the editor did not believe that unusual and rigorous legislation directed at this class would promote the true interests of the state. "It is evidently the best policy to stimulate their industry, show that we desire their improvement, and satisfy the most skeptical that our laws afford them protection and security."[17]

[16] Governor Humphreys' inaugural address may be found in *Senate Journal, 1865*, pp. 14–17.

[17] Jackson *Clarion*, November 12, 1865. See also the November 8 and 9 issues of the *Clarion*.

The Jackson *Clarion* editor was not alone in supporting a policy of moderation toward the freedmen; other leading newspaper editors of the state thought that the intractable position of the radicals was unwise, both from an economic and a political standpoint.[18] The Natchez *Democrat* claimed that the real reason for Negroes refusing to contract for the new year was not their illusions of securing land, but, rather, the uncertainty of their place in Mississippi society. Their disposition to work, a characteristic of the Negroes in slavery, had not been changed by emancipation, it was argued in the *Democrat*. And as soon as the position and rights of the freedmen were determined by the legislature, so soon would they seek regular employment and become responsible members of society. "It will only require kind treatment, a fair recompense for faithful labor, and a disposition to make the Negroes happy and comfortable, to restore a healthy and permanent system of labor," the editor avowed. "Negroes under this system will become permanent fixtures of the plantations." [19]   C. B. Manlove, of the Vicksburg *Journal* and a former Confederate officer, declared that the freedman could not be protected outside the courts; "and we care not whether any respectable lawyer in the State sustains us or not, common sense and reason does [*sic*]. The negro of Mississippi has to be protected by the laws of Mississippi or by Federal bayonets." [20]

Yet, in fact, many "respectable lawyers" and private citizens did advise the legislature to provide adequate safeguards for the rights of the Negroes. Sharkey exhorted the assembly to grant "full and perfect protection" to their property and personal rights, pointing out that for it to do otherwise would be in contravention of the state

[18] *Ibid.*, October 10, 1865, gives a list of several newspapers which supported a policy of moderation, although of a varying degree, toward the Negroes.

[19] Natchez *Democrat*, November 18, 1865.

[20] Vicksburg *Journal*, November 17, 1865. See also the remarks of the editor of the Brandon *Republican* as reported in the Meridian *Clarion*, October 7, 1865. Editor H. P. Reid of the Friar's Point *Coahomian*, October 27, 1865, was a very reluctant moderate. Reid declared that the question of Negro testimony "is repugnant to our feelings," but it was necessary to accept it, since "negro equality in the courts is not as nauseating a dose as negro equality in all political privileges. If we reject it, it may be forced upon us at the point of a bayonet." Reid, however, adamantly opposed permitting freedmen to own land, since, he said, they could not be protected if they secured this privilege. Issue of October 20, 1865.

constitution, as amended by the August convention.[21] Walker Brooke, an antebellum Whig leader and a former United States Senator, was "gratified to know that the intellect of the State is enlisted on the side of the freedmen's rights and privileges, and in favor of maintaining, to the fullest extent, the pledge of the Convention, that the Legislature shall provide, by law, for the protection and security of the person and property of the freedmen of this State." [22] One writer to the Meridian *Clarion* believed that the legislature should go further than the reconstruction convention and "repeal all incompetency for color." Another wrote that, in effect, state laws concerning free Negroes had been abolished by the convention, and now freedmen were *ipso facto* occupying a higher position under the law than had free blacks during the antebellum period.[23]

In formulating a comprehensive system for regulating the freedmen, legislators undoubtedly were influenced more by contemporary conditions in Mississippi, and their interpretation of these conditions based upon experience and prejudice, than by outside forces and precedents. Yet many precedents, other than those rooted in antebellum practices, were available as guides for perplexed legislators. Many of the members of the assembly probably made no effort to find these guides; but some, like Simrall, the learned chairman of the Joint Committee on Freedmen, sought precedents for their actions.[24] Both the ordinances of Northern states and regulations of the Freedmen's Bureau provided pertinent and often harsh examples for the legislators to follow in devising their regulative system. For example, several Northern statutes contained stringent vagrancy measures, and at least in one case any citizen of the state was permitted on his own authority to arrest wanderers. As to court testimony, five Northern states prohibited blacks from giving evidence in favor of or against any white person. Oregon forebade Negroes to hold real estate, make contracts, or maintain lawsuits. Apprenticeship laws were quite harsh in some Northern states, and persons enticing apprentices away from their masters were subject to severe punishment. Moreover, extralegal

[21] "Report of the Joint Committee on Reconstruction," *House Reports*, 39th Cong., 1st Sess., No. 30, Pt. III, 133.

[22] Vicksburg *Journal*, November 17, 1865.

[23] Meridian *Clarion*, October 1, 12, 1865.

[24] See Simrall's speech on the civil rights bill before the house, as reported in the Jackson *Clarion*, November 14, 1865.

codes—enforced by public opinion—provided "Jim Crow" restrictions on the social activities of Negroes.[25]

The Freedmen's Bureau in Mississippi also had instituted certain practices and procedures for managing the Negroes that could have served as precedents for the legislature. The pass system was employed by bureau officials in some areas during the summer of 1865 to regulate the movements of the freedmen.[26] Written contracts between planters and laborers that were to be rigidly enforced were insisted upon by the bureau. At the suggestion of General Oliver O. Howard, Colonel Samuel Thomas, the assistant commissioner for the state, indicated in late October while the Joint Committee on Freedmen was preparing its report that the old state vagrancy laws could be enforced by the civil authorities against idle Negroes. In July, 1865, Thomas made provision to bind out orphans, deserted children, and those whose parents were unable to keep them properly. The desire of the child was to be considered to a certain extent in choosing a master, Thomas directed, but "the judgment of the officers will, of course, have to decide such matters when the children's choice is unwise." Thomas suggested in October that the new civil officers might be reluctant to enforce the apprentice law, in which case, he said, bureau agents were to take action to bind out needy children.[27]

On the other hand, Colonel Thomas made it clear that no state legislation would be recognized that attempted to limit the Negro's right to hold property. Negro lessees, sponsored by the bureau, occupied abandoned plantations in the river counties, and Colonel Thomas hoped to secure other holdings for freedmen.[28] Thomas, moreover, insisted that the freedmen receive justice in the civil courts

[25] The best account of the free Negro in Northern society during the late antebellum period is Leon F. Litwack, *North of Slavery: The Negro in the Free States, 1790–1860* (Chicago: The University of Chicago Press, 1961). See especially pp. 64–112, for a discussion of the political and legal restrictions placed on the free Negro.

[26] Canus, "The Freedmen's Bureau in Mississippi," 199.

[27] "Report of the Commissioner of the Freedmen's Bureau," *House Executive Documents*, 39th Cong., 1st Sess., No. 70, p. 174; Natchez *Democrat*, October 17, 1865. In at least one case a circuit court intervened to prevent local bureau officers from binding out two Negro boys. The court ruled that the boys should be returned to their homes, since their mother and father were able to show evidence that they could support the children. Colonel Thomas endorsed the court's decision in the case. Natchez *Weekly Courier*, March 21, 1866.

[28] "Report of the Commissioner of the Freedmen's Bureau," *House Executive Documents*, 39th Cong., 1st Sess., No. 70, p. 158.

and that they particularly be given the privilege of testifying against whites.[29] Nevertheless, the probable effect of the bureau's policies, except in regard to property ownership and justice, was to suggest to the legislature that Thomas and his officers would not interfere to prevent the passage or enforcement of a strict state code to regulate the activities of the blacks.

With such a broad and extensive background of precedents, suggestions, and demands to draw upon, the Joint Committee on Freedmen compiled its report and presented it to the assembly on November 6. The most comprehensive and most controversial of the measures which collectively became known as the "Black Code" was the bill entitled, "An Act to confer Civil Rights on Freedmen, and for other purposes." This bill, in twelve sections, sought to define the place of the Negro in Mississippi society. The first four sections granted the freedmen certain civil or legal privileges. Section one specified that blacks could sue in all of the courts of the state and could acquire property: "Provided, That the provisions of this section shall not be so construed as to allow any freedman, free negro, or mulatto to *rent or lease* any lands or tenements, except in incorporated towns or cities in which places the corporate authorities shall control the same." [30]

Although section one did not specifically prohibit freedmen from acquiring land, even in the country, it was interpreted after passage by federal authorities and newspapers, as well as by at least one leader in the legislature, as a restriction against Negroes' owning farm property.[31] Giles Hillyer, representative from Adams County and editor of the Natchez *Courier,* believed the proviso meant an outright prohibition of landownership by Negroes and later indicated this as his reason for supporting the measure. The policy of blacks becoming

[29] See Chap. 5, pp. 86–88.

[30] The italics have been added for emphasis. The civil rights bill as passed may be found in the *Laws of Mississippi, 1865,* pp. 82–86.

[31] For examples of the later belief that the property proviso meant an outright prohibition of landownership for Negroes except in towns, see the Port Gibson *Standard,* December 9, 1865, the Jackson *Clarion,* April 10, 1866, and the New York *Times,* February 4, 1866. Some historians have also assumed that the proviso prevented colored persons from owning land in the country. For example, see Francis B. Simkins, *A History of the South* (3rd ed. rev.; New York: Alfred A. Knopf, 1963), 267, and William B. Hesseltine and David L. Smiley, *The South in American History* (2nd ed. rev.; Englewood Cliffs, N. J.: Prentice Hall, Inc., 1960), 365.

freeholders "would be most destructive, except under permission," Hillyer asserted. "Nests of negro colonies would at once be formed around every city, town and village, whose occupants would alone be supported by theft or other crime." Potential laborers would flock to these "colonies," whether near towns or in the country. The property proviso of section one, according to Hillyer, was therefore designed to return and to keep the Negroes on the plantations of the whites.[32]

Nevertheless, at the time when the civil rights bill was being debated before the legislature, it appears that the property proviso was not generally regarded as restricting Negro ownership of land in the country. Simrall in a long speech defending the bill in the house declared that section one did in fact give the Negroes full property rights. "These people are free," he declared. "We need them as laborers, and should stimulate their industry by permitting them to invest their earnings in any kind of property they choose."[33] Notwithstanding Simrall's manifestations, some conservatives probably supported the property proviso because they realized that Negroes would not soon be in a position economically to own farmlands, despite their legal right to do so. On the other hand, they probably believed that if they did not prohibit the leasing and renting of lands in the country, some freedmen might secure such properties and convert these into havens for idle, and even rebellious, Negroes.

The ambiguity in the legislature concerning the property proviso, accentuated by increased racial tensions while it was meeting, made it easy to include this clause in the final act, with little opposition. The implication, however, was clear to federal authorities—section one of the civil rights act was designed to prevent Negroes from holding land. After its passage Bureau Commissioner Howard in Washington immediately sent instructions to Colonel Thomas that no attention was to be paid to this proviso.[34]

It is difficult to understand why conservative legislators, who apparently saw the necessity for dealing justly with the Negroes and for sustaining President Johnson's program, would agree to the property clause, which plainly contained discriminatory features. Evidently many conservatives genuinely feared, like Giles Hillyer, that "nests

[32] As reported in the Vicksburg *Journal*, December 19, 1865.
[33] Jackson *Clarion*, November 22, 1865.
[34] *Ibid.*, December 6, 1865; Natchez *Democrat*, December 7, 1865.

of negro colonies" would form on property held by freedmen. They probably believed, almost incidentally, that the property proviso, couched in ambiguous terms, would be accepted by the national administration and would still in fact prevent the holding of lands in the country by Negroes. It is true that the free Negro of the antebellum period was permitted to possess land without restriction, provided that he had been properly freed in the state. Yet the problem of idle freedmen was insignificant before the war since only 773 were free in 1860. Furthermore, most of these free Negroes lived in the towns and probably had little desire to settle on farmlands.[35] Legislators, who were fearful of Negro disorders as the Christmas of 1865 approached, believed that in passing the property proviso they were acting to reestablish law and order and to prevent a possible freedman's uprising. In their deliberations and action on this matter, conservatives, like their radical colleagues in the legislature, reacted naturally to the problem and with little real concern for the attitude of President Johnson or Northerners toward their work.

From the beginning section four of the civil rights bill, dealing with Negro testimony in court, elicited the greatest amount of debate in the legislature and tended to minimize and confuse other issues.[36] By this provision freedmen were granted the right to testify in the courts, although only in cases in which they or other members of their race were parties. The success or failure of the moderate civil rights bill in the assembly depended upon the action of the legislature on this section. Several members had won election on a platform pledged to oppose Negro testimony; and others, inflamed by Samuel J. Gholson, James H. R. Taylor, and William D. Lyles to oppose the provision, had come to believe that the admission of Negro evidence in court would be the first step toward political equality.[37] When the bill was introduced, Gholson made a fiery speech in which he exclaimed that a conciliatory policy toward the North, as embodied in the testimony proviso, to the exclusion of the practical interests of Mississippians, would not work. He denounced the Jackson *Clarion* and other

[35] Sydnor, "The Free Negro in Mississippi before the Civil War," 782, 787.

[36] See the comments of a Mississippian, who was disgusted with the long "quibbling over the negro testimony bill," in the Memphis *Appeal*, December 14, 1865. Section two of the civil rights act provided for the legalizing of Negro common law marriages, and section three made intermarriage between the races a felony. *Laws of Mississippi, 1865*, p. 82.

[37] *Laws of Mississippi, 1865*, p. 83; Jackson *News*, October 22, 1865.

conservative newspapers for "threatening" the legislature on the issue.[38] Simrall in reply reiterated his position that economic reasons made it imperative that the Negro be made a contented laborer again, and the privilege of his seeking protection and redress in the courts was necessary for his security and happiness. Discounting arguments that passage of the testimony measure would lead to political privileges, Simrall asserted that the freedman would never be even a citizen of the United States, much less be enfranchised.[39]

After two days of debate on the measure, the Negro testimony proviso was defeated in the house by a vote of 50 to 40, and even friends of the civil rights bill agreed to its tabling.[40] Immediately, conservatives throughout the state denounced the action of the house and called for a reconsideration of the bill. Editor Manlove of the Vicksburg *Journal* confronted the legislators and declared: "We tell you plainly, gentlemen, that in less than a year you will be compelled to do that which you have refused voluntarily to do. . . . The negro is in the Courts now [as a result of Sharkey's proclamation of September 25], and he will stay there, whether the Legislature acquiesce or not." [41] On November 17 President Johnson telegraphed Governor Humphreys, informing him that troops would not be withdrawn from the state until it gave protection to the person and property of freedmen. Meanwhile, Johnson dispatched General George Thomas, the district commander, to talk with state officers and evidently to attempt to gain their cooperation for the passage of measures to secure justice for the Negroes.[42]

Whether due to outside or domestic pressures, or both, Humphreys on November 20 at last asserted positive executive leadership in the freedman controversy. In a special message to the legislature he denounced those who proposed to return the Negro to some form of slavery. The state constitution, as amended by the August convention,

[38] Jackson *Clarion,* November 14, 1865; Natchez *Weekly Democrat,* November 27, 1865.

[39] Jackson *Clarion,* November 14, 18, 1865.

[40] *House Journal, 1865,* pp. 212–13; Natchez *Democrat,* November 21, 1865.

[41] Vicksburg *Journal,* November 17, 1865. For another example of an editor's denunciation of the house for its failure to pass the Negro testimony proviso, see the Jackson *Clarion,* November 19, 1865.

[42] Johnson to Humphreys, November 17, 1865, in Governors' Correspondence, E-77; Raymond *Hinds County Gazette,* November 25, 1865; Vicksburg *Journal,* November 19, 1865; New Orleans *Picayune,* November 28, 1865.

and justice entitled him to protection and security in his person and property. Humphreys continued: "No person, bond or free, under any form of government, can be assured of protection in either person or property, except through an independent and enlightened judiciary. The courts then should be open to the negro. But of what avail is it to open the courts, and invite the negro to 'sue and be sued,' if he is not permitted to testify himself, and introduce such testimony as he or his attorney may deem essential to establish the truth and justice of his case?" [43] The freedman therefore should be permitted to testify for or against both whites and blacks. "Now that the negro is no longer under the restraints and protection of his master," Humphreys said, "he will become the dupe and the 'cat's paw' of the vile and vicious white man who seeks his association, and [the white man] will plunder our lands with entire security from punishment, unless he can be reached through negro testimony."

Yet Humphreys declared that the question of Negro evidence in court "sinks into insignificance by the side of the other great question of guarding them and the State against the evils that may arise from their sudden emancipation." These evils were crime, vagrancy, and pauperism, which already were afflicting the state. The governor recommended that the legislature enact three measures to curb these tendencies. First, he urged that Negro testimony be admitted in the courts of the state. Second, he suggested that the freedmen be encouraged "by laws assuring him of friendship and protection" to go to work and to support his family and the education of his children. At the same time Negroes should be taxed for the support of the indigent and helpless members of their race. Finally, Humphreys recommended the passage of an effective militia law for protection against the expected insurrection, "or any possible combination of vicious white men and negroes." [44]

Pressed to reconsider the civil rights bill, the legislature revived the measure on November 22 after Speaker Gholson, the leader of the

[43] Humphreys' November 20 message to the legislature may be found in the Memphis *Appeal*, November 28, 1865.

[44] Four days before Humphreys' November 20 message, a letter from Judge Robert S. Hudson, who had shown considerable intemperance earlier in recommending changes to state laws in view of the new position of the freedmen, was published in the Jackson *Clarion*. Hudson now encouraged the legislature to pass the civil rights bill with the Negro testimony proviso included.

radicals, agreed to support reconsideration.[45] But the extremists were not to be subdued easily. They switched their tactic from that of denouncing the bill, especially the Negro testimony proviso, to that of offering a comprehensive substitute for the whole measure, entitled "An act to protect freedmen, free negroes or mulattoes in person and property." This substitute, introduced by Senator M. D. L. Stephens, a Whig of north central Mississippi, was apparently the only plan the radicals in the legislature proposed as a settlement for the Negro problem.[46] And when compared with the old bill, it is obvious that Stephens' proposal recommended a far more extreme settlement than the relatively conservative civil rights measure. The Stephens substitute provided for the appointment of agents, primarily from members of the county boards of police, to serve as guardians of the freedmen and to administer, if not regulate, their affairs. Negroes under this plan actually would have no legal privileges except through their agents. All suits for or against freedmen would be brought in the name of the agent as the Negro's "next friend," and only white testimony would be permitted in court.[47] The agents, furthermore, were "to confirm and ratify all trades and contracts for hire, or the performance of labor made by any freedman." Finally, agents were to arrest vagrants in their communities and to have writs issued to secure the return of absconding laborers.

Stephens' ingenuous proposal was tabled by a vote of 17 to 12 in the senate, and the calendar was cleared for the passage of the civil rights bill.[48] This comprehensive measure passed on November 24 by a vote of 16 to 13 in the senate and 58 to 31 in the house.[49] The vote in the senate on the two plans, and amendments, indicates the cohesiveness of the radical-conservative alignment in that body. Only one senator who favored the Stephens substitute joined the conservatives in the final ballot on the civil rights bill, whereas no senator who op-

[45] Jackson *Clarion*, November 26, 1865.

[46] The Stephens substitute may be found in the *Senate Journal, 1865*, pp. 223–24.

[47] Agents under the Stephens proposal were to report all assaults upon Negroes to justices of the peace, who would issue writs of arrest against the offenders. Agents were to appear in court on behalf of the freedmen, and they could employ an attorney if necessary.

[48] *Senate Journal, 1865*, p. 226.

[49] The votes on the civil rights bill may be found in *ibid.*, 232, and in the *House Journal, 1865*, p. 284.

posed the radical plan voted against the civil rights bill. Party lines were not as sharply drawn as on other issues. Ten Whigs and six Democrats voted for the civil rights proposal in the upper chamber, while eight Democrats and five Whigs opposed it. In the lower chamber, of those whose party preferences have been identified, thirty-five Whigs and twenty Democrats favored the bill, whereas sixteen Democrats and thirteen Whigs voted against it.

A vague sectional pattern appeared in the voting on the civil rights bill. Members from the river counties, including the alluvial bottoms, voted overwhelmingly for the bill. Of the twenty-nine legislators from these counties in both houses, only five voted against the measure. Their vote strongly suggests that the more substantial planters of the state, who were quite anxious for an arrangement that would insure a stable labor supply, believed that the moderate plan proposed by the Simrall committee offered greater hope for a permanent return of the Negroes to the field than that of the radicals.

Although the piney woods section as a whole was split on the issue, the southern group of counties tended to oppose the conservative measure. Only three of the nine legislators in this area voted for the bill. No sectional pattern is evident in the votes of the legislators from the north and central counties; however, county delegations tended to vote in bloc, either for or against the measure. For example, Marshall and Tippah, populous white counties with a total of nine representatives in the legislature, voted unanimously with their Democratic senate leaders, James H. R. Taylor and Francis Wolff, against the conservative plan for the freedmen. On the other hand, legislators of the northern hill counties of Pontotoc and Tishomingo voted, with one exception, for it. In general, however, it may be concluded that the whites of the plantation counties supported the moderate settlement, whereas the small farmers and poor whites of the hills and piney barrens opposed it.[50]

The civil rights act, approved by Governor Humphreys on November 25, contained far more than a definition of the legal or civil

[50] The evidence that is used in this study refutes the conclusion by some historians that the Black Code represented a triumph of the radical small farmers and poor whites of the hills and piney barrens over the conservative planters. Actually, the moderates in the legislature were able to block the extreme proposals advanced in that body, although the conservative measure, the civil rights act, was later denounced as the work of radicals. For an example of the traditional interpretation, see Wharton, *The Negro in Mississippi*, 90.

privileges of the freedmen. Actually, the granting of civil rights was only in the first four sections, and a series of economic limitations followed. Section five provided that after the second Monday in January of each year, all Negroes must have homes and occupations, with written evidence to that effect. This evidence must be in the form of a written contract, if the term of employment was for more than a month, or a license from the local authorities, if the Negro was engaged in irregular or job work.[51]

Section six set forth the form and procedure for labor contracts, and the next three sections provided stringent regulations and measures to insure faithful compliance with these contracts on the part of freedmen.[52] Section ten made it legal for Negroes to charge any white or black person with any criminal offense against their persons or property. A supplementary act to this part of the civil rights measure was passed a few days later. This supplement provided that, if it were apparent that a white person had been arrested falsely because of an affidavit sworn to by a freedman, the perjured accuser was to pay all costs of the case, to be fined fifty dollars, and to be jailed for a period not to exceed twenty days.[53] The eleventh section of the act provided that the penal laws of the state, except where specified otherwise, applied to the freedman.

While the comprehensive civil rights bill was being considered by the legislature, other measures that were designed to regulate freedmen were enacted. The first of these, the apprentice law, was intended "to give protection and direction to that large class of black minors who have been recently freed and to prevent this class of persons from becoming a tax upon the public treasury."[54] This act directed all local officers to report to the probate courts of their counties all Negroes under eighteen years of age who were orphans or who were without means of support. The court was instructed to apprentice them to competent and suitable whites, with their former owners having preference if in the opinion of the court they were suitable. Masters were required to furnish bond with the condition that they provide the minor with sufficient clothing and food, treat

[51] *Laws of Mississippi, 1865,* pp. 83–85.

[52] See Chap. 5, p. 99.

[53] *Laws of Mississippi, 1865,* p. 194.

[54] Charles E. Hooker, attorney general of the state, to Governor Humphreys, March 12, 1866, in Governors' Correspondence, E-78.

him humanely, give him medical attention in case of sickness, and teach him to read and write, if under fifteen years of age. Masters were permitted "to inflict such moderate corporal chastisement as a father or guardian is allowed to inflict on his child or ward at common law, [but] in no case shall cruel or inhuman punishment be inflicted." Runaway apprentices were to be apprehended and returned to their masters. If, however, the court believed that the absconding apprentice had good cause to leave his master, it could relieve the minor of the indenture.[55] A subsequent ruling by the attorney general of the state declared that either parent could retain control of his child if the court determined that he or she had the ability and willingness to support him.[56]

The Black Code provision which probably elicited the least debate in the legislature was the vagrant act. On the roll call vote in the house only six representatives opposed the bill, all but one being from predominantly white counties.[57] This measure was designed to put the idle of both races to work. The first part of section two, however, applied solely to Negroes and provided that all freedmen found on the second Monday in January, or thereafter, with no lawful employment or business would be subject to prosecution under the act. In addition to establishing the machinery for its enforcement, the act levied a poll tax, not to exceed one dollar annually, to constitute the "Freedmen's Pauper Fund" for the support of Negro indigents. Failure to pay this tax was to be considered prima facie evidence of vagrancy.[58]

Meeting at the time of the Negro insurrection scare, the legislature on November 29 passed an act providing that no freedman, except in military service or licensed by the board of police of his county, should be permitted to possess firearms. Upon arrest and conviction freedmen were to be fined a sum not exceeding ten dollars. Moreover, any Negro

committing riots, routs, affrays, trespasses, malicious mischief, cruel treatment to animals, seditious speeches, insulting gestures, language, or acts, or assaults on any person, disturbance of the peace, exercising

[55] *Laws of Mississippi, 1865,* pp. 86–88. The act further provided that persons enticing away apprentices would be punished as if they had induced hired laborers to leave their employers.

[56] Hooker to Humphreys, March 12, 1866, in Governors' Correspondence, E-78.

[57] *House Journal, 1865,* p. 247. The vote in the senate on the vagrant law was not recorded in the journal of that chamber.

[58] The vagrant act is found in *Laws of Mississippi, 1865,* pp. 90–93.

the function of a minister of the Gospel without a license from some regularly organized church, vending spirituous or intoxicating liquors, or committing any other misdemeanor, the punishment of which is not specifically provided for by law, shall, upon conviction thereof in the county court, be fined not less than ten dollars, and not more than one hundred dollars, and may be imprisoned at the discretion of the court, not exceeding thirty days.[59]

A futile effort was made in the house of representatives to prohibit Negroes from migrating to Mississippi. Surprisingly, thirty-two of the eighty members voting on the measure favored its passage, although the planters of the large cotton-producing counties were anxious to secure laborers from any source, regardless of race.[60] The relative closeness of this vote suggests that many legislators in enacting the Black Code may have viewed the problem of the freedmen more as a social problem than as a labor one.

The enforcement and administration of the Negro settlement obviously was expected to place an unusual, if not impossible, burden upon the existing public agencies and courts.[61] By the acts of the legislature responsibility for the discipline and regulation of the Negroes had in effect been transferred from the plantation to public authorities. Already the county jails were crowded with accused criminals of both races who had been in confinement for five or six months awaiting the action of the overburdened circuit courts. The Joint Committee on Freedmen reported that a solution to these problems, and to the general problem of crime, was to establish a court in each county inferior to the circuit courts. As a result of this report, the county court system was instituted, modeled after the old Virginia local judicial arrangement.[62] Each tribunal under this act consisted of the probate judge and two justices of the peace of the county, and it was authorized to try all criminal cases below felonies

[59] Ibid., 165-66.

[60] House Journal, 1865, pp. 338–39. "Jim Crow" laws were not generally a feature of the Black Codes of the Southern states. C. Vann Woodward, Origins of the New South, 1877–1913 (Baton Rouge: Louisiana State University Press, 1951), 210–12. The Mississippi legislature enacted one such measure. This act made it unlawful for Negroes to ride in first-class passenger cars used by whites, and offenders were to be deemed guilty of a misdemeanor. Laws of Mississippi, 1865, p. 231.

[61] Natchez Democrat, October 24, 1865; Friar's Point Coahomian, September 29, 1865.

[62] Raymond Hinds County Gazette, December 23, 1865.

and all civil suits where the value of the property did not exceed $250. Indictment by grand jury was not necessary, and jury trial for accused offenders was replaced by the court, which acted as both judge and jury. Appeals from the decisions of the county courts were to be made to the circuit courts.[63] A few days before the passage of this act the legislature increased the authority and discretion of town officials, permitting them "to pass such laws as shall seem to them expedient for the suppression of vice and immorality, and the preservation of good order and morality, and for the suppression of vagrancy and trespasses."[64]

With the passage of these measures Mississippi became the first of the Southern states to attempt to define the place of the Negro in its postwar society and to enact rules and regulations for his conduct. The Mississippi settlement actually represented a victory for the conservative or moderate plan in the legislature, although it is evident that some of its features, particularly the one prohibiting the leasing of country properties to freedmen, were unduly harsh and unwise. Even the conservatives, who desired to do justice to the Negroes and to sustain the policies of the national administration, were reluctant to support measures that departed too far from traditional ideas and methods of managing the blacks. Moreover, social and economic conditions in the state during the fall of 1865, when the legislature was meeting, were unpropitious for the sober reasoning necessary for the formulation of a truly moderate program for the Negroes. Those who were well-disposed to enact such a program were affected, as were others, by the forces and pressures resulting from such conditions as the insurrection scare and the labor crisis, and were prone to support proposals more related to antebellum experiences than attuned to the hard realities of postwar adjustment. The reaction to the Black Code in the North and in the state, in addition to that of federal officials, would determine the extent of its enforcement.

[63] The provisions of the county court act are found in *Laws of Mississippi, 1865*, pp. 66–79.
[64] *Ibid.*, 157–58.

8

The Fate of the Black Code

T HE WORK of the Mississippi legislature immediately aroused a storm of protest in the North. To the philosophical abolitionist group these laws were severe violations of the freedom of the Negroes. Radical Republicans saw evidence that Mississippians were attempting to restore slavery in fact.[1] The Chicago *Tribune* on December 1, 1865, revealed the sentiments of Radical journals toward the code when it declared: "We tell the white men in Mississippi that the men of the North will convert the State of Mississippi into a frog pond before they will allow such laws to disgrace one foot of soil in which the bones of our soldiers sleep and over which the flag of freedom waves."[2] It is evident that in the Mississippi laws the Republicans found an effective instrument with which to sway opinion in the North and to work for the repudiation of the President's plan of reconstruction.

Even conservative Democrats in the North were unhappy with the Mississippi acts regulating the freedmen. A factor in creating this response to the laws was the cavalier way in which the legislature refused to ratify the Thirteenth Amendment, despite the President's admonitions. In a strongly worded dispatch, Johnson had exhorted retiring Provisional Governor Sharkey on November 1: "it is all important that the Legislature adopt the amendment to the Constitution abolishing slavery. The action of the Legislature of Mississippi is looked to with great interest at this time, and a failure to adopt the amendment will create the belief that the action of the Convention, abolish-

[1] James G. Randall and David Donald, *The Civil War and Reconstruction* (2nd ed. rev.; Boston: D. C. Heath and Co., 1961), 571–72; Ezell, *The South Since 1865*, p. 49.

[2] Coulter, *The South during Reconstruction*, 39.

ing slavery, will hereafter be revoked. . . . I trust in God that the Legislature will adopt the Amendment, and thereby make the way clear for the admission of Senators and Representatives to their seats in the present Congress."[3]

Opposition to the ratification of the amendment, however, was quite strong. One writer to the Jackson *Clarion* asserted that the second section of the amendment, giving Congress power to enforce it "by appropriate legislation," would "open the door for congressional legislation concerning our domestic affairs," particularly regarding the Negroes. This correspondent's explanation for rejecting the amendment indicates the nature of resistance to national pressures that characterized many in the state during the hectic days of late 1865. He proclaimed:

To adopt the amendment is to gain admittance to Congress for our Representatives, while we surrender all of our rights as a State to the Federal Congress. . . . To refuse to adopt the amendment precludes all hope of admission for our Representatives, weakens the strong arm of him who has shown himself to be our friend, and raises a howl of intense satisfaction among the radicals at the North; but it will show the world that there is still preserved among us the spirit of liberty, without which a republican government is a mobocracy. [We] are not willing to sharpen the sword that is to sever the arteries of our political life.[4]

A majority of the legislators were not so emotional in their approach to the Thirteenth Amendment, but most came to the conclusion that if this change were made to the Constitution it would result in further encroachments on state rights.[5] In one of the last actions of this session of the legislature, the house rejected the amendment by a vote of forty-five to twenty-five.[6]

Reaction in Mississippi to the acts of the legislature varied consid-

[3] Copy of a telegram from Johnson to Sharkey, November 1, 1865, in Johnson Papers. The President might have been more successful in securing the support of state officials had he addressed his dispatch to Governor Humphreys rather than to Sharkey.

[4] Jackson *Clarion*, November 8, 1865.

[5] See in the *Laws of Mississippi, 1865*, pp. 272–74, the arguments set forth by the Joint Committee on State and Federal Relations urging the rejection of the amendment by the legislature.

[6] *House Journal, 1865*, p. 327. The Alabama legislature ratified the Thirteenth Amendment, but at the same time showed its misgivings concerning the second section by asserting that ratification did not extend to this part.

erably. Immediately upon the passage of the laws regulating the activities of Negroes almost all of the newspapers either indicated their approval of the measures or withheld their opinions. Perhaps to try to head off Northern negative reactions, the leading conservative editors expressed the belief that the laws would secure justice for the freedmen and would lead to the restoration of agricultural prosperity. When passage of the civil rights bill appeared imminent, C. B. Manlove, editor of the Vicksburg *Journal*, declared: "We trust that the advocates of negro suffrage and equality are satisfied. The Legislature of Mississippi has provided freely and fully for the protection of the Freedman in his person and property—and that these provisions will be faithfully and conscientiously carried out, no sane man will doubt. We have met the issue presented us, in good faith, and in Mississippi today, the Freedman is as well protected as he is in any State in the Union."[7]

Editor H. P. Reid of the Friar's Point *Coahomian*, although admitting that some of the measures were harsh, claimed that these laws were "as good as could be framed at this time, for while they seize with an iron hand the vagrant and lawless and compel them to work and conform to law and order, they give protection and hold out inducements to the frugal and industrious in the rights of person, property, and pursuit of happiness." Furthermore, these ordinances sought to restrain "those vicious whites who may be inclined to decoy the negro from the path of honest industry." Reid denounced Edward M. Yerger of the Jackson *News* and other radical editors for their vituperations against the legislators who voted for the civil rights bill.[8] Upon the adjournment of the legislature, the Jackson *Clarion*, without commenting specifically on the Negro settlement, declared: "There was a very respectable amount of ability in both Houses, and no Legislature, we have ever seen, appeared more anxious to discharge their duties or worked more assiduously at the business before them."[9]

[7] Vicksburg *Journal*, November 12, 1865.

[8] Friar's Point *Coahomian*, December 1, 1865.

[9] Jackson *Clarion*, December 7, 1865. The often-quoted comment by a Mississippi editor that the house was composed of "a motley crew" serving their own interests, was actually made prior to the time that the Joint Committee on Freedmen made its report and did not reflect an early opposition to the settlement as an extreme plan. The Raymond *Hinds County Gazette*, November 18, 1865, reported this statement several days after it was made.

The attitude of the state press toward the work of the legislature, however, began to change when Northern hostility became pronounced, when Congress refused to seat the elected Mississippi representatives, and when federal officials indicated their disapproval of some of the provisions of the Black Code. After the publication of General Howard's sharp telegram of November 30 to Colonel Thomas instructing him to disregard the property proviso of the civil rights act, the editor of the Jackson *Clarion* arraigned the legislature for its narrowmindedness. The legislature, the editor declared on December 9, in its great anxiety "to feed the prejudices of a certain class of our people, and its indifference to the wholesome sentiment of the sober, reasonable men of the State, in its insane proclivity to strain at gnats after having swallowed the camel, has succeeded in fastening upon us indefinitely the negro bureau, placed us in imminent danger of another provisional government, and doubtless secured the rejection of our members in Congress, and caused its own legislative authority to be treated with contempt; thus paralysing the industrial energies of our people, and throwing us back into uncertain chaos."[10] The *Clarion* editor chose not to remember that only a few days before he was supporting many of the same provisions that he was now condemning the legislature for passing.

By January, 1866, most of the leading newspapers of the state, with the notable exception of the two Natchez newspapers, the *Courier* and the *Democrat,* were vigorously denouncing the work of the legislature. The editors of the Vicksburg *Journal* and the Friar's Point *Coahomian* now took the position that the Negro had been denied justice by the acts of the legislature.[11] The Vicksburg *Herald* also

[10] Jackson *Clarion*, December 9, 1865. The *Clarion* further commented: "If the laws of the present Legislature were regarded, slavery would be restored in a far worse form than it was before. The negro would not only be deprived of the protection of a humane master who was pecuniarily interested in his health and comfort, but if unable to find a white man to hire him, would be mercilessly turned over to the vagrant commissioner of each county, to be treated as a vagrant. It is easy to see what this system will lead to. Rather than become vagrants many negroes would be compelled to labor for nothing."

[11] Vicksburg *Journal*, December 14, 20, 1865; Friar's Point *Coahomian*, January 26, 1866. One of the first criticisms of the Black Code came from a group of Negroes meeting in convention at Vicksburg. In a petition to President Johnson to secure his nullification of the acts, they claimed that if the Mississippi code was permitted to go into effect, "it will be virtually returning us to slavery again.

described the legislation as unwise.[12] The Columbus *Sentinel*, denouncing both the economic and racial policies of the assembly, accused the legislators of being "far more anxious to make capital at home than to propitiate the powers at Washington. They were as complete a set of political Goths as were ever turned loose to work destruction upon a State."[13]

On the other hand, the editor of the Natchez *Democrat* maintained that the legislature had generally shown a spirit of liberality toward the freedmen, although it should have gone a step further and granted them the right to purchase and lease lands in rural areas. "We are not disposed to find fault with the members of our legislature," the *Democrat* editor said. "As pioneers they approximated wonderfully near to full justice to the negro."[14]

As the impolitic nature of the Mississippi plan became more apparent, Governor Humphreys received requests from influential citizens asking him to reconvene the legislature to repeal the obnoxious laws. Benjamin G. Truman, President Johnson's representative, reported from Jackson that numerous legislators soon after returning home had written letters to the governor and to other prominent persons in the capital admitting that their work had found little favor with their constituents.[15] One legislator, William D. Lyles, a radical leader in the senate, had been home from Jackson for only a few days when he reversed his position toward the regulation of the freedmen. "We can now begin to understand the defects of our recent legislation," he wrote Humphreys. And, possibly facetiously, he added, "if you do not think of calling us together for several months, I would be glad to know it as I am thinking seriously of going to Mexico."[16]

To this we will not submit in any form, and you may know what that means." G. W. Blackwell, convention chairman, to Johnson, November 24, 1865, in Johnson Papers.

[12] As reported in the Vicksburg *Journal*, December 19, 30, 1865.

[13] As quoted in the Raymond *Hinds County Gazette*, December 23, 1865.

[14] Natchez *Democrat*, January 6, 1866. The editor reminded those who criticized the work of the legislature that the assembly "has amply protected his [the freedman's] person, and it has sufficiently protected such property as he is permitted to acquire. It has admitted him to testify in all cases where a negro is a party to the record. It has granted him the right to absolute property in personal estate; and has permitted him to lease real estate within the corporate limits of our towns and cities."

[15] New York *Times*, February 4, 1866.

[16] William D. Lyles to Humphreys, December 31, 1865, in Governors' Corres-

Then, too, Senator-elect Sharkey criticized the Black Code, and declared that the property proviso, besides being unconstitutional, never had the support of the people of the state.[17] A planter friend of Humphreys thought that the Negro settlement was too comprehensive, and that, even if the legislature immediately rectified its mistakes, it would take several years to restore a stable labor system in Mississippi.[18] In a letter to Humphreys a former Confederate congressman summed up the feelings of apprehension shared by many regarding the work of the legislature and concluded by declaring: "I wish that Legislature had never assembled, or that you had closed their acts in mass and vetoed the whole concern."[19]

State newspapers also joined the chorus for the repeal or modification of undesirable portions of the code, although not all of them could agree as to which laws should be abrogated or softened. Probably most of them believed, with the editor of the influential Jackson *Clarion,* that the freedmen should be granted the unrestricted right to own and lease property and should be given equal legal rights with whites, including the privilege of testifying in all cases in court.[20] Editor Reid of the Friar's Point *Coahomian,* upon reflection, urged the immediate ratification of the Thirteenth Amendment. Regarding the acts of the legislature, Reid declared: "We do not propose to discuss the right or wrong attached to the laws, but what we do propose is to show that their repeal or modification is necessary if Mississippi would regain her position in the Union."[21]

pondence, E-77. Writing in May, 1866, another legislator said that some of the work of the legislature was a mistake, but that it met under "unfavorable circumstances. The minds of the people have undergone a great change since last year, especially in regard to the rights of the freedmen." Jackson *Clarion,* May 8, 1866.

[17] "Report of the Joint Committee on Reconstruction," *House Reports,* 39th Cong., 1st Sess., No. 30, Pt. III, 136; Friar's Point *Coahomian,* April 27, 1866.

[18] George Torrey to Humphreys, March 29, 1866, in Governors' Correspondence, E-78. Many thought that other acts of the ill-starred legislature needed repealing or modifying, especially the laws staying the collection of overdue debts and exempting certain properties from seizure for defaulted debts. Jackson *Clarion,* January 3, 1866.

[19] William D. Holder to Humphreys, February 16, 1866, in Governors' Correspondence, E-78.

[20] Jackson *Clarion,* April 10, 1866; Natchez *Democrat,* January 6, 1866.

[21] Friar's Point *Coahomian,* January 26, 1866. Some persons suggested that the reconstruction convention be reconvened, but this received little encouragement from influential newspapers and leaders. Natchez *Weekly Courier,* March 12,

WILLIAM L. SHARKEY

MAJOR GENERAL THOMAS J. WOOD

MAJOR GENERAL HENRY W. SLOCUM

JAMES LUSK ALCORN

SAMUEL J. GHOLSON

BENJAMIN G. HUMPHREYS

Governor Humphreys, however, refused to recall the legislature. He generally approved its acts concerning the freedmen;[22] furthermore, he knew that if the legislature were reconvened, it might not only legislate for the freedmen but insist on passing laws to relieve debtors. As an adamant foe of repudiation in any form, Humphreys had no desire to hasten a confrontation with a hostile legislature bent on debtor relief. The governor probably believed also that what disagreeable measures federal officials did not invalidate the courts of the state would declare unconstitutional. He did dispatch two commissioners, William Yerger and J. M. Acker, to Washington to ask President Johnson which laws the federal government would allow to be enforced. Humphreys later said that Johnson indicated to the commissioners that none of these acts would be nullified except by the civil courts.[23]

From the time of the introduction of the civil rights bill, officials of the Freedmen's Bureau in the state were extremely wary of the proceedings in the legislature.[24] Yet after the passage of the Black Code, the bureau and the military invalidated only a very small portion of it. On November 30, 1865, General Oliver O. Howard ordered that the provision prohibiting Negroes from leasing or renting lands in the country be disregarded.[25] After the enactment of the federal civil rights bill in April, 1866, General Thomas J. Wood gave his opinion that the state law preventing freedmen from possessing arms without permission and the proviso requiring them to make contracts before the second Monday in January of each year were illegal. But apparently he did not specifically declare these two measures to be null and void.[26] Only one circuit court evidently followed Wood's "opinion"

1866; Raymond *Hinds County Gazette*, January 13, 1866; Jackson *Clarion*, January 3, 1866; Friar's Point *Coahomian*, February 2, 1866.

[22] Rainwater (ed.), "Autobiography of Benjamin Grubb Humphreys," 248.

[23] New Orleans *Picayune*, October 17, 1866; McNeily, "Mississippi's Provisional Government," 233.

[24] Lieutenant Colonel R .S. Donaldson to Captain J. H. Weber, November 17, 1865; Colonel Thomas to General Oliver O. Howard, November 21, 1865, in Johnson Papers.

[25] Copy of a telegram from General Howard to Colonel Thomas, November 30, 1865, in Governors' Correspondence, E-77. Prominent lawyers of the state thought that the property proviso would have been declared unconstitutional by the courts without military intervention. Jackson *Clarion*, February 3, 1866.

[26] As reported in the Jackson *Clarion*, December 16, 1866. See also Wood to Humphreys, January 28 and March 12, 1866, in Governors' Correspondence, E-78.

and declared the law prohibiting unlicensed Negroes from bearing arms to be unconstitutional. However, from the beginning the extent of the enforcement of this law varied throughout the state, depending upon the discretion of the local officials. And by the fall of 1866 few of them persisted in enforcing it.[27]

Although federal officers were extremely reluctant to annul acts of the legislature, they insisted in principle that the laws of the state be applied equally to both races. The remedy for correcting the oppressive features of the code, Wood believed, "is not to nullify the laws of the state, for this would make a practical outlaw of the Freedmen, when beyound [sic] the reach of Military protection, by leaving them in many parts of this State without the protection of municipal or State laws." Wood's policy was to correct individual cases of abuse and to promote a spirit of good will on the part of the whites toward the Negroes that would result in the modification of the harsh acts of the legislature.[28] Yet only in a few cases did the military actually attempt to secure equal treatment for the Negroes.[29]

The extent of the enforcement of the laws pertaining to the freedmen varied throughout the state. Influential citizens attempted to prevent the enforcement of the vagrancy act in Jackson and Vicksburg, while in smaller towns mayors generally insisted on carrying out the letter of the law.[30] The section of the civil rights act requiring Negroes to secure a certificate of employment or a license to do job work apparently was rigidly enforced in most areas of the state. Encouraged by the vague wording of this provision, some unscrupulous local officials took advantage of the freedmen. General Wood complained to Humphreys that in many places civil officers were charging Negroes from one to five dollars for issuing work certificates or for recording labor contracts. Since freedmen were usually not able to pay the fee, they were denied the proper licenses and were therefore subject to the

[27] Raymond *Hinds County Gazette*, October 5, 1866; Albert T. Morgan, *Yazoo; or on the Picket Line of Freedom in the South* (Washington: Published by the author, 1884), 115–16; New York *Times*, October 26, 1866; Henry B. Whitfield to Governor Humphreys, May 1, 1866, in Governors' Correspondence, E-79; Will S. Bailey to Humphreys, April 21, 1866, *ibid.*, E-78.

[28] Wood to Humphreys, January 28, March 12, 1866, in Governors' Correspondence, E-78.

[29] See, for example, Wood to Humphreys, March 14, 1866, *ibid.*, and "Freedmen's Affairs," *Senate Executive Documents*, 39th Cong., 2nd Sess., No. 6, pp. 96–97.

[30] Jackson *Clarion*, April 13, 1866; New York *Times*, July 7, 1866.

vagrant law.[31] As a result of Wood's complaint, Humphreys directed officials to cease making Negroes pay for job certificates. The attorney general further instructed civil officers that the inability of a person to produce written evidence of work was not a sufficient reason for declaring him a vagrant, although it could be included as evidence to that effect.[32]

Irregularities also occurred in the administration of the apprentice law; however, these activities were confined largely to the interior counties of the state. In many cases, able-bodied Negro boys sixteen years of age and above, who were willing to work under contract, were forcibly apprenticed by local officers to labor-starved planters. When this practice was reported to General Wood, he appealed to state officials for civil redress of the wrongs.[33] Although not specifically correcting this abuse, Humphreys and the attorney general insisted that local officers apprentice, in addition to orphans, only those children whose parents plainly were unable to support them or whose parents consented to the indenture. Furthermore, they urged probate judges to give preference in apprenticing minors to their former owners only when they were clearly suitable persons for serving as guardians of the children. For those minors who had been apprenticed arbitrarily or illegally, the proper remedy for annulling their indentures was by writ of habeas corpus. The state supreme court and at least two circuit courts sustained these instructions to local officers and ruled that the oppressive administration of the apprentice law must cease.[34]

White Mississippians only reluctantly accepted freedman testimony in court as provided by section four of the civil rights act.[35] Much less were they ready to convict on Negro evidence members of their own race. A red letter day for Negro justice, however, occurred in September, 1866, when the testimony of only freedmen convicted an alleged white murderer of homicide. Circuit Judge Josiah A. P. Campbell, an influential secessionist in 1860–61, boldly upheld the

[31] Wood to Humphreys, March 12, 1866; Colonel Thomas to Wood, March 12, 1866, in Governors' Correspondence, E-78.

[32] Charles E. Hooker to Humphreys, April 26, 1866; Wood to Humphreys, April 23, 1866, ibid.

[33] Wood to Humphreys, March 1, 1866, ibid.

[34] Humphreys to Hooker, March 6, 1866; Hooker to Humphreys, March 12, 1866; Wood to Humphreys, May 10, 1866, ibid., E-79; Natchez Weekly Courier, March 26, 1866; Jackson Clarion and Standard, June 14 and July 11, 1866.

[35] Wood to Humphreys, March 14, 1866, in Governors' Correspondence, E-78.

principle of Negro testimony in declaring that "every principle of justice and humanity, every consideration of honor and manliness, alike with motives of policy, combine to require even handed justice in vindication of the unfortunate negroes against the brutal outrages of the lawless white man. The courts of the country are solemnly bound to protect all alike in the enjoyment of life and liberty, and this can be done only by a faithful and fearless execution of the laws."[36] Campbell then sentenced the white man to twelve months in jail. Although General Wood thought that the sentence was wholly inadequate, he believed that the decision, since it was based on Negro testimony, would have a wholesome effect upon public sentiment.[37] In fact, two months later Wood reported that prejudice against the freedmen was discernible only in the lower courts and that the higher courts were determined that the blacks receive justice at their hands. It should be mentioned, however, that almost all cases involving freedmen were settled in the lower courts, specifically in the county courts.[38]

At the same time, the national Civil Rights Act of 1866, designed to protect Negro rights in the Southern states, was being "religiously observed" in many parts of Mississippi, according to federal district Judge Robert A. Hill. Judge Hill, who was soon to support the Republican party in the state despite his appointment to the bench by President Johnson, wrote his friend Chief Justice Salmon P. Chase: "There is an increasing feeling of sympathy for [the Negroes], and as we leave the period of their liberation from slavery the feeling of hostility against them as a class is very preceptiably [sic] diminishing, and [there is] an increased disposition upon the part of both people and officers to give them Justice and their civil rights. Experience is convincing the people that such a course is not only just to the black man but to the white man [as well]."[39]

[36]"Autobiography of J. A. P. Campbell" (MS in Josiah A. P. Campbell Papers, Southern Historical Collection, University of North Carolina Library, Chapel Hill).

[37] Ganus, "The Freedmen's Bureau in Mississippi," 252; Jackson *Clarion*, September 26, 1866.

[38] "Freedmen's Affairs," *Senate Executive Documents*, 39th Cong., 2nd Sess., No. 6, pp. 96–97; Wharton, *The Negro in Mississippi*, 135–36.

[39] Robert A. Hill to Chief Justice Salmon P. Chase, November 14, 1866, in Salmon P. Chase Papers, Manuscripts Division, Library of Congress. See also Hill to Chase, February 20, 1867, *ibid*.

In October, 1866, Governor Humphreys called a special session of the legislature for one purpose, to adjust the laws of the state pertaining to the Negroes. In his message of October 15 to the legislature Humphreys declared that the conduct of the freedmen had been excellent and that therefore justice and honor demanded that full protection be given to them. In view of this, the legislature should "relax the rigidity of our law" and remove the discriminating features of the Black Code.[40] The assembly, however, failed to act on the governor's recommendation during this session, preferring apparently to wait until after the crucial national elections in November—elections that would determine the future course of political reconstruction.

The triumph of the anti-Johnson Republicans in the 1866 congressional elections and the continuation of the postwar economic recession in Mississippi motivated the legislature when it reconvened in January, 1867, to repeal or modify the obnoxious measures passed by the 1865 session. The property proviso of the civil rights act was the first of the undesirable laws to be discarded by the legislature. Although this measure had never been enforced because of federal action, the legislature believed that it would be expedient to repeal it.[41] The section of the vagrancy law which placed a capitation tax on blacks for the support of their indigent was modified to include only a levy on adult male Negroes.[42] This change did not make the provision palatable to Major General Edward O. C. Ord, who in March, 1867, became commander of the fourth military district charged with the implementation of the congressional plan of reconstruction in Mississippi and Arkansas. Ord in June declared that the poll tax was discriminatory and therefore null and void.[43]

On February 21, 1867, Governor Humphreys approved a bill of the legislature repealing the special law on freedmen apprentices and

[40] Humphreys' message to the legislature may be found in the New Orleans *Picayune*, October 17, 1866, and in the *Appleton's Annual Cyclopaedia*, VI, 520–21.

[41] Natchez *Courier*, February 9, 1867.

[42] *Laws of the State of Mississippi, Passed at a Called Session of the Mississippi Legislature, Held in the City of Jackson, October, 1866, and January and February, 1867* (Jackson: J. J. Shannon and Co., State Printers, 1867), 232, hereinafter cited as *Laws of Mississippi, 1866–1867*.

[43] General Order number 15, June 27, 1867, in *General and General Court Martial Orders, Circulars and Circulars Civil Affairs, Headquarters, 4th Military District, 1867* (Vicksburg: Government Printing Office, 1868).

applying to Negro orphans the same laws which covered whites. At the same time, the section of the civil rights bill which restricted Negro testimony in court was removed from the statute books. Negroes still could not serve as jurors. The last section of the February 21 act repealed all laws which provided discriminatory punishment for blacks, and declared that Negroes were to be tried in the same courts, by the same procedures, and subject to the same penalties as whites.[44]

Thus ended the Mississippi Black Code, except for the essential features of the vagrancy law. A product of the economic and social uncertainty of the autumn of 1865, the Black Code had been designed to define the place of the Negro in the postwar society and to regulate his economic activities. A stringent settlement of the freedman problem, legislators of 1865 believed, would result in returning the Negro to the field, stabilizing the society of the state, and restoring the economic prosperity of the people. The Mississippi plan of 1865 did not completely fail to achieve these objectives. Although basic economic factors were at work to restore an adequate labor system for the planters, the enforcement of the acts of 1865, with the assistance of federal officers in the state, undoubtedly speeded the return of the Negroes to work.

The Black Code, on the other hand, did not succeed in ending strife and lawlessness in the state, which was generally linked by whites with the Negro problem, but which actually was a part of a broader problem of violence virtually inherent in a frontier society of the type that existed in Mississippi after the war. Because of the confusion and uncertainty concerning the enforcement of specific acts, the code complicated and probably accentuated the difficulties of arriving at an equitable settlement for the blacks. Both the national and local reaction to the Mississippi laws promoted the belief that the Black Code was the work of extremists who desired to return the Negroes to a form of slavery, when actually, although harsh, it represented at least partially a triumph for the conservatives in the legislature. The effect was to discredit greatly the work of the legislature and to continue the uncertainty regarding the status of the freedmen. Finally, the Black Code of 1865 did not bring about the desired economic salvation of the state; the existence of favorable conditions other than

[44] Meridian *Semi-Weekly Gazette,* March 27, 1867; *Laws of Mississippi, 1866–1867,* pp. 232–33.

civil tranquility and the devising of a viable replacement for the ante-bellum labor system were necessary before a degree of the prosperity of the 1850's could be regained. Money or credit had to be extended, the levees needed to be reconstructed, and transportation means had to be restored before the agricultural economy of the state could be completely revived.

9

Problems of Agricultural Recovery

THE SUCCESSFUL procurement of operating funds and the rapid recovery of trade media were as essential to the reconstruction of the cotton economy of Mississippi as the restoration of an adequate labor supply. Credit was necessary to replace worn-out implements, to purchase draft animals, to pay laborers and supply them with provisions, to rebuild the levees, and to restore the transportation facilities of the state. When the war ended the state was almost completely devoid of liquid assets, and formidable obstacles had to be overcome before local funds could be accumulated or Northern money would be invested in the state.

One barrier to recovery was the great scarcity of currency, and without an adequate medium of exchange economic restoration would have indeed been difficult. With local paper almost completely worthless at the end of the war, the demand for federal currency, particularly greenbacks, was tremendous. Greenbacks had circulated in the river counties since the Union forces had occupied the area in 1862 and 1863, and some had entered the cotton-producing region of central Mississippi through trade, both legal and illegal, with Federal-held towns. When peace came, and for several months thereafter, interior residents found themselves at a decided financial disadvantage in comparison with merchants and planters of the river counties because of their lack of federal currency. Furthermore, the specie that once had circulated in the state had been driven out during the war or had been seized by Federal forces, although a few people had managed to hoard some gold or silver. A few planters and merchants had placed some of their funds in Europe expecting to withdraw these after peace was restored. Some funds were held in Europe from the proceeds of cotton sold in Liverpool before and during the early part of the war. After the war, however, the amnesty proclamation, excluding persons with wealth of more than twenty thousand dollars, caused many who held these accounts to fear that their money might be confiscated if it were returned to the state.[1]

Railroad notes and some state issues of "cotton money" were not completely worthless after the war. In 1861 the legislature had authorized the railroads to issue notes in denominations of one to three dollars to circulate as money until one year after the war. These notes, totaling $350,000, were to be redeemable on demand in specie, Confederate currency, or bank notes.[2] As the fortunes of the Confederacy waned, holders of the notes became extremely reluctant to present their bills for redemption, for fear that the railroad companies would insist on meeting their obligations in depreciated paper. When the war ended, these notes, like other wartime issues, appeared valueless. "We have known the negroes to refuse to hold a horse for five minutes for five dollars in Railroad money," one newspaper editor remarked.[3]

But in November, 1865, the legislature ordered the railroads to redeem their wartime notes in passenger or freight service. The legislature in taking this action was cognizant of the state's need for currency and apparently aware that the railroads were in a more favorable position than any other economic institution in Mississippi, with assets that could serve as one basis for an important, although temporary, source of circulating medium. No company, however, under this 1865 act was required to receive the bills of another railroad. These railroad notes immediately appreciated in value, and by January, 1866, one newspaperman reported that unredeemed notes were selling at par with greenbacks.[4] Then, too, the 1867 session of the legislature,

[1] Moore, "Social and Economic Conditions in Mississippi during Reconstruction," 78, 80–81. For the general condition of Southern finances after the war, see George L. Anderson, "The South and Problems of Post-Civil War Finance," *Journal of Southern History*, IX (1943), and Theodore Saloutos, "Southern Agriculture and the Problems of Readjustment: 1865–1877," *Agricultural History*, XXX (1956).

[2] *Laws of the State of Mississippi, Passed at a Regular Session of the Mississippi Legislature Held in the City of Jackson, November and December 1861, and January 1862* (Jackson: Cooper and Kimball, State Printers, 1862), 78–79, 81.

[3] Raymond *Hinds County Gazette*, January 20, 1866.

[4] *Ibid.; Laws of Mississippi, 1865*, p. 213.

meeting at a time when prospects for financial assistance for cotton growers appeared bleak, further provided that the railroad companies could issue, or reissue, their notes until 1875, for an amount not to exceed one million dollars for all of the roads. Under the provisions of this act, each railroad was required to receive the notes of the other Mississippi companies.[5] These postwar measures undoubtedly contributed, beginning in late 1865, to alleviating the great need for a stable and valuable medium of exchange for the state.

Cotton money had been placed in circulation in 1861 to aid planters who could not ship their cotton and at the same time to increase the medium of exchange for Mississippi. The act of 1861 had authorized the state treasurer to issue notes not exceeding five million dollars, to be advanced on cotton at the rate of five cents per pound. Planters were required to execute bond for double the amount of notes secured in this manner and to assume all risks for the safekeeping of the stored cotton. The cotton bonds were to be held by the state treasurer. When the blockade might be lifted, the governor was required by the act to issue a proclamation calling for the redemption of the bonds with either cotton notes, specie, or the staple itself. These notes became the chief circulating medium of the state during the war.[6] After the surrender many believed that cotton money, like other Confederate and state issues, was worthless and would not be redeemed. But some thought that, since these notes were not tied to the state's military effort, cotton money should not be repudiated as being "in aid of the rebellion."[7]

The state might have used cotton money in an effective way to provide a makeshift circulating medium until federal currency could become available throughout the state. The uncertainty of its status, however, prevented its use as currency and gave rise to speculation in cotton notes, which was conducted mainly from outside the state and especially from New Orleans. The speculators evidently understood the Whig, anti-repudiationist background of Governor Humphreys, for on January 6, 1866, the governor issued a proclamation

[5] *Laws of Mississippi, 1866–1867*, pp. 408–10.

[6] Friar's Point *Coahomian*, January 26, 1866; Raymond *Hinds County Gazette*, January 20, 1866; Marce C. Rhodes, *History of Taxation in Mississippi* (Nashville: George Peabody College for Teachers, 1930), 48; Garner, *Reconstruction in Mississippi*, 43.

[7] Port Gibson *Standard*, November 25, 1865; Raymond *Hinds County Gazette*, December 2, 1865.

directing that the bonds held by the state treasurer for cotton notes be redeemed within ninety days.[8]

A significant feature of Governor Humphreys' three-year administration was his intractable opposition to repudiation in any form, which was a traditional policy of Mississippi Whigs. His action regarding the redemption of cotton bonds is an excellent illustration of his persistence in this policy, despite exceedingly strong opposition.[9] The governor's proclamation affected primarily the planter class, which was generally left with few assets as a result of the war, but which was now obligated for the redemption of the cotton bonds. A large planter himself, Humphreys in taking this action dealt a blow to the hopes of his class for immediate recovery. In their complaints planters pointed out, with a great deal of truth, that the stored cotton either had been burned or stolen and that, since they had no money, there was no possible way in which they could redeem the bonds without increasing their debts.[10] Even some Whig leaders who resisted repudiation during the antebellum period opposed the proclamation. Senator-elect Sharkey, a leading anti-repudiator of the prewar era, believed that the cotton issue was invalid from the beginning; besides, he pointed out sarcastically, "our former history shows that we are not very much inclined to pay our debts."[11] Only a few die-hard Whigs supported Humphreys' action in calling for the redemption of the cotton bonds.[12]

Governor Humphreys persisted in the enforcement of his January proclamation and initiated suits against delinquents. But not until after

[8] Humphreys' proclamation may be found in the Canton American Citizen, January 13, 1866.

[9] During the 1840's the Democratic-controlled state government repudiated the state bonds that had been sold to capitalize the Mississippi Union and the Planters' banks. The Whig party of the state vehemently opposed this action, and for the remainder of the antebellum period Whigs, including Humphreys, sought to reverse the action of the repudiators and to renew payments to the bondholders. Whigs, however, were frustrated in their efforts, since the Democrats maintained control of the state government until the latter part of the Civil War. Dunbar Rowland, History of Mississippi; The Heart of the South (Chicago: S. J. Clarke Publishing Company, 1925), I, 621–23, 626, 636, 646.

[10] Port Gibson Standard, January 20, 1866; Raymond Hinds County Gazette, February 2, 1866; Friar's Point Coahomian, January 26, 1866.

[11] "Report of the Joint Committee on Reconstruction," House Reports, 39th Cong., 1st Sess., No. 30, Pt. III, 135.

[12] For example, see the Raymond Hinds County Gazette, January 20, February 23, 1866, and the Canton American Citizen, January 13, 1866.

he left office and after more than $1,300,000 cotton notes were paid to the state treasurer for the redemption of bonds did the state supreme court rule on the validity of the money. The court declared that the cotton issues were in effect "in aid of the rebellion" and therefore were illegal and void.[13]

The cotton money imbroglio did not injure the faith of the state or the credit reputation of individual planters, since repudiation of the obligations imposed by the act of 1861 could easily have been justified as a result of the state's failure in the war. The controversy does indicate the desperation, in order to attract capital, with which some leaders worked to sustain the faith of the state and to remove the stigma of repudiation from its reputation. One significant result of the controversy was the siphoning out of the state of funds to buy from speculators cotton notes with which to redeem the bonds held by the state treasurer.[14] Planters who were responsible for the redemption of the bonds were forced in many cases to sacrifice what assets they could salvage from the war to pay off this indebtedness. And much of the hope for the economic recovery of the state lay with this class.

During the war, while Mississippi and the other Southern states were not represented in Washington, Congress had passed certain measures that, if not directly hostile to agrarian interests, served as barriers to the accumulation of money in Mississippi and to the economic reconstruction of the state. Wartime federal banking legislation gave special privileges to Northeastern financial and commercial interests, while discriminating against other sections. The last of these national banking acts during the war put a 10 per cent annual tax on all state bank notes, which practically eliminated them as a source of currency after the war.[15] Bank notes were available in Mississippi in

[13] Humphreys to John Hammond, February 7, 1866, in Governors' Correspondence, E-78; Jackson *Clarion*, April 10, 1866; Vicksburg *Times*, October 28, 1866; *Thomas v. Taylor*, 24 Miss. 651 (1869); New Orleans *Picayune*, October 18, 1866; Natchez *Courier*, April 12, 1868.

[14] Speculators undoubtedly profited from the appreciation in the value of cotton money as a result of Humphreys' proclamation. Cotton money that they were able to buy at fifteen cents on the dollar in late 1865 was selling for more than thirty cents after the governor's edict. Raymond *Hinds County Gazette*, December 2, 1865, January 20, 1866.

[15] For discussions of the national and sectional effects of these banking acts, see George R. Woolfolk, *The Cotton Regency: The Northern Merchants and Reconstruction, 1865–1880* (New York: Bookman Associates, 1958), 108–109, and

1865 at greatly depreciated values, but without the discriminatory federal laws these issues might have increased in value and might have met to a great extent the needs of the state for a medium of exchange. Furthermore, the federal acts by weakening state banks made it almost impossible for most local banks to begin business after the war. Then, too, the national bank currency was brazenly maldistributed in favor of the Northeast. This misapportionment was arbitrarily done by the United States comptroller of the currency during the latter part of the war; and, when the Southern states renewed their economic ties with the North in 1865, they found themselves at a significant disadvantage in the accumulation of this form of currency. For example, in 1866 the per capita circulation of ten Southern states averaged $1.70, with Mississippi's being only $.38, against a per capita average of $33.30 for New England and New York. The unequal distribution of these notes not only hindered the financial reconstruction of Mississippi but it also injured the overall development of the state, since the underdeveloped areas of the country, like Mississippi after the war, needed more currency for economic growth than the advanced regions where checks and credit instruments could be used instead.

Finally, the national banking legislation prevented banks organized under it from lending money on real estate. With an economy based on land, although, to be sure, this land was reduced in value, Mississippi could not sustain many such financial corporations, notwithstanding the lucrative privileges that accumulated to the holders of national banking charters. This partially explains why only two national banks were chartered in the state during the period of Presidential Reconstruction, and both of these had forfeited their charters by 1874.[16] In fact, one traveler during 1873 found no banking accommodations in most districts of Mississippi,[17] which is some evidence at least of the discriminatory effects that the Civil War banking legislation had on the state.

Federal policies also prevented Mississippians from securing full

---

especially Robert P. Sharkey, *Money, Class, and Party: An Economic Study of Civil War and Reconstruction* (Baltimore: The Johns Hopkins Press, 1959), Chap. 5. See the *Bankers' Magazine and Statistical Record*, June, 1866, p. 953, for the per capita circulation of these notes in the states.

[16] Jackson *Clarion*, December 1, 1865; Friar's Point *Coahomian*, December 8, 1865; Raymond *Hinds County Gazette*, September 14, 1866; *Appleton's Annual Cyclopaedia*, XIV, 575.

[17] Saloutos, "Southern Agriculture and the Problems of Readjustment," 64.

use of cotton as a source of funds with which to finance a new start. The London *Index* estimated that two hundred thousand bales of cotton were on hand in the state at the end of the war, and with upland cotton selling for as much as forty-five cents a pound in the market centers in May, 1865, this war-grown cotton could have served as an immediate and fairly substantial source of money.[18] Much of this cotton, however, was seized by federal officials either legally or illegally, as Confederate property, although the Treasury Department could account for only 20,240 bales that were collected by its officers in the state after June 1, 1865.[19]

The greatest encumbrance placed by the federal government on the profitable marketing of cotton was the burdensome taxes on the staple. Designed to provide a means by which the Southern states would pay a sizable share of the cost of the war, these levies included mainly at their inception a revenue tax of two and one-half cents a pound on cotton, no matter by whom it was raised. This tax was increased to three cents a pound in July, 1866, only to be restored to the original rate in 1867. Apparently none of this tax was collected in Mississippi prior to the end of the war, although the river counties had been under Federal control since 1863.[20] For the fiscal year ending June 30, 1866, Mississippi farmers paid $756,629 in duties on cotton, most of which had been accumulated during the war. Federal officers collected $4,464,664 in 1867 and $3,521,702 in 1868. The total amount collected in the state during the three years in which the cotton levy was effective was $8,742,993.[21] The loss of such a large sum of revenue, coming at a time when the economy of the state suffered from an acute lack of money, hindered greatly the process of economic, if not political and social, reconstruction.

In order to secure the repeal of the obnoxious tax, various argu-

[18] Moore, "Social and Economic Conditions in Misssissippi during Reconstruction," 80. The price of cotton did not drop below thirty-three cents a pound on the New Orleans market during the first six months after the war. Boyle, *Cotton and the New Orleans Cotton Exchange,* 180.

[19] "Seizure of Cotton," *Senate Executive Documents,* 43rd Cong., 2nd Sess., No. 23, p. 58. See pp. 63–68 above for a discussion of the seizure of this cotton.

[20] James L. Watkins, *King Cotton: A Historical and Statistical Review, 1790 to 1908* (New York: James L. Watkins and Sons, 1908), 117; "Report of the Commissioner of Internal Revenue, June 30, 1866," *House Executive Documents,* 39th Cong., 2nd Sess., No. 55, p. 26.

[21] Watkins, *King Cotton,* 177. Furthermore, the method of collecting the tax only at certain points of concentration was a hindrance to normal trade.

ments were advanced in both the North and the South against it. Mississippians, for example, hoped to gain the support of the Northwest for repeal by asserting that after paying the cotton levy they would have nothing with which to purchase meat and grain from that section.[22] As the price of cotton declined precipitantly during 1867, planters argued strenuously for an end of the tax, claiming that the levy would amount to 20 per cent of the price they would receive for the staple—a sum that they could not afford to pay without suffering a loss for the year. Yet without the growing opposition to the cotton tax of Northeastern merchants, particularly those engaged in the export traffic, repeal of the measure might have been delayed indefinitely. When influential Boston businessmen joined New York merchants in petitioning Congress to repeal the levy, Congress responded and ended its collections in 1868.[23]

Of less concern to most Mississippians than the cotton tax, after initial fears had subsided, was the direct property tax levied during the war by Congress. Under this revenue law each state of the Union, including the Southern states, was given a quota of the twenty million dollars to be raised, the apportionment being based on population. Mississippi's share of the tax was $413,184, but only a small portion of this was paid before the federal government ceased to collect it.[24] Apparently only in Hinds County did federal officials manage to collect very much of this tax, and residents of the county were probably motivated to pay by newspaper admonitions that if they failed to honor the levy their lands would be forfeited. Actually, those who paid the duty found that it was not very burdensome. The tax amounted to only one third of 1 per cent of the value of land based on an assessment made in 1857. Furthermore, property owners in communities in Mississippi where the tax was collected were required to pay for 1865 only.[25]

Conditions purely local in nature also worked to hamper the exten-

[22] Friar's Point *Coahomian*, June 15, 1866.

[23] Milton M. McPherson, "The Federal Cotton Tax in the South, 1862–1868" (M.A. thesis, University of Alabama, 1959), 55, 58, 65; Woolfolk, *The Cotton Regency*, 82–85, 87; *Commercial and Financial Chronicle*, October 12, 1867, p. 455.

[24] Randall and Donald, *Civil War and Reconstruction*, 344; New Orleans *Picayune*, December 2, 1865.

[25] Raymond *Hinds County Gazette*, January 20, 26, April 13, 1866; Jackson *Clarion*, January 14, 1866.

sion of money for capital investments in Mississippi. Political and labor uncertainties undoubtedly discouraged some from lending money or investing in commercial enterprises in the state, notwithstanding professions to the contrary by Mississippians. Northern capitalists could find less risky enterprises for investments in the West than in the cotton kingdom.[26] Unstable civil and political conditions also caused some local planters to be reluctant to engage in the cultivation of cotton on the scale practiced during the antebellum period, even though they might have had the means at their disposal to do so.[27] Moreover, as soon as peace was restored, creditors began to press planters and farmers for payment of their debts; and, since they were not able to pay, many cotton growers found it difficult to secure sufficient advances for the purchase of provisions and work stock. In the Delta the cultivation of the rich bottom lands was retarded by the overflow of the Mississippi River. The temporary inability of the state and the reluctance of federal authorities to provide for adequate levee repairs discouraged potential investors in alluvial plantations, especially after the failure of Northerners who had early invested in these lands.[28]

The need for large tax revenues to be used to restore and administer state institutions, to support the elaborate court system, and to provide relief for indigent and incapacitated citizens placed an unusual financial burden upon the people and thus hindered the recovery of the cotton economy of Mississippi. The state penitentiary, the insane asylum, and the university at Oxford survived the war either partially destroyed or in a dilapidated condition. With makeshift facilities the university re-opened its doors to sixty students in the fall of 1865, and the other state institutions were also functioning by the late spring of 1866.[29] To support these services and activities the legislature of 1865 passed both a general and a special revenue measure which imposed duties upon practically every taxable object within the state. Of these

[26] Memphis *Appeal,* December 14, 1865; Jackson *Clarion,* February 23, 1867; Francis W. Loring and C. F. Atkinson (eds.), *Cotton Culture and the South, Considered with Reference to Emigration* (Boston: A. Williams and Company, 1869), 114; Walter Goodman to Governor Humphreys, November 19, 1865, in Governors' Correspondence, E-77.

[27] See, for example, the Raymond *Hinds County Gazette,* December 16, 1865.

[28] [Benham], *Year of Wreck,* 459.

[29] Friar's Point *Coahomian,* November 3, 1865; Jackson *Clarion and Standard,* May 30, 1866.

duties a two dollar tax on each bale of cotton grown in Mississippi produced the most revenue as well as the most controversy.[30] At the same time the county boards of supervisors were levying duties ranging in many communities from 150 to 600 per cent of the state tax. These local levies were not only used to support the present county governments but also to pay debts which had accumulated before and during the war. In order to prevent fiscal disaster and the mass confiscation of land for taxes, the legislature in early 1867 passed a bill which prohibited county officials from levying a tax of more than 100 per cent of the state one.[31]

An effort was made to restore the infant common school system of the state which had been disrupted by the war. In October, 1866, Senator William D. Lyles, a Democrat, introduced a bill in the legislature that would set aside 25 per cent of the state's revenue for the purpose of restoring and expanding the white public schools. The proposal also provided for the appointment of county superintendents of education. Mainly because of a lack of funds, and despite vigorous support from two of the leading newspapers of the state, Lyle's bill failed to pass at this time and again in 1867. A state teachers' convention, meeting in Jackson in January, 1867, when the legislature was in session, applauded Lyle's efforts and further urged the lawmakers to provide common schools for Negroes as well as whites and to provide for a state superintendent to administer the program.[32]

State revenue measures for the fiscal year ending September 30, 1866, were adequate to meet the needs of the makeshift public services that the cautious Whig administration had instituted when it came to power in 1865. In a message to the legislature in October, 1866, Governor Humphreys claimed a balance in the treasury of $61,922 after public officials had disbursed $507,086 of the $569,048 collected by the state.[33] Nonetheless, the condition of state institutions con-

---

[30] *Laws of Mississippi, 1865,* pp. 186–89, 216–25; Port Gibson *Standard,* December 9, 1865. Included among these taxes was a poll tax of one dollar on all males between the ages of twenty-one and sixty years of age and without distinction of race.

[31] Jackson *Clarion,* February 2, 1867.

[32] *Ibid.,* September 28, 1866, January 18, 30, February 2, 20, 1867; Vicksburg *Times,* October 21, 1866; Meridian *Semi-Weekly Gazette,* April 24, 1867.

[33] *Appleton's Annual Cyclopaedia,* VI, 520; New Orleans *Picayune,* October 18, 1866. To stop the drain on state revenues for the support of the penitentiary, the convict lease system was introduced in 1866. From the beginning this arrangement was controversial, not on humanitarian grounds, but because the

tinued to be deplorable, and it was not until the Republican administrations of the 1870's that these facilities were properly restored and expanded to accomodate the unusual postwar demands for state services.[34]

Local accumulations of money were also restricted by the necessity for state revenues to provide relief for indigent citizens and disabled Confederate veterans. Centered in the piney woods and in the predominantly white counties of the northeast, the destitution that prevailed in 1865 continued during the next year. Not only did suffering occur as a result of poor cotton yields, but corn crops also generally failed. Pushed further into debt by these failures, many yeoman farmers and planters found it extremely difficult to secure credit with which to buy meat and other foodstuffs.[35] Some communities dispatched agents to the Northwest to obtain food, and funds were provided by Northern charitable associations for the purchase of corn for destitute persons. The Freedmen's Bureau gave provisions for distribution among both races, but even these were discontinued in August, 1866.[36]

The legislature that met in the fall of 1865 took steps to furnish relief for persons in a condition of extreme poverty and for incapacitated Confederate veterans. A bill was passed and approved by Governor Humphreys which provided that 20 per cent of the revenue of the state, but not more than sixty thousand dollars, was to be reserved annually by the state treasurer for the relief of disabled veterans and destitute persons, with preference being given to widows and children of Confederate soldiers. In each county boards of police were to

interests of mechanics and others were allegedly injured by it. Jackson *Clarion*, November 3, 1866, January 29, 1867.

[34] Adelbert Ames to James W. Garner, January 25, 1900, in James W. Garner Papers, Mississippi Department of Archives and History, Jackson.

[35] Citizens of Lawrence County to Governor Humphreys, April 3, 1866, in Governors' Correspondence, E-78; Meridian *Semi-Weekly Gazettte*, April 10, June 30, 1867; Jackson *Clarion*, February 13, 1867. The *Clarion* reported in the late fall of 1865 that "much distress will exist in the winter of 1865 and the following year, and thousands of families heretofore in comfortable circumstances, are so reduced as scarcely to be able to provide for themselves the necessities of life." Moore, "Social and Economic Conditions in Mississippi during Reconstruction," 333.

[36] Meridian *Semi-Weekly Gazette*, June 13, 30, 1867; Jackson *Clarion*, August 17, 1866; Jackson *Clarion and Standard*, August 4, 1866; New Orleans *Picayune*, November 4, 1865; Raymond *Hinds County Gazette*, September 7, 1866.

compile a list of people who would be qualified for aid, and they were to submit these lists to the state treasurer. Their reports were to serve as the basis for a pro rata distribution of the indigent fund. The act also provided that impecunious children of deceased or disabled soldiers, and maimed veterans themselves, were entitled to free education at any state institution of learning.[37]

Many boards of supervisors were slow to submit their lists of indigent persons, and until all of the counties made their reports the state treasurer refused to distribute any of the money that had accumulated. When the legislature met in early 1867, one fourth of the counties were still delinquent in forwarding reports, and the fund of sixty thousand dollars had been lying idle in the treasury since May, 1866.[38] The legislature immediately authorized the treasurer to distribute the complete fund to the 13,630 indigent persons who had been reported by their county officials and to all others who were reported by May 1. During the same session the legislature appropriated thirty thousand dollars to provide artificial legs for maimed Confederate veterans.[39]

Obstacles to the recovery of the agrarian economy appeared insurmountable to many, and this pessimism contributed to a conspicuous decline in the value of land from that of antebellum days. Land depreciated generally from one third to one half of its prewar value, and, if valued in terms of greenbacks, the depreciation was even greater. Good land in areas remote from transportation facilities was reported to be selling for as little as thirty-five cents an acre. In the cotton belt of central Mississippi plantations valued at twenty to twenty-five dollars an acre in 1860 were being purchased for ten dollars an acre in late 1865.[40] Some expected a large turnover of farm ownership as a result of the decline in land values; however, this failed to materialize primarily because prospective buyers simply lacked

---

[37] *Laws of Mississippi, 1865*, pp. 149–52.

[38] Port Gibson *Standard*, November 25, 1865; Jackson *Clarion*, April 22, 1866; *Journal of the Senate of the State of Mississippi, at a Called Session, October, 1866 [and January–February 1867]* (Jackson: J. J. Shannon and Co., State Printers, 1866 and 1867), 273; Natchez *Courier*, February 14, 1867.

[39] *Senate Journal, 1866–1867*, Appendix, 109, 126–29.

[40] *Commercial and Financial Chronicle*, May 9, 1868, p. 583; "Report of the Joint Committee on Reconstruction," *House Reports*, 39th Cong., 1st Sess., No. 30, Pt. III, 135; "Affairs in the Late Insurrectionary States," *House Reports*, 42nd Cong., 2nd Sess., No. 22, p. 531; Natchez *Weekly Courier*, June 1, 1866; Raymond *Hinds County Gazette*, November 25, December 2, 1865.

money. Moreover, sellers who were financially able to retain their property often refused to sell at the depreciated levels, preferring to lease their plantations to Northerners or to cultivate only a portion of their improved lands. In the river counties the large-scale entrance of Northerners during late 1865 and early 1866, looking for cotton plantations either to lease or to buy, made real estate prices rise in that region, at least in communities that were not flooded.[41] But with the disastrous crop failure of 1866 the value of these lands declined to the level of those in other areas of the state.

One consequence of the depreciated value of land was that money could hardly be borrowed with land as the only basis for security. Critically handicapped in the use of real estate as collateral for sound credit, planters in many cases were forced to borrow money on almost any conceivable terms to carry on operations.[42]

Despite barriers and unsettled conditions, as long as the price of cotton remained high, the prospects were good that money from some source would be extended to restore the productivity of the farmlands of the state. Since Mississippi was nearly destitute of financial assets, the main sources of funds would have to be in commerical centers near the state and in the North. Newspapers carried a number of advertisements in 1865 and 1866 by Memphis, New Orleans, and Mobile cotton factors, grocers, and dry-goods dealers offering to provide credit for enterprising planters. Many planters took advantage of these opportunities and renewed old business connections. But with the poor crops of 1866 and 1867 and the decline in the price of cotton in the latter year to a low of fourteen cents a pound on the New Orleans market, these sources became quite limited. In the general ruin that followed the crop misfortunes of these years, the factorage system, which had shown signs of continuing after the war, virtually collapsed.[43]

[41] Jackson *Clarion*, December 21, 1865, January 5, 1866; Raymond *Hinds County Gazette*, November 30, 1866; Henry M. Crydenwise to his parents, March 3, 1866, in Crydenwise Papers; Reid, *After the War*, 414, 455, 480–81, 579; Theodore Saloutos, *Farmer Movements in the South, 1865–1933* (Berkeley: University of California Press, 1960), 7.

[42] Reid, *After the War*, 414; Jackson *Clarion*, January 11, 1866.

[43] Moore, "Social and Economic Conditions in Mississippi during Reconstruction," 84; Loring and Atkinson (eds.), *Cotton Culture*, 75; Friar's Point *Coahomian*, September 22, 1865; John Watt and Company to Mrs. Nancy Richey, January 9, 1867, in Mrs. Nancy Richey Papers, Mississippi Department of Archives and History, Jackson.

From the beginning the most important source of funds for Mississippi planting operations came from the North. Even before the end of the war, Federal soldiers, travelers, and local promoters were sending glowing accounts to the North of the economic opportunities for cultivating cotton in the rich soils of Mississippi. They specifically encouraged Northerners to secure government leases to the numerous abandoned plantations in the western part of the state. In their letters, many Union soldiers indicated their resolve to stay after they were mustered out. A correspondent to the New York *Herald* wrote that everywhere he went with the army in the Mississippi Valley men were casting "longing eyes at the prospective wealth around them."[44] One veteran wrote home of his enthusiasm for the Delta: "There is no place where I could do better than here. Had I a farm all stocked at the North I could not, with good success, make beside expenses more than a few hundred dollars a year, while here, with no capital invested and my money at interest, I can probably make three or four times as much."[45]

Although not antagonistic to Northerners settling in the state, influential Mississippians were more interested in the extension of Eastern capital to finance agricultural enterprises than in immigration. Editor George W. Harper of the Raymond *Hinds County Gazette* admonished his readers to encourage the introduction of Northern money, despite past animosities. "There is capital at the North," he said, "which is deeply interested in the cultivation of a Southern crop. This capital will be alive to its own interests" if Mississippians would publicize the profits to be made from lending money to planters and merchants. The Friar's Point *Coahomian* urged Northern capitalists to invest in Mississippi bottom lands, where from four to seven hundred pounds of lint cotton could be produced on one acre.[46] After the poor crops of 1865 and 1866 and the subsequent retrenchment of outside money, Albert G. Brown, a former governor, United States Senator, and Southern nationalist, proclaimed to a meeting in his home county: "We want Yankee capital, Yankee ingenuity, Yankee enterprise, and to get all of this, we must agree to accept Yankee politicians. [However], after the

[44] Watkins, *King Cotton*, 177; David H. Overy, Jr., *Wisconsin Carpetbaggers in Dixie* (Madison: The State Historical Society of Wisconsin, 1961), 17; Knox, *Camp-fire and Cotton-field*, 493–94.

[45] Henry Crydenwise to his parents, November 11, 1866, in Crydenwise Papers.

[46] Raymond *Hinds County Gazette*, January 20, June 15, 1866; Friar's Point *Coahomian*, November 10, 1865.

Yankee comes, his politics won't be much in his way. When he sees the dollar, he will throw [meta]physics to the dogs."[47] In 1866 William J. Barbee, a De Soto County physician, wrote a book on the techniques of the cultivation and harvesting of cotton. The book was designed to encourage Northerners to come to Mississippi and to invest in cotton lands. He pointed out to prospective buyers that bottom lands in the state could be purchased for as little as five dollars an acre, although a large portion of these, Barbee admitted, was inundated and unimproved.[48]

Various schemes were proposed for securing operating funds for the cultivation of cotton in the state. One plan was advanced by Walter Goodman, a former railroad president with financial contacts in the East. He went to New York after the war and organized a company to lend money to cotton producers. Then he wrote Governor Humphreys that, if the legislature would charter his proposed loan company immediately and repeal the obnoxious usury laws of the state, he could raise one million dollars in ten days. With these funds he would establish an agency in the state to lend money to planters with nothing but their plantations as security. The legislature, however, was not in session when the governor received the letter; when it reconvened in the fall of 1866, Goodman was dead and outside capitalists had already soured on Mississippi investments.[49]

Another scheme, evidently promoted by New England textile manufacturers, called for the establishment of a large investment-loan company which would purchase or lease lands in the South or advance money to local planters. Where money was advanced, the planter would be required to mortgage his land as security, to ship his cotton to Boston, and to give one half of the proceeds to the company after expenses were paid. The planter would still have to pay off his mortgage from his share of the profits. Although admitting that its terms were hard, the editor of the Jackson *Clarion* believed that under the circumstances the plan was "the fairest proposition made to the planters by any body of capitalists of which we have heard. The

[47] Meridian *Semi-Weekly Gazette*, August 21, 1867.
[48] William J. Barbee, *The Cotton Question: The Production, Export, Manufacture, and Consumption of Cotton* (New York: Metropolitan Record Office, 1866), 80–81, 249.
[49] Walter Goodman to Humphreys, December 11, 1865, in Governors' Correspondence, E-77; Jackson *Clarion*, May 1, 1866.

planters want money to commence with. They can get it only by mortgaging heavily and paying large interest."[50]

Other companies, or "associations," were also formed to invest in Mississippi enterprises. Little money was extended to local planters by these associations, except possibly through agencies in New Orleans and Memphis. These companies were more successful in leasing or selling farm lands to prospective immigrants from the North.[51]

The greatest amount of money came to Mississippi with Federal soldiers and Northern immigrants. Military occupation proved a blessing in disguise as soldiers spent their pay in the state; furthermore, many of these men remained in Mississippi after being discharged and invested their mustering-out money in agricultural and commercial endeavors. Former Federal soldiers settled in large numbers in the river counties near Natchez and Vicksburg. The Northern editor of a Vicksburg newspaper estimated that approximately ten thousand Union veterans remained in or returned to Mississippi after the war, of whom four thousand settled in Warren County (Vicksburg) alone.[52] Even by making allowances for exaggeration on the part of this editor, it is evident that hundreds of Northerners recognized the opportunities for quick profits in the cultivation of cotton for men who had money; and, immediately upon being discharged from the army, they sought out destitute and disillusioned landowners to buy or to secure leases to their plantations.[53] Colonel Samuel Thomas reported that by the spring of 1866 the best lands along the Mississippi River were being cultivated by Northern men who had the money to pay laborers and to purchase the necessary provisions.[54]

Of those who settled in the interior, apparently most bought farmlands in the fertile cotton belts and especially along the Mobile and Ohio Railroad. Many of these Northern settlers were not Federal veterans.[55] Then, too, many Confederate veterans, especially from the border states, settled in this area after the war.

[50] Jackson *Clarion*, January 11, 1866.

[51] *Ibid.*, December 21, 1865, January 5, February 14, 1866; Raymond *Hinds County Gazette*, December 16, 1865.

[52] Vicksburg *Weekly Republican*, August 31, 1868.

[53] For brief accounts of this Northern penetration into Mississippi, see the Jackson *Clarion*, August 21, 1866; Reid, *After the War*, 414; and Morgan, *Yazoo*, 121.

[54] Raymond *Hinds County Gazette*, June 22, 1866.

[55] The United States Census does not give any information as to the number of

The fact that many Northerners believed that profitable opportunities existed in Mississippi does not completely explain their large migration into the state. Young men of the mid-nineteenth century, especially of the farmer class of the old Northwest, were thoroughly imbued with the frontier spirit and anxious to seek their fortunes in distant places when attractive opportunities appeared. They saw Mississippi as a new and exciting frontier and as an area awaiting only enterprise and capital for exploitation. Army life had conditioned many of them to change and to hazards. For them to seek economic opportunity in an unfamiliar and possibly hostile land was not too risky a venture for hard-bitten veterans of months of campaigning. One former soldier wrote from the Mississippi bottoms: "It seems so strange that I should be settled down away off here so far from all my kindred and friends. Yet such has been the wild, strange life I have lived for the past few years that I am at home anywhere and contented wherever I happen to be."[56] Few were merely "soldiers of fortune" seeking wealth by whatever means possible, although many were quick to speculate on land and cotton.[57]

Most Northerners settled in Mississippi as farmers or planters, since they were usually of the agrarian class in the North, and the high price of cotton influenced them to continue in the occupation of their fathers. Some, however, with nominal sums of money found excellent opportunities in business and the professions; these hopeful individuals located mainly in Natchez and Vicksburg. One Northern businessman, for example, came to Natchez before the end of the war, leased

---

Northerners who entered Mississippi during this period. Statistics on the nativity of the people living in the state in 1870 included both antebellum and postbellum settlers. Although there are no pertinent statistics available, newspapers and private correspondence give some indication of the most popular locations for Northern settlements after the war. See, for example, the New York *Times,* July 2, 1866; the Raymond *Hinds County Gazette,* March 9, 1866; F. Salter to Governor Humphreys, March 29, 1866, and F. T. Stackweather to Humphreys, March 30, 1866, in Governors' Correspondence, E-78.

[56] Henry M. Crydenwise to his parents, March 3, 1866, in Crydenwise Papers.

[57] One such "soldier of fortune" was J. R. Parsons, a Union army veteran who came to Mississippi soon after the war and reportedly commenced making "a mean article of soda water, which he sold to the negroes." He later was a prominent Union League organizer in Hinds County. Raymond *Hinds County Gazette,* March 17, 1869. Civilians who came to the state were often prominent men in their counties in the North; also, many former soldiers had been field grade officers in the Union army. See *ibid.,* March 9, 1866; [Benham], *Year of Wreck,* 169; and the Hernando *Weekly Press,* September 16, 1869.

three plantations from the government, and soon, anticipating the needs of a cotton boom, established the Agricultural Bank of Natchez with capital assets of one-half a million dollars.[58] A few Northerners were willing to come as overseers on plantations and even as laborers. Those who worked as overseers hoped to learn the planting and marketing techniques of cotton farming before embarking on careers as planters.[59]

The crop disasters of 1866 and 1867 dashed the hopes of Northern settlers for large and quick profits in cotton planting. One disillusioned farmer doubted whether many Northern men were successful in cultivating the staple, believing that they had only planted their money.[60] Former Governor John A. Andrew of Massachusetts, for example, had invested thirty thousand dollars in a plantation in the Mississippi bottoms, only to lose it in 1866. Another large investor estimated in the spring of 1866 that he and his partner would make approximately nine hundred bales of cotton, with a gross income of $108,000. But their plantations produced only sixty-five bales, which sold for $6,564 and which represented a sizable loss to the partners after expenses were deducted.[61]

Many Mississippians were quick to point out that Northern planters failed because of their impractical notions concerning Negro labor.[62]

[58] Horace S. Fulkerson, *A Civilian's Recollections of the War Between the States* (Baton Rouge: Otto Claitor, 1939), 241; Morgan, *Yazoo*, 121; Overy, *Wisconsin Carpetbaggers in Dixie*, 13, 19.

[59] Morgan, *Yazoo*, 82; [Benham], *Year of Wreck*, 233; Charles S. Lease to Governor Humphreys, November 20, 1865, in Governors' Correspondence, E-77. Almost all of the Northern settlers sought to make friends with their Southern neighbors, and they refrained from participating in local politics during the first two years after the war. Mississippians, however, did not always reciprocate the good-will expressions of these settlers. Reid, *After the War*, 560, 579; [Benham], *Year of Wreck*, 134; Morgan, *Yazoo*, 85; S. L. James to Governor Humphreys, January 12, 1866, in Governors' Correspondence, E-78.

[60] Warren, *Reminiscences of a Mississippi Carpetbagger*, 22.

[61] Jackson *Clarion*, August 17, 1866; [Benham], *Year of Wreck*, 459.

[62] For example, see Hiram Cassedy to William Whitehurst, December 16, 1866, in Whitehurst Papers, and the Raymond *Hinds County Gazette*, August 31, 1866. Northern planters did not always eschew the traditional methods of operating a plantation. Henry Crydenwise wrote, as if the system employed on the plantation where he worked in the Mississippi bottoms was characteristic of the area, that freedmen worked in field gangs, including Negro women. Overseers were used and the Negro laborers continued to live in the slave quarters. Crydenwise to his parents, March 3, 1866, in Crydenwise Papers. See also Warren, *Reminiscences of a Mississippi Carpetbagger*, 28.

However, labor problems, which were common to most planters, were not the main reasons for the failures of 1866 and 1867. Defective seed, excessive rain during the spring and severe droughts during the summer, the work of the destructive caterpillars, and a drop in the price of cotton in 1867, all contributed to the ruin of planters during these years.[63] In the Delta, lands that had been reclaimed, mainly by Northerners, continued to be subject to floodings. Northern planters suffered more than local producers because they had more invested and therefore had more to lose when disaster struck; furthermore, their lack of experience in the cultivation of cotton made them ill-prepared to cope with the calamities of 1866 and 1867.

Many disappointed Northerners returned home or moved West to seek new opportunities. One planter who remained claimed that nine tenths of the wartime or early postwar immigrants left the state during this period; however, this estimate is probably exaggerated.[64] Contrary to traditional interpretations, many enterprising Northerners probably remained in the state and refused to be discouraged by temporary setbacks. Unable now to secure credit in New Orleans or Memphis, some went North and made arrangements for financial assistance.[65] When Congressional Reconstruction was implemented in Mississippi, many of the remaining Northern settlers, somewhat reluctantly at first, entered politics. Meanwhile, those who returned home, embittered by the failures of 1866 and 1867, inveighed against the inhospitable climate and the rebellious spirit of Mississippians.[66]

The state government of 1865–67, dominated by Whigs who generally appreciated the need for policies that would attract capital, made major efforts, either directly or indirectly, to secure money for the state. While prospects were good for the extension of credit, Governor

[63] Jackson *Clarion*, August 17, 1866, September 19, October 9, 1867; Friar's Point *Coahomian*, June 1, 1866.

[64] [Benham], *Year of Wreck*, 461.

[65] *Ibid.*, 463. A brief survey of biographical information on some who remained and later participated in politics in the state gives an indication of the relatively high qualifications and persistence of these men. See especially Warren, *Reminiscences of a Mississippi Carpetbagger*, 36 *et passim*. For an example of the traditional interpretation, see Richard W. Griffin, "Problems of the Southern Cotton Planters After the Civil War," *Georgia Historical Quarterly*, XXXIX (1955), 109.

[66] Warren, *Reminiscences of a Mississippi Carpetbagger*, 33, 48, 63–64; Robert F. Futrell, "Efforts of Mississippians to Encourage Immigration, 1865–1880," *Journal of Mississippi History*, XX (1958), 64.

Humphreys and the legislature hesitated to act directly in the matter, although the governor was quick to aid indirectly by insisting on strict compliance with credit arrangements or contracts. Furthermore, in view of the amorphous condition of the economy in 1865 and 1866, it was very difficult for state leaders to determine specifically what measures were necessary to attract capital investment funds. But the poor crop of 1866 and the curtailment of outside investments brought pressure for state assistance. At the same time the failure of local planters and the decline in the value of their lands made it exceedingly hard, if not impossible, for them to satisfy their creditors. And under these unfavorable circumstances, cotton growers were fearful that they would not be extended credit for provisions, unless some plan was arranged to make loans secure.[67]

To the legislators who convened at Jackson on January 21, 1867, the main purpose for their meeting was to devise some scheme to facilitate the extension of money in the state. The most significant result of their work was the passage of a bill entitled "An Act for the Encouragement of Agriculture," which gave to first liens on crops the force of state law. The act was designed to protect primarily merchants and capitalists in furnishing provisions to planters and farmers, but it also gave landowners a lien on the crops of their tenants where they had made advances for supplies. The law further provided that all liens should be filed in the office of the circuit court.[68] Governor Humphreys immediately dispatched agents to the Northeast for the purpose of informing financiers and merchants of the new law and to secure consignments of goods for Mississippi planters. These goods were to be secured by the first lien on the crop.[69]

The crop-lien bill passed the legislature with little opposition. Many Mississippians hopefully believed that the law would open the gates for an abundant flow of money in the form of credit and goods to sustain the agricultural economy of the state.[70] This flow never ma-

[67] Jackson *Clarion*, December 9, 1866.

[68] *Laws of Mississippi, 1866–1867*, pp. 569–72. Even before the passage of the crop-lien bill, many farmers had pledged their anticipated crops to merchants for provisions. See, for example, the Jackson *Clarion*, April 22, 1866, and I. M. Moore to Humphreys, September 1, 1866, in Governors' Correspondence, E-80. Crop mortgages, although not too common, had been employed since colonial days in cases where the value of land was not sufficient to secure credit.

[69] A. J. Withers to Humphreys, March 5, 1867, in Governors' Correspondence, E-81.

[70] Jackson *Clarion*, January 22, February 15, 1867.

terialized. Yet the crop-lien arrangement did provide a means by which cotton growers could continue as commercial farmers, though for many it soon meant that they were hopelessly mired in a position of tenancy. By the 1870's the crop-lien law, which was continued by the Republican regimes, had become in the minds of the small farmers the most unpopular measure enacted by the restoration legislature.

The legislature of 1867 took other direct measures to entice money to the state and to provide for investment of funds available in Mississippi. Usury laws were repealed and savings associations were chartered, which, however, were never capitalized. Probably the most unique scheme to attract capital investment funds for the state was the incorporation of the Mississippi American Industrial Agency.[71] This company was established to invest in bonds and stocks of substantial corporations, especially railroad companies, "which being placed in Europe or elsewhere, may be sold or held as the basis of credit, enabling the company to obtain money and credit upon such time and upon such terms as will enable them advantageously . . . to make loans and advances to Railroad companies, farmers, planters, manufacturers, and others, upon terms more favorable than such loans are usually made by banks." The corporation was required to deposit bonds with the state treasurer or some other person as security for repayment of deposits that were subject to withdrawal. This provision was designed to give greater confidence and security to potential investors or depositors in the company and thus secure a lessening of interest rates. Unlike the savings associations, whose supporters were limited to local merchants and planters, the Mississippi American Industrial Agency was promoted by many of the most influential business and professional men of Mississippi. Nonetheless, this scheme also failed to materialize for want of financial backing.

The insuperable problem of the indebtedness of the people was the most vexatious issue, with the possible exception of the freedmen question, facing the state during the period immediately after the war. With creditors clamoring for payment in full of antebellum and wartime obligations, insolvent planters and farmers found it virtually impossible to arrange a settlement. Many who were demanding payment were only links in a chain of indebtedness that ran to New Orleans, Memphis, Mobile, and in many cases to New York. Pressed by

[71] The act of incorporation may be found in the *Laws of Mississippi, 1866–1867*, pp. 659–60.

their creditors, merchants of Natchez, Vicksburg, and other commercial centers wanted no scaling down of debts or stay laws which would prevent or delay their collecting from interior merchants and planters. Unless they could show good faith toward their creditors by paying at least some of their indebtedness, these merchants believed, correctly, that it would be extremely difficult for them to re-establish their lines of credit with New Orleans, Memphis, and Northern centers. Payment from their debtors was the only way in 1865 that merchants could meet the demands of their creditors and regain their commercial contacts.[72]

Yet the need for some relief for debtors was admitted by most state leaders. The real issue concerned what form the relief should take. Many were demanding a complete repudiation of all private and public indebtedness, whereas others wanted the legislature only to postpone the collection of private debts until the cotton economy was revived.[73] To former Whigs who had bitterly fought repudiation before the war, relief had to be such that it would in no way further impair the credit standing of the state, especially at a time when great care needed to be taken not to offend potential investors in Mississippi enterprises.[74] In fact, so strong was this feeling among a few Whigs that when the legislature met in October, 1865, these conservatives proposed that the state appropriate 25 per cent of its revenue to pay the public debt, apparently regardless of whether or not the obligation was made in support of the Confederate cause. However, President Johnson's insistence that the other former Confederate states repudiate their war debts gave the Mississippi legislature a convenient, if not desirable, excuse to disclaim this obligation without damaging anew the credit reputation of the state.[75]

[72] Francis W. Henry to B. E. Wofford, April 15, 1867, in Henry Papers; Natchez *Democrat*, November 9, 14, 1865; Natchez *Courier*, December 16, 1865; Vicksburg *Journal*, November 12, 1865.

[73] I. W. Watson to Governor Humphreys, November 2, 1865, in Governors' Correspondence, E-77; Jackson *Clarion*, April 5, 1866; Friar's Point *Coahomian*, September 29, 1865.

[74] George W. Harper of the Raymond *Hinds County Gazette* in an editorial, January 26, 1866, called for former Whigs to stand firm and not to agree to any debt adjustments. "Our life-long position on these questions (the very basis on which the old Whig party was built) should not be regarded as a position proper to be abandoned now, or at any other time."

[75] New Orleans *Picayune*, October 25, November 4, 1865; Port Gibson *Standard*, November 9, 1865; Jackson *Clarion*, December 1, 1865.

To stifle radical proposals to wipe out all indebtedness, Whigs in the legislature agreed to a bill, sponsored by Democrats Samuel J. Gholson and James H. R. Taylor, which suspended all legal processes for the collection of debts until January 1, 1868. Governor Humphreys promptly vetoed the measure as unconstitutional and as an infringement on the sanctity of contracts.[76] He later explained his veto by asserting that a stay law would not alleviate any of the effects of the economic dislocation of the state. "Temporary relief from debt often tends only to additional embarrassments," Humphreys declared. "Patient industry, strict economy and 'long suffering' are now our destiny and our duty, and the only means of restoring our lost fortunes and re-establishing our prosperity and happiness."[77] The governor was in no mood to compromise basic principles of Mississippi Whigs which upheld the interests of creditors.

The legislature immediately reconsidered the stay bill, and on December 1, 1865, it passed the measure over the governor's veto.[78] Party lines were not clearly drawn because of the compromising policy of many Whigs. A few die-hard Whig anti-repudiators in the senate, however, opposed any law which modified contractual obligations, despite forebodings of a wholesale disavowal of debts if the legislature did not provide some relief. In the house, on the other hand, a majority of the Whigs accepted the compromise arrangement as embodied in the stay bill. Democrats were not as divided as Whigs on the issue, and the great majority of them in both houses followed antebellum party policies and voted for the measure.

At the same time, the legislature passed a property exemption measure designed to prevent the seizure for debts of a certain amount and type of property. The measure exempted from court seizure for each white family head 240 acres of land, four thousand dollars worth of real or personal property, and necessary farming equipment, including draft animals, or tools of a mechanic. When Humphreys vetoed the bill, its supporters on November 28, 1865, easily secured the necessary votes of two thirds of the members of the legislature to enact the measure.[79] Actually, this law may have been more of a

[76] New York *Times*, February 4, 1866.
[77] New Orleans *Picayune*, October 18, 1866.
[78] *Senate Journal, 1865*, p. 210; *House Journal, 1865*, pp. 361–62.
[79] *Laws of Mississippi, 1865*, pp. 137–38; *House Journal, 1865*, pp. 345–46; *Senate Journal, 1865*, p. 169. The governor was more successful in his opposition to other legislative proposals to aid debtors. Memphis *Appeal*, December 7, 1865.

bane than a blessing for the people of the state, as one editor later claimed after observing its workings for more than four years. "Credit is the honest poor man's only help," he declared, "and so long as the exemption laws cover more property than 99 out of every 100 of our citizens have, so long will liens and mortgages be required, which pile up costs and which cover all descriptions of property."[80]

A chorus of bitter denunciation greeted the passage of the stay and exemption bills. Generally from the older generation of Whigs or from the commercial centers of the state, these anti-repudiators claimed that the legislature in enacting the relief measures had ignored the lessons of the past and that capital would now be even more reluctant to come to Mississippi than it had been before the passage of the acts. One embittered Whig editor suspected that many of the legislators who voted for the bills would profit directly as a result of their action.[81]

Opposition to the debtor relief measures was not limited to the state. New Orleans and New York newspapers reflected the anger of the merchants of those cities who were creditors in Mississippi. The New York Times avowed that the stay law was "ruinous to State credit, odious to every principle of justice, and must seriously retard the restoration of commercial and business prosperity" in Mississippi.[82] Walter Goodman, a Mississippian then in New York attempting to organize an investment company, wrote Governor Humphreys that millions of dollars might have gone to the state but for the legislature's bent toward repudiation.[83]

Opponents called specifically for the invalidation of the stay measure by the High Court of Errors and Appeals. The court acted, and within three months of its passage the stay law was declared null and void. Chief Justice Alexander H. Handy delivered the opinion, ruling that the act violated both the national and state constitutions respecting the obligation of contracts. Handy, an old Democrat, who during the campaign of 1865 had been accused of being a repudiator, sought to

[80] Raymond Hinds County Gazette, April 27, 1870.

[81] Ibid., February 2, 1866; Natchez Courier, December 16, 1866; Jackson Clarion, August 25, 1866; Port Gibson Standard, November 25, 1865; Vicksburg Journal, November 12, 1865.

[82] New York Times, February 24, 1866. See also the Raymond Hinds County Gazette, February 28, 1866, for comments by New Orleans newspapers on the stay laws.

[83] Goodman to Humphreys, November 19, 1865, in Governors' Correspondence, E-77.

soften the blow of the decision by declaring that the ruling was especially painful to the court, since the stay law proceeded "from the well-meant policy of relieving, as far as might be, the pecuniary distresses and prostration of a people unparalleled in all our history."[84]

Immediately after the court declared the stay law unconstitutional, creditors flooded the courts of the state with suits for the collection of debts. Probably fearful that the next session of the legislature would enact a comprehensive measure for debtor relief that would meet the approval of the high court, creditors demanded payment in full from those who owed them money.[85] One Mississippian described their activities: "The dockets groan under the weight of his [the creditor's] notes and accounts. The sons of a certain character in Shakespeare's *Merchant of Venice* are abroad in the land seeking their pound of flesh."[86] Reporting that some persons were being sued in Hinds County without being asked for payment, Editor James J. Shannon of the Jackson *Clarion* commented that creditors had become "quite blood-thirsty." In a neighboring county almost four hundred suits for the collection of outstanding debts were brought in one week. A member of the state house of representatives from a north Mississippi county near Memphis reported that between twelve hundred and fifteen hundred suits were initiated at the spring session of the circuit court in his district. In turbulent Choctaw County officials resigned their offices and refused to qualify when subsequently re-elected, in order to prevent creditors from processing suits in the county. A large meeting of debtors of another county, called by prominent citizens of the communities, resolved that they would boycott the businesses of persons who insisted on collecting on overdue accounts in the county.[87] The results of the wholesale suing in the

[84] *Coffman et al.* v. *The Bank of Kentucky*, 40 Miss. 29 (1866). Several Whig circuit judges had already declared the stay law unconstitutional when the high court rendered its decision. During the same term the high court ruled that the exemption law did not violate the obligation of contract, and therefore it was constitutional. *Mosely* v. *Anderson*, 40 Miss. 49 (1866). When Congressional Reconstruction was imposed upon the state, the military commander extended to the Negroes the benefits of the exemption law. Major General Alvan C. Gillem to Theodore Wiseman, January 8, 1866, in Freedmen's Bureau Records, Mississippi.

[85] Jackson *Clarion*, April 10, 14, 1866.

[86] Raymond *Hinds County Gazette*, November 2, 1866.

[87] Jackson *Clarion*, April 10, 14, 29, 1866; William T. Cole to Governor Humphreys, June 7, 1866, in Governors' Correspondence, E-79; Natchez *Weekly Courier*, June 1, 1866.

courts were evident to all, one writer asserted. Property was being sold at a great sacrifice to settle debts, and this condition, he claimed, was "rapidly bringing many of the best men in the State to beggary."[88]

In spite of demands for state action, Governor Humphreys at first refused to call the legislature into session, preferring to believe that "the creditor would be a stay law unto himself, in this, the hour of his country's calamity, and that he would keep aloof from the dockets of the courts until the debtor could catch his breath." Nevertheless, faced with growing pressure, Humphreys capitulated to the demands and assembled the legislature on October 15, 1866.[89]

Apprehensive lawmakers during this session, however, could not devise a relief measure that Humphreys would approve. When the legislators met again in January, 1867, they were concerned almost exclusively with proposals to entice money to Mississippi, and they feared that if they enacted a relief law the flow of funds to the state would be impeded.[90] Thus, with the exception of the exemption act, no law was passed by the restoration legislature and sustained by the courts which gave succor to debtors.

Ironically, the relief that debtors sought during the restoration period became, to a certain extent, a reality as a result of the policies of the federal government during the early days of the period commonly referred to in the South as Radical Reconstruction. At the same time that Radicals in Congress were busy passing reconstruction measures, they enacted a general bankruptcy law. This act provided a voluntary means whereby a debtor could be adjudged insolvent by a federal court and could arrange to pay off his obligations in accordance with his ability to do so.[91] Mississippians who had been frustrated in their efforts to secure relief locally hailed the bankruptcy legislation. The Port Gibson Standard declared: "Congress, though ungenerous and unjust in some things, has seen and admitted [the need for relief], and with an eye to the interest of northern men, who are, more than any body else, affected by it, have sought" to aid

[88] Jackson Clarion, September 7, 1866.

[89] Raymond Hinds County Gazette, August 10, November 2, 1866; citizens of Carroll County to Humphreys, April, 1866; a Crystal Springs planter to Humphreys, May 10, 1866, both in Governors' Correspondence, E-79; Vicksburg Times, October 21, 1866.

[90] Raymond Hinds County Gazette, November 2, 1866; Jackson Clarion, January 29, 30, 1867; Natchez Courier, February 5, 1867.

[91] Meridian Semi-Weekly Gazette, March 19, 1867.

depressed debtors.[92] The Jackson *Clarion* editor thought that the federal law wonderfully approximated the desires of Mississippi debtors and was "the only refuge to which we can point," since state legislative efforts to secure relief had failed.[93] Yet the relief granted by this act was limited, since insolvent landowners lost land by taking bankruptcy.

The military commander, Major General Edward O. C. Ord, who had been sent to implement the Radical program in Mississippi, also acted to aid hard-pressed debtors. To provide immediate relief and to prevent foreclosures before the federal bankruptcy law became effective, General Ord on June 12, 1867, proclaimed a stay law against forced sales of property until January 1, 1868.[94]

The effect on the extension of capital of stay measures and other schemes to relieve debtors was undoubtedly exaggerated by those who had long sought to remove the stain of repudiation from the reputation of the state. Anti-repudiators apparently chose not to accept the basic economic explanation that the securing of operating funds by cotton growers and merchants and the subsequent accumulation of capital was largely dependent upon the production of cotton and upon the price that it would bring on the market.

During the first two years after the war the price of cotton was quite high, never dropping below thirty cents a pound on the New Orleans market.[95] Mississippians, however, were unable to take full advantage of these lofty prices to accumulate money. In 1865 labor problems and the general economic dislocation of the state resulted in small yields. Although the Negroes had generally been returned to the fields by the spring of 1866, a series of disasters, including a mass destruction of the bolls by caterpillars, occurred in that year and greatly limited the yields. Only 306,389 bales were produced in 1866, as compared to 859,285 in 1860.[96] Yet the value of the 1866 crop ex-

[92] As reported in the Jackson *Clarion*, May 10, 1867.

[93] As reported in the Meridian *Semi-Weekly Gazette*, November 5, 1867. See also the Vicksburg *Herald*, March 27, 1867.

[94] Meridian *Semi-Weekly Gazette*, May 25, 1867; "Correspondence Relative to Reconstruction," *Senate Executive Documents*, 40th Cong., 1st Sess., No. 14, p. 146; Jackson *Clarion*, May 10, 1867.

[95] Boyle, *Cotton and the New Orleans Cotton Exchange*, 180.

[96] Raymond *Hinds County Gazette*, August 10, 1866; Henry M. Crydenwise to his parents, June 20, 1866, in Crydenwise Papers; Watkins, *King Cotton*, 176. Statistics are not available for the 1865 yields. A significant reason for the small

ceeded that of 1860 by more than five million dollars because of the higher price for the staple in 1866. Cotton growers, nevertheless, netted less in 1866 than in 1860. The cost of producing cotton after the war had increased to twice that of 1860, according to the *Commercial and Financial Chronicle*. Included in these added expenses were increased outlays for Negro labor and for provisions, which were more expensive in 1866 than in 1860. In addition to these increased costs, planters after the war saw their profits curtailed by the federal tax on cotton and by high interest rates for credit.[97] Furthermore, some of the net profits left the state when disillusioned Northern planters returned home.

Disappointed and with little means to secure credit for the new year, farmers planted less cotton in 1867 than in 1866. And this cotton before harvesting was subject to some of the same natural disasters, although not as extensively, which had affected the crop the year before.[98] The yield for the state was approximately the same as in 1866, but the monetary value was almost one-half less. The reason for this tremendous difference in the worth of the two crops was a major decline in the price of cotton, from a low of thirty cents in December, 1866, to a low of fourteen cents twelve months later.[99]

Prices improved somewhat in 1868, as did yields, but the total value of the cotton crop on the market was still less than that of 1866. Costs of production, however, were doubtless considerably less than during the preceding three years. Large outlays for replenishing draft animals and farm equipment destroyed during the war were no longer necessary, and the burdensome cotton tax had expired in early 1868. Then, too, a decline in wages due to the scarcity of money and the increasing dependence of planters on the relatively inexpensive sharecrop system resulted in landowners' retaining more of what they received for their cotton than previously.[100] In effect, for the first time since the

crop of 1866 was that much of the seed planted in the spring was defective. Friar's Point *Coahomian*, June 1, 1866.

[97] The general inflationary trend that had begun during the war must be considered in any comparison of 1860 and 1865–67 prices.

[98] Jackson *Weekly Clarion*, October 9, 1867; Meridian *Semi-Weekly Gazette*, October 9, 1867; New York *Times*, April 21, 1867.

[99] Watkins, *King Cotton*, 176; Boyle, *Cotton and the New Orleans Cotton Exchange*, 180.

[100] Captain William Shields to Lieutenant Merritt Barber, January 31, 1868; report of Captain Allen B. Higgins, April 30, 1868; and report of P. P. Bergevim, June 30, 1868, all in Freedmen's Bureau Records, Mississippi.

war, Mississippi cotton growers in 1868 made money, most of which was probably used to pay outstanding debts. Prospects now appeared good that money would begin to accumulate in the state. This development, nevertheless, would be slow as long as the economy of the state depended upon an agricultural staple, cotton. Local producers in an agrarian economy dependent upon outside markets have nearly always been handicapped because of their lack of control over the price their product brings.

Because of the risks involved for investors and merchants, cotton growers found it increasingly difficult to secure operating funds or credit for each year, much less to accumulate money for extending their farming operations or for other investments. The planters' main need for money was to pay and to sustain Negro laborers and their families, many of whom were dependent upon the landowners for sustenance.[101] When planters were unable to procure sufficient operating funds, the sharecrop technique was employed as a substitute for the wage system.

Apparently most planters paid their laborers wages in 1865 and 1866. Payments in the former year were probably made only after the cotton crop was marketed, since a crucial shortage of currency existed in the state during the first few months after the war. In 1866, when a relatively large amount of operating money was extended to cotton growers in the state, most planters evidently were able to make partial monthly payments to their workers. The great demand for laborers made it possible for freedmen to insist on and to secure these monthly payments. Planters, however, preferred to withhold as much of the workers' wages as possible to insure labor stability during the harvesting season.[102]

[101] Barbee, *The Cotton Question*, 82. For an example of the continuing dependence of Negroes on whites for housing and provisions under the wage system, one planter in 1866 agreed to pay a field worker $15 and his wife $10, plus to provide "good and comfortable quarters and wholesome rations," that is, four pounds of mess pork and a peck of meal each week. Furthermore, the planter agreed to furnish a small vegetable garden and adequate material for one summer and one winter suit of clothes for both the Negro laborer and his wife. He was to give them "kind care and attention in case of sickness," but the freedmen would have to pay for other medical expenses. Contract between Jonathan Rucker and John and Sarah Nelson, freedmen, March 1, 1866, in Whitehurst Papers.

[102] [Benham], *Year of Wreck*, 118; contract between Jonathan Rucker and John and Sarah Nelson, freedmen, March 1, 1866, in Whitehurst Papers; Barbee, *The Cotton Question*, 82.

By 1867 sharecrop arrangements had generally replaced wage payments as the means for compensating workers. The sharecrop technique had been common in the state in 1866; in fact, in that year in some districts the system had already replaced the wage arrangement on a majority of the plantations.[103] The crop failure of 1866 and the subsequent difficulty of securing operating funds or credit for the new year resulted in an even larger number of cotton growers trying the sharecrop technique in 1867.[104] In addition to the financial reason for preferring this arrangement, planters believed that labor stability would be promoted by it. Since blacks would receive no compensations above subsistence until the crop was marketed, planters believed that they would be motivated to remain on the plantations and to work during the difficult and crucial harvesting period. Yet by withholding some of their pay under the wage system, planters were generally able to keep their laborers until the end of the cotton season, and thus they probably achieved somewhat the same results regarding labor stability as planters who divided their lands among sharecroppers.

In cases where Negroes worked for a share of the crop, they secured supplies for the year from planters under the crop-lien arrangement. When the poor crop of 1867 was harvested, it was found that in most cases the share that laborers received was not sufficient to pay their indebtedness for provisions advanced. This created a great deal of dissatisfaction among sharecroppers and a determination on their part to work only for wages in 1868.[105] Their insistence on cash might have been successful but for the rapid decline in the wage rate throughout the state, caused by the crop misfortunes of 1867 and a subsequent lack of operating funds for the new year. Under these circumstances most Negroes believed, according to Freedmen's Bureau officers, that the sharecrop arrangement would be more remunerative and desirable than the wage system. Many, however, still contracted with planters for wages in 1868.[106]

[103] Barbee, The Cotton Question, 82; Loring and Atkinson (eds.), Cotton Culture, 114.

[104] Jackson Clarion, January 1, 1867.

[105] Report of General Alvan C. Gillem, December 10, 1867, in Appleton's Annual Cyclopaedia, VII, 518.

[106] Report of Captain J. R. Webster, May 1, 1868; report of Andrew Thomas, May 3, 1868; report of J. H. Chapman, May 1, 1868; report of Captain Loyd Wheaton, July 31, 1868; report of P. P. Bergevim, June 30, 1868; report of W. H. Eldridge, April 30, 1868, all in Freedmen's Bureau Records, Mississippi.

The sharecrop system did not solve the planter's problem of money deficiencies, nor did it insure him a highly stable source of labor. The Negro, on the other hand, protested about oversupervision and claimed that he was cheated in his contracts.[107] Yet the sharecrop system, along with the crop-lien technique, made it possible, if not compulsory, for cotton growers of all classes in a region virtually devoid of financial assets to continue as commercial farmers. Planters were able to obtain labor without paying current wages, and dependent farmers were able to obtain land without buying it or paying cash rent.

Formidable indeed were the barriers to economic recovery that confronted Mississippians during the years immediately following the Civil War. Federal policies, especially the cotton tax and the surreptitious confiscation of wartime-grown cotton, restricted their use of this valuable staple as a means of restoring the economy of Mississippi and of accumulating capital for expansion purposes. Southern nationalists and radical state rights advocates had been quieted by the results of the war. Their place as spokesmen for the state had been taken by conservatives, who, although not all were former Whigs, expressed attitudes and formulated policies that followed the antebellum position of the Whig party. Their economic policies were divorced from the emotionalism of the earlier period of sectional conflict and war and were designed to provide for the first needs of the state.

To these conservatives, the first need for economic recovery was money; and it was obvious to them that local sources, including those located in commercial centers near the state, were inadequate for their purposes. They readily concluded that Northern sources of money held the key to the restoration and expansion of the cotton economy. In order to entice this Northern capital, including Northern settlers, it was necessary, men of the Whig persuasion believed, to make it clear to all that the government of Mississippi was no longer in the hands of debt repudiators or of men who were not sophisticated on matters of finance. In their zeal to erase the stigma of repudiation from the reputation of the state, these conservative leaders and spokesmen acted as if there had been no destructive war that had disrupted the economic life of the state. Especially did Governor Humphreys believe that a strict regard for the contractual rights of creditors was necessary before money would be extended to cotton growers and

[107] See, for example, the report of George S. Smith, February 10, 1868, *ibid*.

merchants in the state, notwithstanding the general insolvency of most of the people and their need for some relief. Evidently many Mississippi leaders did not understand that the extension of operating funds and the eventual accumulation of capital depended largely upon the production of cotton and upon the price that the staple would bring on the market.

Yet those persons who did place their confidence in king cotton as the main means for recovery were soon disappointed. The small yields of 1865 and 1866 canceled the benefits that would have been gained from marketing while the price was high. After the price of cotton dropped 50 per cent in 1867, most farmers and merchants found themselves further mired in debt, with little hope for relief in the immediate future. Cotton yields for 1868, however, restored their confidence somewhat in the ability of king cotton to provide a degree of the prosperity they had known before the war.

10

Vicissitudes of Levee Reconstruction

THE LACK of capital resources was in no way more evident than in the frustration of Mississippians in their efforts to rebuild the levees along the river. The reconstruction of these embankments was necessary to restore the productivity of the greater portion of the lands of the rich Delta. The problem was not simply one of repairing the levees deteriorated and damaged during the war but also, if permanent recovery were to be achieved, of constructing a new and more durable system for controlling the river and for draining the basin. In December, 1865, Brigadier General Andrew A. Humphreys of the United States Corps of Engineers surveyed the region and reported that it would cost approximately $1,500,000 to build a complete and durable levee system. Even to repair the major breaks in the existing levees would require $817,000.[1] Financial resources for the restoration of the old levees, much less for the construction of a new system to drain the Mississippi bottoms, were simply not available in the state after the war.

The old levee system had been built during the 1850's, mainly as a result of the resourcefulness of the planters whose lands fronted on the river. Using well-organized gangs of slaves, planters were able to construct makeshift embankments to protect their lands from overflows. They hesitated, however, to build levees that would protect lands that had not been occupied, and it was not until December, 1858, that the state legislature passed an act organizing a levee district

[1] For a summary of Humphreys' report, see "Report on the Levee on the Mississippi River," *Senate Reports*, 39th Cong., 1st Sess., No. 126, pp. 1–2. He made no recommendations concerning the drainage of the overflow areas caused by periodic floodings of the narrow channels of the Yazoo River and its tributaries.

board and authorizing a tax on residents of the district to complete the embankments. Under the supervision of James Lusk Alcorn, a large Delta landowner, the gaps in the levees were closed before the outbreak of the war.[2]

The irregular and uncoordinated way in which this system was built suggested from the beginning that it would not withstand unusual floodings and that its effectiveness under ordinary conditions would be temporary. Most of the levees constructed during the 1850's averaged about four feet in height, whereas they should have been at least five or six feet to have been able to contain severe floods. Furthermore, a great many of the embankments had been constructed of sand, with logs, stumps, and brush often added, which proved centers of weakness in the line when the river rose.[3] By 1861 Mississippi had a system of levees, although of questionable effectiveness, from below Memphis to near Vicksburg, a distance of approximately three hundred miles.[4]

Although this levee system served only as a temporary expedient, its completion opened the fertile Mississippi bottoms for large-scale exploitation by cotton growers during the late 1850's. When the war temporarily checked this development, large tracts of the lowlands were still unclaimed, since transportation facilities had not yet been extended into some areas of the hinterland of the basin. Furthermore, the fear of chills and fever prevented many from settling in the bottoms.[5] Then, too, the problem of floods had not been completely solved by the construction of the levees.

During the war no effort was made by authorities to improve the levee system or to provide needed repairs. Delta planters, left to shift for themselves, were unable to secure the money and labor necessary to save their fields, and many were forced to abandon their lands. When the war ended, the old system of levees was virtually in ruin, and much of the Delta was subject to floodings.[6]

[2] New York *Times,* April 10, 1867; Loring and Atkinson (eds.), *Cotton Culture,* 113; Arthell Kelly, "Levee Building and the Settlement of the Yazoo Basin," *Southern Quarterly,* I (1963), 290.

[3] New York *Times,* April 29, 1867.

[4] Memphis *Appeal,* November 23, 1865; Halsell, "Migration into Leflore County," 223.

[5] Halsell, "Migration into Leflore County," 221, 223.

[6] Memphis *Appeal,* November 23, 1865; Sillers, "Flood Control in Bolivar County," 6–7; Montgomery, *Reminiscences,* 258–59.

Even before the restoration legislature met in the fall of 1865, interested persons and groups began to demand that plans be made for the reconstruction of the levees. Most of these parties had little faith in the ability of the state to provide the needed funds and enterprise to restore the embankments.[7] The reconstruction convention meeting in August took cognizance of these demands and dispatched four commissioners to Washington to seek aid. These agents had broad authority. They could secure laborers to work on the levees and could negotiate loans, to be based on taxes that would be levied by the legislature when it met.[8] The traditional conflict arose in the convention as to whether the state as a whole, or only those counties that would benefit from the restoration of the levees, should pay for the work. As in 1858 representatives from the alluvial basin were unable to secure statewide support for the levee project, and the convention specifically directed that the legislature could place taxes only on the planters in the counties and districts that would be protected by the embankments. Under no circumstances was the faith of the state to be pledged for the payment of money that might be borrowed by the commissioners.[9]

When the legislature met, it acted to implement the program outlined by the convention. In November, 1865, the assembly passed an act establishing a board of levee commissioners for Bolivar, Washington, and Issaquena counties. The commissioners were given authority "to rebuild, strengthen or elevate the old levees, or make new embankments or levees," and to provide for this work the legislature levied an annual tax of ten cents per acre on land in these counties. In addition to the land tax, the legislature placed a duty of one cent per pound on all cotton produced in the levee district. The board also was granted the authority to borrow money and issue bonds, as long as the faith of the state was not pledged for payment. The provisions of the act could be extended to other Delta counties, if the voters approved.[10] The landowners of these counties, however, declined to participate in the program, since they were almost completely without means to pay the required taxes and were divided concerning the

[7] Natchez *Democrat*, October 10, 1865; Friar's Point *Coahomian*, November 24, 1865; Memphis *Appeal*, November 23, 1865.

[8] *Mississippi Constitution As Amended, 1865*, p. 44.

[9] *Ibid.*, 44; *Convention Journal, 1865*, pp. 267–68.

[10] *Laws of Mississippi, 1865*, pp. 51–52.

nature of the levees to be constructed. Many desired to restore the old levees, while others wanted to build durable and more extensive embankments several miles from the river.[11] Furthermore, Alcorn, the most influential promoter for an effective levee system, adamantly opposed the use of Delta resources alone to build the levees.

The board of levee commissioners found it difficult to secure outside financial assistance until the debts of the 1858 levee board were paid. These debts amounted to more than $1,500,000. Accordingly, the legislature meeting in 1867 established the Liquidating Levee Board to settle prewar claims against the old board. The new board was authorized to quiet valid claims for from one half to two thirds of the amount by issuing bonds to the claimants. To finance these bonds, the legislature placed an annual tax of five cents an acre on all lands in the antebellum district.[12] This property tax imposed an additional financial burden on landowners in these counties; in fact, the virtual insolvency of most planters of the region made it impossible for most of them to pay their taxes. In Bolivar County at least three fourths of the land was reported to have been forfeited because the owners were unable to pay the duties.[13] Most of the revenue collected by the Liquidating Levee Board during its nine-year existence probably came from the reduced sale of forfeited Delta lands.

Claims on the land by the state, the levee board, county boards of supervisors, and creditors resulted in incredible confusion and in a staggering number of land title cases. It was not until the 1880's that the problem of debts and the confusion of land titles were resolved. The agricultural development of the Delta then regained its prewar momentum.[14]

It seemed obvious to many in 1865 that no state agency would be capable in the near future of raising the necessary funds to restore the levees.[15] Almost immediately after the war interested persons and groups began to press federal officials to take action to control the

[11] Friar's Point *Coahomian*, January 12, February 16, 1866.

[12] *Laws of Mississippi, 1866–1867*, pp. 237–48; Jackson *Clarion*, February 21, 1867; Gray, *Imperial Bolivar*, 28; Lillian A. Pereyra, "James Lusk Alcorn and a Unified Levee System," *Journal of Mississippi History*, XXVII (1965), 34.

[13] Many of these planters had already abandoned their lands when the state seized their properties for delinquent taxes. Sillers, "Flood Control in Bolivar County," 9; Gray, *Imperial Bolivar*, 28.

[14] Kelly, "Levee Building," 299.

[15] See, for example, *De Bow's Review*, V (April, 1868), 423–24.

river. At first, since Congress was not in session, these parties urged President Johnson to use his war power and dispatch army engineers to supervise the rebuilding of the levees. Even the anti-Johnson New York *Tribune*, reflecting the keen interest of the merchants of that city in the revival of the cotton trade, demanded that the President act immediately and without regard to Constitutional niceties. "To wait the action of Congress," the editor declared, "is to have the peril of a destructive, desolating flood next spring, which will derange the [cotton] industry of the Mississippi lowlands for years, and inflict untold misery on their cultivators."[16] Mississippi newspapers likewise urged the President to assume the responsibility for protecting the lands of the Delta, since, as Editor George W. Harper of the *Hinds County Gazette* somewhat erroneously explained, "it was a war measure that most of the Levees were destroyed, and it is certainly but fair that they should be repaired by the General Government."[17] Editor H. P. Reid of the *Coahomian,* a spokesman for the Delta planters, sought unsuccessfully to get federal officials to rebuild the Mississippi embankments immediately, with landowners of the region repaying the government over a period of twenty or more years at 6 per cent interest.[18]

Meanwhile, the four agents dispatched to Washington by the reconstruction convention of 1865 were singularly unsuccessful in their efforts to secure financial support for the restoration of the levees. When the state's congressional delegation arrived in the national capital in December, 1865, it became a virtual lobby for federal aid for reclamation of the Mississippi bottoms. Led by Senator-elect Alcorn, members of the delegation talked to President Johnson and Secretary of War Edwin M. Stanton and urged them to order army engineers to commence the work of levee reconstruction immediately. Already Cincinnati merchants, who were interested in the expansion of the foodstuffs trade in the Mississippi Valley, had proposed that dislocated freedmen be put to work on the levees.[19] Pressed by these influential groups, Johnson sent General Humphreys and his engineers to the Delta to survey and report on the condition of the levees, preparatory to providing federal aid for the speedy repair of the principal

[16] New York *Tribune*, October 9, 1865.

[17] Raymond *Hinds County Gazette,* December 23, 1865.

[18] Friar's Point *Coahomian,* November 24, 1865.

[19] Jackson *Clarion,* December 15, 1865; Natchez *Courier,* December 16, 1865; Meridian *Clarion,* October 13, 1865.

breaks in the system.[20] At the same time Stanton ordered seven Negro regiments, then stationed in Mississippi and scheduled to be discharged in January, 1866, to be retained in the service and to be put to work to rebuild the embankments. The War Department, however, did not possess the financial means to repair even the major breaks, and therefore the Negro troops assigned for that purpose were never employed in the bottoms.[21]

When the Republican-controlled Congress met, a select Senate committee was appointed to study the problem of the Mississippi River overflows. The committee reported in the summer of 1866 that the people of Mississippi had neither the money nor the labor to rebuild the levees and that "unless the resources of the nation be promptly interposed, a large extent of country, supporting a numerous population of both races, must be abandoned and will speedily relapse into its original wild and uncultivated condition." The committee suggested that the federal government could assist in the work of reclamation under the generally accepted constitutional authority of Congress to improve harbors and rivers since, unless the Mississippi River was limited to its channel, alluvial deposits would accumulate, filling up the mouths of tributaries and causing an increase in the number of bars.[22] Acting upon the committee's recommendation, the Senate passed a bill which provided $1,500,000 in aid to Mississippi and Louisiana for the repair of the most important breaks in the levees. The House of Representatives, however, rejected the measure. According to the New York *Times*, the main reason was that Thaddeus Stevens, the Radical leader of the House, was "dissatisfied with the political attitude" of these states.[23]

[20] Raymond *Hinds County Gazette*, December 23, 1865; Jackson *Clarion*, December 15, 1865; "Report on the Levee on the Mississippi River," *Senate Reports*, 39th Cong., 1st Sess., No. 126, p. 1.

[21] "Report of the Commissioner of the Freedmen's Bureau," *House Executive Documents*, 39th Cong., 1st Sess., No. 70, p. 176; "Message of the President of the United States and Accompanying Documents to the Two Houses of Congress, at the Commencement of the Second Session of the 39th Congress," *House Executive Documents*, 39th Cong., 2nd Sess., No. 1, p. 52; "Report on the Levee on the Mississippi River," *Senate Reports*, 39th Cong., 1st Sess., No. 126, p. 1.

[22] "Report on the Levee on the Mississippi River," *Senate Reports*, 39th Cong., 1st Sess., No. 126, pp. 1–4.

[23] New York *Times*, April 4, 14, 1867. The interest of congressmen in levee repairs may have also been motivated by their desire to aid Northern planters who had invested heavily in Mississippi bottom lands. *Convention Journal, 1865*, p. 270.

Allowing for the powerful Stevens' political reservation, the willingness of many Republicans to support the levee bill of 1866 caused
Alcorn to conclude that the Republican party offered the surest and
quickest hope for the extension of federal resources to restore the
levees. It seemed to Alcorn that President Johnson and the Democratic
party would be politically impotent for the next several years and
would be in no position to assist the hard-pressed planters of the
Mississippi lowlands.[24] Furthermore, Johnson's Democratic friends,
reflecting their party's antebellum predilections against internal improvements, were urging a policy of retrenchment in government expenditures for such programs.[25] Although Alcorn's strong feelings
against the Democratic party had their origins during the antebellum
period, the comparative position of the two major parties on the issue
of the levees was probably the determining factor in convincing him
that it would be wise for Mississippi to shun the party of the President
and to assume a "political attitude" acceptable to Thaddeus Stevens.
Alcorn believed that by cooperating with the Republicans not only
would Mississippi secure levee repairs, but also that its representatives
to Congress would be seated, the cotton tax would be repealed, and
the state would receive political preferment from the party in ascendancy in the nation.[26] Mississippians, including Delta planters,
were not disposed at this time to accept Alcorn's advice, for to do so
would have meant the repudiation of the moderate Presidential Reconstruction plan and the acceptance of Negro suffrage.

Continual inundations, climaxed by the destructive flood of the
spring of 1867, brought the influential New York *Times* into the campaign to secure the reclamation of the bottom lands. In a series of edi-
torials the *Times* called for a comprehensive program of flood control
for the alluvial plains of Mississippi, Louisiana, and Arkansas; simply
repairing the old levees would not bring about a permanent restoration of cotton production in these lowlands.[27] "The subject is of ut-

[24] See an address by Alcorn to the people of Mississippi, July 29, 1866, printed
in the Jackson *Clarion*, August 21, 1866. See also James L. Alcorn, *Views of the
Honorable J. L. Alcorn on the Political Situation of Mississippi* (Friar's Point,
Mississippi: n.p., 1867), 5.

[25] Howard K. Beale, *The Critical Year: A Study of Andrew Johnson and Reconstruction* (New York: Harcourt, Brace, and Company, 1930), 225, 227, 229.

[26] Jackson *Clarion*, August 21, 1866; Alcorn, *Views on the Political Situation*,
4–5.

[27] New York *Times*, April 4, 10, 14, 29, 1867.

most importance," the *Times* editor declared, "and nothing less than a broad and carefully matured system of construction and supervision will meet the difficulties of the future; those of the present are beyond control."[28]

In 1867 another levee bill was introduced in the Senate. This measure, designed specifically for Louisiana but with the condition that it would be subsequently applied to Mississippi, provided for federal endorsement of bonds to the amount of six million dollars to be issued by the state for the purpose of reclaiming the flooded alluvial lands. A special state tax was to be levied for the redemption of the bonds at maturity. The state, moreover, was to convey to the federal government, as security against possible loss, five million acres of rich alluvial lands, which were held by the state as swamplands. State commissioners under the direction of army engineers were to administer the program. Finally, and very significantly, the measure would not become effective until the restoration government had been superseded by one in conformity with the reconstruction acts of Congress.[29]

The bill of 1867 also failed to pass, and demands for the federal government to rebuild the levees subsided somewhat. The surprising success by the Mississippi board of levee commissioners in constructing by 1869 a temporary, but continuous, levee from the lower part of Coahoma County to the Issaquena-Warren border, a distance of approximately 225 miles, was probably the main factor in the abatement of these demands.[30] Yet the problem of overflows had not been solved, and the development of the fertile Mississippi bottoms continued to be impeded. It was not until the militant Alcorn went to the United States Senate in 1871 that the next phase began in the efforts of Delta planters and cotton merchants to secure federal aid for the reclamation of the Yazoo Basin.

[28] *Ibid.*, April 10, 1867. Meanwhile, Carlos Chapman, a Northern engineer who had settled in Mississippi, made what was apparently a new proposal for restoring the bottom lands to productivity. He suggested that the overflows be drained off through every natural channel in the basin, rather than spending millions of dollars to confine the waters to the Mississippi River. Vicksburg *Herald*, April 30, 1867. Such a program, in itself, would not have been sufficient, since much of the water in the flat lowlands of the Delta could not have been drained without some mechanical force being applied. Interview with Wendell B. Johnson, associate professor of geology, Millsaps College, Jackson, Mississippi, February 8, 1965.

[29] New York *Times*, April 4, 1867; "Levees on the Mississippi," *Senate Reports*, 40th Cong., 1st Sess., No. 2, pp. 1–2, 7.

[30] Loring and Atkinson (eds.), *Cotton Culture*, 116.

11

Restoration of the Railroads

For MOST sections of Mississippi the revival and expansion of commercial agriculture after the war depended upon the rapid restoration of the railroads of the state. Good wagon roads were few in number, and during the war even these had been allowed to deteriorate. Without improvements the upper Tombigbee and several tributaries of the Mississippi and Yazoo rivers were generally not navigable into the interior, and where navigable the circuitous and lengthy routes of these rivers made the transportation of cotton on them extremely difficult.[1] Therefore, when the war ended, the railroads were the main, if not only, hope for interior farmers to obtain immediate and convenient means of transporting their valuable staple to market.

The basic pattern of the railroad system of the state that would be retained virtually intact for several years after the Civil War had been formed in the last two years of the antebellum era. The New Orleans, Jackson, and Great Northern Railroad had been completed in 1858; and the whole north-south line from the Louisiana port to Jackson, Tennessee, had been opened in January, 1860, with the completion of the Mississippi Central Railroad. Using the Mobile and Ohio road from Jackson, Tennessee, to Columbus, Kentucky, the new trunkline furnished cotton growers of central Mississippi relatively cheap access to the foodstuffs-producing region of the Midwest. Another connection with the Midwest was via Memphis with Louisville, Kentucky. The Mobile and Ohio Railroad, running north and south through most of east Mississippi, was opened from Mobile to Columbus, Kentucky, in

[1] Jackson *Clarion*, December 22, 1866; Halsell, "Migration into Leflore County," 221.

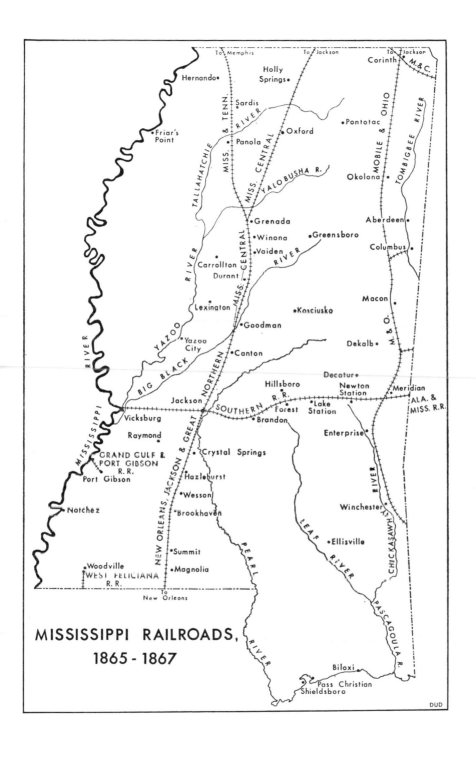

To Memphis   To Jackson   To Jackson

Corinth •M. & C.

Hernando•   Holly
                Springs•

              •Sardis   •Pontotac
                        •Oxford

         •Panola

                                    •Okolona

                      •Grenada
                      •Winona   •Greensboro
                      •Vaiden
          Carrollton   Columbus•
          •Durant

          •Lexington   Macon
                        •Kosciusko

                •Goodman   Dekalb•
        •Yazoo
         City
              •Canton

                              Decatur•
                  Hillsboro•   Newton   Meridian
        Jackson•   •Forest Station• •ALA. &
                              •Lake   MISS. R.R.
        Vicksburg•   Brandon• Station
        Raymond•   Enterprise•

   GRAND GULF &
   PORT GIBSON   •Crystal Springs
        R. R.
   Port Gibson•   •Hazlehurst

        •Natchez •Wesson   Winchester•
                  •Brookhaven
                                  •Ellisville

        •Woodville •Summit
        WEST FELICIANA •Magnolia
           R. R.
              To
           New Orleans

        MISSISSIPPI   RAILROADS,
              1865 - 1867

                              Biloxi•
                                  Pass Christian
                              Shieldsboro

DUD

TALLAHATCHIE   RIVER
YAZOO   RIVER
BIG BLACK
MISSISSIPPI   RIVER
MISS. & TENN. R. R.
MISS. CENTRAL   R. R.
YALOBUSHA R.
MISS. CENTRAL   RIVER
MOBILE & OHIO
TOMBIGBEE RIVER
M. & O.
SOUTHERN   R. R.
NEW ORLEANS, JACKSON & GREAT NORTHERN
PEARL   RIVER
LEAF   RIVER
CHICKASAWHAY   RIVER
PASCAGOULA R.

April, 1861. The Southern Railroad, extending from Vicksburg to Meridian, was not completed until two months after the firing on Fort Sumter; and the last rail on the Mississippi and Tennessee road, running from Grenada to Memphis, was laid on July 20, 1861.[2] Therefore in 1861, with the recent completion of these roads, many interior farmers and merchants were eagerly anticipating a period of promising economic development and expansion when the war temporarily crushed their hopes.

In 1865 the condition of the railroads of the state was far from encouraging. All of the companies came out of the war with extensive damage to their properties, with large outstanding debts, and virtually without operating funds. The work of restoration required large sums of money, or other assistance; however, the extension of the necessary aid to reconstruct the roads appeared unlikely in the spring of 1865 because of the disruptive effects of the war and of the presence of golden investment opportunities elsewhere.

Yet the railroad companies of Mississippi had not been ruined by the war. Transportation requirements immediately after the cessation of hostilities put traffic demands upon the roads that astute railroad managers and creditors could visualize as offering a way for the speedy recovery of the railroads. Confederate soldiers and refugees needed to be transported home. The accumulated cotton supply of the country, whether of private or government ownership, had to be hauled to ports, and the high price of cotton justified the action of the companies in increasing freight rates in order to procure more revenue. Furthermore, there was a need for every sort of provisions in the state, although a deficiency of money would restrict the trade that developed to supply this demand. Federal military traffic also offered lucrative financial returns for railroad companies.[3] Finally, not everyone failed to see an advantage in the movements of freedmen in the "year of jubilee." President Morris Emanuel of the Southern road estimated that the freeing of the slaves would double passenger travel on the railroads.[4] In fact, the reduced facilities of the companies, even when

[2] *Report of President Emanuel, 1866,* p. 3; Clark, *A Pioneer Southern Railroad,* 111; Stover, *The Railroads of the South,* 11.

[3] Most of these factors which placed traffic demands on the Southern railroads after the war are pointed out in James F. Doster, "The Georgia Railroad and Banking Company in the Reconstruction Era," *Georgia Historical Quarterly,* XLVIII (1964), 3. See also the *Report of President Emanuel, 1866,* p. 12.

[4] *Report of President Emanuel, 1866,* p. 12.

the roads were repaired, were taxed by the traffic requirements upon them.

Actually, one of the most important boosts toward recovery for the railroads came from the federal government. When the roads under army control were ordered restored to their owners, the bulk of the government-owned rolling stock was made available for purchase by railroad companies either for cash or on credit. Lacking money and unable to borrow it, these roads accepted the credit terms and bought the materials and equipment at a much higher price than otherwise could have been obtained by the government in the North.[5] All of the Mississippi railroads, except the Southern, took advantage of this opportunity. With only 29 pieces of rolling stock in operation and without a dollar in the treasury, the New Orleans, Jackson, and Great Northern Railroad used government credits and purchased 5 locomotives, 102 box cars, and 50 flat cars from the army at Nashville at a cost of $200,865.[6] The Mobile and Ohio company purchased more rolling stock from the government than any other Mississippi railroad— a total of $505,143 worth of equipment. The Mississippi and Tennessee road and the Mississippi Central procured from federal officials rolling equipment valued at $127,750 and $78,460, respectively. None of these companies was able to pay when the amounts became due, and despite the opposition of Radicals in Congress, extensions on their credit were granted after one year.[7]

The federal government aided also in the actual rebuilding of damaged and deteriorated portions of the railroads. During the war Federal commanders in Mississippi attempted to restore those roads

[5] Carl R. Fish, *The Restoration of the Southern Railroads* (Madison: University of Wisconsin, 1919), 14–16; James F. Doster, "Were the Southern Railroads Destroyed by the Civil War?" *Civil War History*, VII (1961), 317–18. The army found itself after the war the possessor of large stocks of equipment designed for the five-foot gauge of the Southern railroads. The need to dispose of this equipment quickly influenced federal officials to sell to local companies at relatively attractive prices and terms. The property was appraised by competent but disinterested men before it was offered for sale.

[6] "Railroad Property," *House Executive Documents*, 39th Cong., 1st Sess., No. 155, pp. 518–19; Jackson *Clarion*, February 2, 1866; *Commercial and Financial Chronicle*, January 25, 1868, p. 107.

[7] *Merchants' Magazine and Commercial Review*, February, 1867, p. 127; "Railroad Property," *House Executive Documents*, 39th Cong., 1st Sess., No. 155, pp. 518–19; Fish, *The Restoration of the Southern Railroads*, 22. The government agreed to accept mail carrying and other services in payment for the rolling stock. *Annual Report of the Mississippi Central Railroad Company, 1865*, p. 7.

that came under their control and had tactical significance, but this work was very incomplete and impermanent.[8] In 1865 the army of occupation made a substantial contribution to the reconstruction of the Southern Railroad. Wanting a quick and convenient means for transporting troops between Vicksburg and Jackson, Major General Peter J. Osterhaus, temporary commander of the department, undertook to rebuild thirty-two miles of track, including bridges, between the Big Black River and the capital city.[9] President Emanuel of the Southern agreed to reimburse the government for its expense in the form of transportation for troops and supplies. The company, however, did not pay for the labor or subsistence provisions of the twelve hundred Negro troops that were employed in the repair of the railroad. By September, 1865, army engineers had the road in running order from Jackson to the Big Black River, and by October, with the use of pontoons over the Big Black, service was restored over the entire route of the railroad, from Meridian to Vicksburg. A permanent bridge across the Big Black was completed by the army in early 1866.[10]

Notwithstanding government assistance, the great desideratum for the restoration of the railroads of the state was still money, or credit, to repair the roads and to make satisfactory arrangements with creditors. For the work of physical recovery the major source of money came from traffic receipts that were collected during the period when the roads were actually being reconstructed. And this remarkable achievement of the companies, along with the evident potential for railroad earnings in postwar Mississippi, was a significant factor in the decision of creditors to be liberal in making arrangements for the payment of the outstanding debts of the roads. But not to be overlooked in the successful efforts of these railroads to regain their financial integrity was the determination and enterprise of the railroad managers themselves.

[8] "Report of Brevet Brigadier General D. C. McCallum," *House Executive Documents*, 39th Cong., 1st Sess., No. 1, Appendix, 24–25. Confederate forces gave some assistance toward the restoration of these roads; however, their lack of resources and the disruptive raids of both sides probably did much to offset this work. Bettersworth, *Confederate Mississippi*, 142.

[9] *Report of President Emanuel, 1866*, p. 10.

[10] *Ibid.*, 11; Meridian *Clarion*, August 13, 1865; Vicksburg *Journal*, November 15, 1865. The New Orleans, Jackson, and Great Northern company in August, 1865, secured the assistance of the army quartermaster at Jackson in rebuilding a two and one-half mile portion of the road below the capital city. Jackson *Clarion*, February 2, 1866.

The New Orleans, Jackson, and Great Northern was probably the first railroad in the state to begin the work of reconstruction on a large scale. During the spring of 1865 and before the road had been officially returned to its owners, the company energetically commenced to repair and rebuild the damaged portions of the line.[11] President C. C. Shackleford soon after the end of the war appointed former General Pierre G. T. Beauregard, of Confederate military fame, as chief engineer and general superintendent; and it was Beauregard who pushed rapidly to completion the restoration of the road. By September, 1865, the railroad was opened from Canton to Brookhaven, a distance of seventy-eight miles.[12] The first through trip since 1862 from New Orleans to Canton was made on the line in October, and in March, 1866, daily service was re-established over the road.[13]

In financing the physical restoration of the New Orleans railroad, the management attempted first to secure subscriptions of fifty thousand dollars from businessmen along the line. This was unsuccessful, due to the shortage of money in the region. The company then resorted to paying for the work of reconstruction entirely from traffic receipts. In fact, total earnings of $2,920,977 for the first two years after the war enabled the company to pay off a large portion of its outstanding debts, to replace worn-out equipment, and to anticipate the day when it would be in a position to pay dividends.[14]

The significant task of satisfying creditors and restoring the financial standing of the New Orleans railroad became entangled in a struggle between local groups for control of the road. This conflict developed, in part, as a result of the efforts of James Robb of New Orleans, who was a former president and early organizer of the company, to regain control of the road from Mississippi interests, as represented by President Shackleford. Before the war New Orleans interests had controlled the railroad for the benefit of the port; in fact, the main reason for its construction was, in conjunction with other lines, to give the Louisiana city a railroad connection with the old Northwest.[15] Missis-

[11] Natchez Tri-Weekly Courier, May 11, 1865.

[12] Jackson Clarion, February 2, 1866.

[13] New Orleans Picayune, October 5, 1865; Moore, "Social and Economic Conditions in Mississippi during Reconstruction," 123.

[14] Meridian Clarion, June 21, 1865; Commercial and Financial Chronicle, January 25, 1868, pp. 106–107.

[15] For the prewar development of the New Orleans railroad, see Clark, A Pioneer Southern Railroad, 56.

sippians, although desirous of maintaining quick and cheap access to the foodstuffs producing region of the Northwest, were primarily interested in using the railroad as a means of developing the interior of their state and of transporting their cotton to a favorable market, which might not be in New Orleans. And, specifically, if New Orleans businessmen controlled the railroad, discriminatory rates might be placed on the commerce of north Mississippi with the design of eliminating Memphis as a market.[16] Then, too, influential Mississippians who managed the Mississippi Central road, the northern portion of the trunkline, viewed New Orleans interests with suspicion. Groups in the city, they correctly believed, were desirous of securing a merger of the entire trunkline, and such a consolidation would probably result in their losing control of the Mississippi Central.[17]

The confusion that accompanied the end of the war and New Orleans' temporary isolation from the interior gave Mississippians an opportunity to end the port city's control of the New Orleans, Jackson, and Great Northern Railroad and to insure the protection of their interests in its future management. On June 6, 1865, they secured the election of Shackleford of Canton to the presidency of the company.[18]

Almost immediately, New Orleans groups, inspired by Robb and Mayor Hugh Kennedy, began to maneuver to replace Shackleford and the six directors from Mississippi. The mayor, in pursuance, he said, of instructions from President Johnson that only loyal men should be on the board of directors of a restored railroad company, called a meeting of the stockholders of the road, but without notifying those from Mississippi. His purpose was to replace "disloyal" directors with "loyal" ones. Provisional Governor William L. Sharkey denounced the mayor's crafty maneuver, declaring that such an election would not be in accordance with the charter of the company. The threat was explicit: "If the charter is violated," Sharkey wrote Kennedy, "I shall feel it my duty to take immediate steps to have it declared forfeited."[19]

[16] Hardly had the war ended when one railroad company, the Mobile and Ohio, sought by discriminatory freight rates to eliminate trade with Memphis along its line. Jackson *Clarion*, November 5, 28, 1865.

[17] Absalom M. West to Governor Humphreys, April 4, 1866, in Governors' Correspondence, E-78.

[18] *Ibid.*; "Affairs of the Southern Railroads," *House Reports*, 39th Cong., 2nd Sess., No. 34, p. 129.

[19] Telegram from Sharkey to Hugh Kennedy, July 19, 1865; Kennedy to Johnson, July 20, 1865, in Johnson Papers; Jackson *Clarion*, August 8, 1865.

Kennedy replied acridly that "what you may do in regard to the charter of the company cannot affect me in this connection."[20] Despite the mayor's bold retort, he wavered in his resolve and permitted Mississippians to participate in the meeting and in the election. The meeting was held in late July 1865, and the six wartime directors from Mississippi were retained on the board.[21] Furthermore, Shackleford continued as president of the company. Thus the first efforts of New Orleans interests to regain control of the railroad failed.

The next phase in the struggle was begun by Robb in New York. Robb devised a plan for the re-organization and consolidation of the New Orleans, Jackson, and Great Northern, the Mississippi Central, and the Mississippi and Tennessee railroads. He hoped to accomplish this by having creditors of the three railroads institute foreclosure proceedings against the companies; and, when successful, all would agree to the merger. Only by such an arrangement, he claimed, would creditors be satisfied and the financial stability of the roads be restored.[22] Robb obviously expected to be selected as president of the new company.

New Orleans merchants and newspaper editors supported Robb's plan, mainly because they believed that a merger of the roads would result in greater efficiency and less conflict in the handling of traffic on the port's trunkline to the Midwest.[23] The basic weakness of Robb's plan was that the railroads which he contemplated merging were showing clear signs of recovery and good prospects for paying their debts individually by the time that he began to seek the cooperation of creditors.

As Robb's scheme became less likely to succeed, vested interests in New Orleans turned again to local means to secure control of the lower portion of the trunkline. This time they advanced General Beauregard of the city for the presidency of the New Orleans, Jackson, and Great Northern Railroad. The candidacy of this Confederate warrior was expected to allay the fears of Mississippians and other stockholders toward the management of the railroad by New Orleans interests.

[20] Copy of a telegram from Kennedy to Sharkey, July 19, 1865, in Johnson Papers.
[21] Kennedy to President Johnson, July 31, 1865, *ibid.*
[22] New Orleans *Picayune*, November 14, 1865; Wirt Adams to Governor Humphreys, June 29, 1866, in Governors' Correspondence, E-79.
[23] See, for an example of this support, an editorial in the New Orleans *Picayune*, November 14, 1865.

Actually, Beauregard was a logical candidate for president, since he had displayed considerable ability in directing the physical reconstruction of the road. In effect, New Orleans groups through Beauregard were hoping to confuse the conflict-of-interests issue and to regain the ascendancy of the city in the management of the railroad.[24]

Since he represented the Mississippi interest in the company, Governor Humphreys held the key to whether Beauregard would be selected to replace Shackleford. President Absalom M. West of the Mississippi Central Railroad, a former Confederate brigadier, urged Humphreys to support only directors favorable to Shackleford at the 1866 meeting of the stockholders. West was fearful that, if Beauregard were selected as president of the New Orleans road, it would be the first step in the direction of incorporating the Mississippi Central with the southern portion of the trunkline into one large company under the control of merchants of New Orleans.[25] Senator-elect Sharkey also interceded for Shackleford, believing that in Beauregard's candidacy "there was a combination against the interests of Mississippi" to subordinate the welfare of the communities along the trunk-line to that of New Orleans.[26]

On the other hand, mutual friends of the governor and New Orleans promoters besought him to support Beauregard. Oscar J. E. Stuart, a close associate and appointee of Humphreys, wrote him that the Confederate hero if elected president of the company would correct abuses in the management of the railroad. Beauregard, Stuart avowed, would work to prevent interference in the affairs of the road from "all of those political bats, or Northern sympathizers, who during our late troubles acted against the South."[27]

The influence of friends like Stuart and the prominence of Beauregard probably persuaded Humphreys to support the Confederate general for president of the New Orleans railroad. Moreover, it might have been suggested to the governor by friends of Beauregard that

[24] Absalom M. West to Governor Humphreys, April 4, 1866, in Governors' Correspondence, E-78.

[25] *Ibid.*

[26] Sharkey to Humphreys, March 16, 1866, *ibid.*

[27] Oscar J. E. Stuart to Humphreys, February 22, April 7, 1866, *ibid.* In supporting the general for president of the company, Stuart said that Beauregard would be favorable to the liability claims of widows of Confederate soldiers who were killed in a major accident on the road in 1863. Stuart candidly told Humphreys that he was the attorney for these claims.

the general as president would not press for the merger of the lines nor would he be subservient to New Orleans interests. At any rate, when the meeting of the stockholders was held in the port city in April, 1866, Governor Humphreys attended and cast the Mississippi votes for directors favorable to Beauregard, who was elected president of the road the next day.[28]

Beauregard's major efforts as head of the New Orleans, Jackson, and Great Northern Railroad, since physical reconstruction had generally been accomplished, were directed toward improving the financial affairs of the company. He immediately went to Europe to negotiate with the bondholders there for a satisfactory arrangement for paying the company's debts. With an able associate, former Confederate brigadier Wirt Adams of Mississippi, the general was able to present convincing proofs of the speedy recovery of the road and of its excellent potential for financial growth. European creditors therefore agreed to permit the conversion of the large interest arrearage, amounting to more than one million dollars, into a second mortgage on the railroad.[29] Following the example of European bondholders, American creditors, despite Robb's efforts to secure their support for the consolidation of the entire trunkline, also quickly accepted the company's funding proposal. The New Orleans road was prompt in meeting its adjusted obligations. From its revenue of 1866 the railroad was able to make its first payment of $141,000 to its creditors.[30]

The Mississippi Central Railroad was somewhat slower than the New Orleans road in restoring service along the entire length of its line. Destructive military raids occurring toward the end of the war and flash floods during the spring of 1866 disrupted the company's plans for a speedy reconstruction of the railroad.[31] Yet, concurrently

[28] Beauregard to Humphreys, April 26, 1866, ibid.; Jackson Clarion, April 19, 1866.

[29] Commercial and Financial Chronicle, October 27, 1866, p. 522; Wirt Adams to Governor Humphreys, June 29, 1866, in Governors' Correspondence, E-79; Moore, "Social and Economic Conditions in Mississippi during Reconstruction," 123.

[30] Commercial and Financial Chronicle, February 2, 1867, p. 134; Jackson Clarion, January 4, 1867. The consolidation of the trunkline that some Mississippians feared did not occur under Beauregard's management.

[31] Annual Report of the Mississippi Central Railroad, 1865, p. 6; Annual Report of the President and Directors of the Mississippi Central Railroad Company to the Stockholders for the Year Ending August 31, 1866 (Jackson, Tennessee: W. W. Gates and Co., Printers, 1866), 14.

with the work of restoration, officers of the Mississippi Central made a greater effort than Beauregard and his assistants to replace deteriorated and outdated equipment and fixtures. This policy, however, also contributed to the delay in completing the actual physical reconstruction of the railroad.[32]

Soon after the end of the war President West secured short-term loans totaling thirty thousand dollars to pay expenses for the repair of the road.[33] With this money and with increasing traffic revenues from the restored portions of the line, West and his energetic superintendent, E. D. Frost, set about to reconstruct the road. A large machine shop was established at Water Valley and smaller ones at Canton and Grenada. These shops, along with the Mississippi and Tennessee Railroad's facility at Memphis which it was allowed to use, permitted the company to repair its own cars and locomotives.[34] However, these repairs and the recovery of cars held by other roads were slow. Under these circumstances, during the first two years after the war the Mississippi Central Railroad was unable to handle a large portion of the available business along its line.[35]

Although the company experienced difficulty in securing adequate rolling stock, the main work of reconstruction on the Mississippi Central was the rebuilding of deteriorated and destroyed bridges and roadbed fixtures. Immediately after the war contracts were made with two Ohio companies to rebuild the large bridges over the Yalobusha and Tallahatchie rivers.[36] At the same time company-employed road gangs were put to work to replace smaller bridges and trestles that had been destroyed and to replace deteriorated ties. Until January 8, 1866, when the bridge over the Yalobusha was completed, the railroad was operated in two divisions.[37] The flash floods of the spring, however, threatened to undo much of the work of reconstruction. But within a week the breaches made by the floods had been temporarily repaired, and trains were again running over most of the road. Finally, on June 17, 1866, connections were made with the Mobile and Ohio

[32] *Annual Report of the Mississippi Central Railroad, 1866,* pp. 14, 16.

[33] *Ibid., 1865,* pp. 7, 16; Friar's Point *Coahomian,* September 22, 1865.

[34] *Annual Report of the Mississippi Central Railroad, 1865,* p. 9; *ibid., 1866,* p. 15.

[35] *Ibid., 1865,* pp. 9, 20, 24; *Commercial and Financial Chronicle,* August 31, 1867, p. 265.

[36] *Annual Report of the Mississippi Central Railroad, 1865,* p. 21.

[37] *Ibid., 1866,* p. 11; Jackson *Clarion,* January 9, 1866.

Railroad at Jackson, Tennessee, thereby making it possible for trains to run over the entire length of the trunkline, from Columbus, Kentucky, to New Orleans.[38]

Clarification of the financial status of the Mississippi Central Railroad was delayed somewhat by conflicts within the company as to the proper course to be pursued in making arrangements with creditors. In June, 1865, President West appointed Walter Goodman to visit Northern bondholders and selected Hugh Torrance, C. M. Vaiden, and W. F. Mason to meet with those from the South.[39] Goodman had been president of the company for several years until he was replaced in 1864 allegedly because of his Unionist activities. Although his relationship with Goodman was cool, if not hostile, West probably selected him for the Northern mission due to his extensive financial contacts in New York.[40]

Goodman arrived in the North during the early fall of 1865, and promptly reported to West that there was a movement among the creditors to foreclose on the road. Impatient bondholders, however, were willing to compromise their demands, if the company would allow them to select one third of the directors of the railroad. It was imperative that the management of the company immediately acquiesce in these terms, Goodman asserted, or else the road would become an easy prey to James Robb's consolidation scheme.[41]

President West rejected Goodman's proposal as inconsistent with the charter of the company and declared that his conduct implied "incapacity or infidelity on our part."[42] Actually, West already knew that the majority of the bondholders did not insist on a share in the management of the company as a condition for a satisfactory settlement of the company's debt. Hugh Torrance had visited Georgia and the Carolinas, where three fourths of the bonds were held, and reported that creditors there desired no change in the management

[38] Annual Report of the Mississippi Central Railroad, 1866, pp. 7, 14; Commercial and Financial Chronicle, August 31, 1867, p. 265.

[39] Annual Report of the Mississippi Central Railroad, 1866, p. 5.

[40] F. G. Barney to J. D. Webster, September 8, 1865, in Amnesty Papers, Mississippi; Alexander M. Clayton, Centennial Address on the History of Marshall County (Washington: R. O. Polkinhorn Printer, 1880), 15; Goodman to Sharkey, September 9, 1865, in Governors' Correspondence, E-72.

[41] Goodman to A. J. M. Torrance, October 3, 1865; Goodman to West, October 21, 1865, in Walter Goodman (or Mississippi Central Railroad Company) Papers, 1859–68, Mississippi Department of Archives and History, Jackson.

[42] Annual Report of the Mississippi Central Railroad, 1865, pp. 11–12.

of the railroad. Furthermore, in view of the excellent prospects for earnings of the road, these Southern creditors agreed to accept West's proposal for the conversion of the outstanding portion of the debt into a second mortgage on the railroad.[43] Northerners later accepted this funding plan.

Revenues from traffic receipts during the first two years after the war justified the confidence of creditors in the ability of the Mississippi Central company to meet its obligations. After expenses were paid from these revenues, the railroad showed a balance of $736,706.[44] By late 1866 the company had made such progress toward rehabilitation that President West was seriously considering the possibility of extending his road to Milan or Paris, Tennessee, in order to secure a connection with the Louisville and Nashville Railroad system. He recommended to the directors that the company borrow $500,000 for this purpose.[45] Although the directors approved the project, assistance was not forthcoming; and, when the Louisville and Nashville rejected his request for aid, West turned to Henry S. McComb in 1868. McComb was a business "carpetbagger" from Wilmington, Delaware, who had made his start in Southern railroading in September, 1865, when he offered his services to the Mississippi Central and was appointed as the company's agent in Washington. Beginning in 1868, McComb, as the lessee of the Mississippi Central Railroad built an extension to Milan.[46]

At the end of the war the Mississippi and Tennessee Railroad, a short line linking Memphis with the Mississippi Central at Grenada, was without money to commence the work of recovery. By pledging future freight receipts its management secured subscriptions for sixty-five thousand dollars from Memphis merchants, and the work of reconstruction began in July, 1865.[47] The rehabilitation of the railroad

[43] *Ibid.* When his work was repudiated, Goodman bitterly resigned his position as agent of the company and remained in New York seeking to organize a corporation to invest in Mississippi lands and enterprises. Goodman to West, October 20, 1865, in Goodman Papers.

[44] This balance was determined from figures given in the *Annual Report of the Mississippi Central Railroad, 1866,* pp. 6, 12, and in the *Commercial and Financial Chronicle,* December 21, 1867, p. 791.

[45] *Annual Report of the Mississippi Central Railroad, 1866,* p. 8.

[46] *Commercial and Financial Chronicle,* May 9, 1868, p. 600; Stover, *The Railroads of the South,* 162.

[47] *Merchants' Magazine and Commercial Review,* May, 1867, p. 342; *Com-*

proceeded rapidly until the fall of 1865. At this time the work on the road was slowed when some Memphis promoters repudiated the balances due on their subscription pledges. These businessmen evidently were fearful that with the opening of the trunkline to New Orleans in October the port city would siphon off the cotton trade of northwest Mississippi, and therefore they would secure little benefit from the restoration of the Memphis line.[48] Traffic receipts, however, soon proved sufficient to finance the repairs necessary to restore traffic along the entire route of the road, although horse cars were put into temporary use on isolated parts of the damaged line. By June, 1866, the railroad was doing a thriving business. Yet, due to the makeshift nature of the repairs, a great deal still remained to be done to make the road durable and safe.[49]

Increasing freight revenues made it possible for the Mississippi and Tennessee company to make satisfactory arrangements with creditors for the payment of its debts. Remarkably, gross earnings of the company for the fiscal year 1865–66 exceeded those of 1859–60, despite the fact that only during the latter part of the 1865–66 fiscal year were trains able to run over the complete route of the road. Revenues for 1865–66 were $367,252, whereas those for 1859–60 were only $233,704. However, it should be remembered that during 1865 Treasury agents and planters were hurriedly shipping wartime-grown cotton to market. Then, too, much of the cotton of central Mississippi was marketed at Memphis via the Mississippi and Tennessee Railroad, since the road to New Orleans was not opened until October, 1865.[50] Furthermore, monetary values were inflated by 1865, and expenses, because of reconstruction costs, were also greater in 1865–66 than before the war. Yet the company could show a small net profit from its operations during the first year after the war; and this fact apparently gave

---

mercial and Financial Chronicle, April 21, 1867, p. 489; Memphis Appeal, November 14, 1865.

[48] Memphis Appeal, November 14, 1865; Annual Report of the Mississippi Central Railroad, 1866, Statement B.

[49] Jackson Clarion, January 9, 1866; Merchants' Magazine and Commercial Review, May, 1867, p. 342.

[50] For a summary of the financial reports of the company for 1859–60 and 1865–66, see the Merchants' Magazine and Commercial Review, May, 1867, p. 343. Until the Mississippi and Tennessee Railroad was opened over its entire route, freight was transshipped around the damaged and deteriorated portions of the road.

creditors confidence in the future of the railroad under its Southern managers.[51]

Until the Mississippi and Tennessee Railroad was restored along its entire line, the Memphis and Charleston Railroad, which intercepted the Mississippi Central road at Grand Junction, Tennessee, gave Mississippians an important connection with Memphis. It also was a part of a through line from New Orleans to New York, especially significant for passenger and express freight. Notwithstanding considerable damage that had been incurred by it during the war, the Memphis and Charleston Railroad by November 6, 1865, was operating along its entire line, except for a missing bridge across the Tennessee River at Decatur, Alabama.[52]

With the aid of army engineers, the restoration of the Southern Railroad was more rapid than that of any of the other roads of the state.[53] Southern trains were operating between Meridian and Jackson by August, 1865, and by October, with the use of pontoons over the Big Black River, service was restored over the entire route of the road, from Vicksburg to Meridian. Machine shops were established along the line, in some cases before the end of the war, to repair damaged and worn-out locomotives and cars. The editor of the Meridian *Clarion* in August, 1865, believed that the Southern's "machinery and rolling stock is perhaps at this moment superior to that of any other road in the South." President Morris Emanuel reported that by September, 1865, the portion of the line between Jackson and Meridian was in a better and more permanent condition than it had been at any time during its brief history.[54]

The huge overdue indebtedness of $1,975,054 might have caused considerable embarrassment for the directors of the Southern Railroad but for the energetic efforts of President Emanuel. During the summer and fall of 1865 Emanuel visited creditors in the United States and in Europe and secured their cooperation for the funding of the whole debt over a twenty-five-year period, with no payment due until January, 1867. Not only did this liberal arrangement relieve the

[51] *Commercial and Financial Chronicle*, April 20, 1867, p. 489.

[52] Doster, "Southern Railroads," 311–12. See also the Annual Report of the Memphis and Charleston Railroad Company for 1865–66 in "Affairs of the Southern Railroads," *House Reports*, 39th Cong., 2nd Sess., No. 34, pp. 711–58.

[53] See above, p. 198.

[54] *Report of President Emanuel, 1866*, pp. 10–11, 20; Meridian *Clarion*, August 13, 1865.

company of considerable financial pressure, it also made possible the rebuilding of a great deal of the road in 1867.[55]

The main reason for the liberality of creditors of the Southern Railroad was probably the optimistic picture painted by President Emanuel concerning the future prosperity of the road once the Vicksburg, Shreveport, and Texas Railroad were completed. Besides serving as an important link in a Mid-South trunkline, the Southern, Emanuel envisioned, would eventually be connected with the coal and iron fields of Alabama.[56] Emanuel's dreams were slow to materialize. The war had prevented the completion of the western portion of the Shreveport road, and the break in the levees in 1862 had resulted in the flooding of an area of some thirty-five miles in width, adjacent to Vicksburg and in an area where the completed part of the railroad ran. Despite the efforts of Vicksburg merchants, Emanuel, and the directors of the Shreveport railroad, permanent levee repairs were not made at this time, and sufficient capital was not extended for the completion of the road.[57]

The Mobile and Ohio company experienced severe financial difficulty in recovering from the effects of the war. Large sums of money were needed to restore rolling equipment and to repair the road, which was a virtual wreck along one portion of the line, from Okolona to Union City, Tennessee, a distance of 184 miles. Furthermore, creditors were clamoring for payments on overdue debts, and some disappointed bondholders sought to take possession of the road to satisfy their claims.[58] President Milton Brown and his superintendent hurried North to halt any such movement to seize the railroad and also to secure financial assistance for the work of reconstruction.[59]

[55] *Report of President Emanuel, 1866,* pp. 7–8; Emanuel to Provisional Governor Sharkey, August 24, 1865, in Governors' Correspondence, E-71; Raymond *Hinds County Gazette,* January 26, 1866; Meridian *Semi-Weekly Gazette,* December 7, 1867.

[56] Report of President Emanuel, 1866, pp. 2, 12, 14.

[57] New Orleans *Picayune,* October 29, 1865; Jackson *Clarion,* December 12, 1865; Vicksburg *Journal,* November 5, 1865. The "carpetbagger" editor of the Vicksburg *Weekly Republican,* writing on April 28, 1868, pointed out the economic rewards that would accrue to the town when the Shreveport road was finished. He predicted that at that time Vicksburg would become "one of the greatest railroad centers of the Southwest."

[58] *Merchants' Magazine and Commercial Review,* February, 1867, p. 126.

[59] Jackson *Clarion,* November 19, 1865; Meridian *Semi-Weekly Gazette,* September 25, 1867. From the sale of almost three thousand bales of cotton by

Anxious to gain some returns eventually from their investments, bond-holders agreed to defer payments on interest arrears. No arrangement was made at this time, however, for the funding of the general debt.

Despite financial problems, the work of physical reconstruction was surprisingly rapid. Applying lucrative freight receipts to pay for repairs, the company had the entire railroad in operation by September 9, 1865.[60]

The financial embarrassments experienced by the Mobile and Ohio Railroad gave its old enemies an excellent opportunity to attack the management and policies of the company. Charges were made that officials and agents were stealing and misusing funds of the company, and even the friendly Jackson *Clarion* reported that there was some truth to these accusations.[61] It is evident that the company at least was loosely managed while President Brown and his superintendent were in the North and preoccupied with reconstruction matters.

The main center for these attacks on the management of the Mobile and Ohio road was Memphis. Hostile merchants and editors in this city were not motivated in their criticism by any altruistic abhorrence of corruption or mismanagement in railroad affairs but rather were anxious to injure a formidable rival for the commerce of northeast Mississippi. Abram Murdock, President Brown's successor, accurately described the basic motivation behind the attacks: "It is not strange that Memphis papers should lend a willing ear to every rumor put forth by designing and disappointed men for the purpose of embarrassing the administration of the affairs of this road, for it has ever been thus with Memphis. Our road has direct influence against that city—cuts off much of its trade and it is natural [that] they should lend themselves to its injury."[62]

---

the Mobile and Ohio company, an important sum of money was made available to pay for some of the costs of reconstruction. "Affairs of the Southern Railroads," *House Reports*, 39th Cong., 2nd Sess., No. 34, p. 838.

[60] Jackson *Clarion*, November 19, 1865; *Merchants' Magazine and Commercial Review*, February, 1867, p. 127; Meridian *Semi-Weekly Gazette*, July 21, 1867. Whitelaw Reid, in reporting on his trip to the lower South after the war, said that the road between Mobile and Meridian in November, 1865, was in a better shape than any of the Southern railroads that he had traveled on. Reid, *After the War*, 401.

[61] Jackson *Clarion*, November 19, 1865.

[62] Meridian *Semi-Weekly Gazette*, September 25, 1867. See also the Jackson *Clarion*, November 28, 1865, September 5, 1867.

Rate policies of the Mobile and Ohio Railroad during the period immediately after the war gave reasonable cause for Memphis interests to be alarmed. In an effort to funnel all the trade of east Mississippi through Mobile, and thus make its southern terminus prosperous, the company sought by discriminatory freight rates to eliminate trade with Memphis along its line. Farmers and merchants as far north as Noxubee County, only 150 miles from Memphis, found that rates to Corinth, where the railroad connected with the Memphis and Charleston road were prohibitive. One Memphis correspondent claimed that it cost the people of Lowndes and Noxubee counties three or four times as much to ship cotton to Corinth as it did to Mobile, although the port city was considerably farther from them.[63]

Individuals and groups in the area affected by the discriminatory rates, along with Memphis merchants, appealed to the Mississippi legislature for redress of their grievances. A writer from Columbus asserted that the management of the Mobile and Ohio Railroad, "like all monopolies, rides rough shod over those who created them."[64] When the legislature failed to act against the company, another disappointed person from Columbus believed that its inaction was due to the influence of Abram Murdock, a prominent merchant and a Whig representative from Lowndes County, and other "old fossils" in the assembly.[65]

Friends and creditors of the Mobile and Ohio were disturbed with Milton Brown's inability to solve the company's monetary difficulties. Large traffic receipts for the latter part of 1865 had probably led many interested persons to believe that the company's finances would soon be put in order. Total earnings for the period May 15, 1865, to January 1, 1866, were an impresive $1,524,676; but, as an indicator of future traffic on the road, this income figure was misleading.[66] Traffic demands on the road were unusual during the first few months after the war, since, after repairs were made, the railroad served as a major thoroughfare for the shipment of interior cotton to Mobile and Memphis. These earnings were not applied to the payment of the outstanding portion of the railroad's debt but were used to meet ordi-

[63] Jackson *Clarion*, November 5, 28, 1865.

[64] *Ibid.*, November 28, 1865; a clipping from the Columbus *Index*, undated, in Governors' Correspondence, E-80.

[65] James T. Blair to Governor Humphreys, September 11, 1866, in Governors' Correspondence, E-80.

[66] *Merchants' Magazine and Commercial Review*, February, 1867, p. 126.

nary expenses and to restore operations. It was hoped that traffic receipts for 1866 would enable the company to make a substantial payment on its debts; however, favorable freight conditions did not exist in that year. The poor crops of 1866 resulted in only one half of the amount of the cotton of 1865 being handled by the Mobile road in 1866. Under these circumstances, President Brown was unable to secure the cooperation of creditors to a funding arrangement for the large indebtedness of the company.[67]

The attacks on the administration of Milton Brown, in addition to his failure to secure a financial settlement for the railroad, convinced the board of directors that it would be wise to replace him as president. The election of officers was held in April, 1867, and the able Murdock was chosen president.[68] Murdock immediately went to Europe to negotiate with bondholders there, and he arranged for the postponement of payments on the railroad's debts to a more convenient time. Prospects were excellent in 1868, when he reached this agreement, that a bumper cotton crop would be produced in the fall and that the company would be able to make a large payment on its debts.[69]

During this period of restoration few new lines were built in Mississippi, and those that were constructed or contemplated were planned mainly as extensions of old lines or were designed to serve interior areas between trunklines. The pattern for railroads traversing the state had developed during the antebellum period, and there was now little need for the building of new trunklines.

Of significance were efforts to lace the interior between the New Orleans-Mississippi Central and the Mobile and Ohio trunklines. One road would have run in a northeasterly direction from Canton on the New Orleans line to Aberdeen, near a point where it would have connected with the Mobile and Ohio Railroad. The New Orleans, Jackson, and Great Northern company had promoted this scheme earlier with hopes that the line could be extended to a place where through connections could be made with the Ohio Valley. At the time it was projected, company officials and New Orleans merchants did not know that the Mississippi Central would be built. Since this road upon

[67] *Ibid.*, June, 1867, p. 463; Meridian *Clarion*, August 19, 1865; Meridian *Semi-Weekly Gazette*, September 27, 1867.

[68] Meridian *Semi-Weekly Gazette*, April 24, 1867.

[69] *Ibid.*, July 21, 1867; Meridian *Chronicle*, April 21, 1868.

completion would insure a connection with the Ohio country, New Orleans promoters lost interest in the Aberdeen project.[70] As a result the cost of constructing the line was assumed by local businessmen and planters. The work of grading the portion of the road between Canton and Kosciusko was pushed during the war, but was interrupted in October, 1864, because of a lack of money and laborers.[71]

After the war, threats were made by some state leaders to secure the revocation of the New Orleans, Jackson, and Great Northern charter if the company did not complete the extension to Aberdeen. These threats, however, never materialized into a formidable movement in the legislature against the New Orleans road. Dominant Whigs were extremely reluctant to tamper with charter privileges; an ominous precedent might easily be established by an act repealing the charter of a railroad. Thus, without legislative support or funds frustrated local promoters were unable to complete the Aberdeen extension during the Reconstruction era.[72]

Another road, the Grenada and Meridian Railroad, chartered in 1867, was designed to serve and develop the interior between these two towns which were located on the north-south trunklines. This proposed railroad, according to a Meridian editor, would "open to the markets of the world a benighted section of the country, where corn and cotton, cereals and poultry, will be raised in an abundance as soon as the road is built." In Jackson, which would not directly benefit from the road, the *Clarion* editor declared that "there is no public improvement better calculated to build up the interior counties" than the Grenada to Meridian enterprises.[73] So high were hopes for prosperity once the railroad was constructed that the Meridian *Gazette* claimed that almost every landowner in the area to be affected by the road was willing to subscribe one half of his land for its construction.[74] The general impoverishment of the region and depreciated land

[70] Clark, *A Pioneer Southern Railroad*, 82.

[71] Correspondent to Meridian *Clarion*, October 18, 1864, in Niles Scrapbook, Vol. XLI; Jackson *Clarion*, December 22, 1866.

[72] Jackson *Clarion*, December 22, 1866, February 13, 1867; New Orleans *Picayune*, December 8, 1865; B. L. Hatch to Governor Humphreys, March 27, 1867, in Governors' Correspondence, E-81. The Aberdeen extension to the New Orleans railroad was finally completed during the 1880's.

[73] Meridian *Semi-Weekly Gazette*, May 13, 1867; Jackson *Clarion*, January 31, 1867.

[74] Meridian *Semi-Weekly Gazette*, June 6, 1867.

values, however, made it impossible for the Grenada and Meridian company to secure the $125,000 required before work could begin on the road.

Despite a lack of capital for such enterprises, a veritable mania developed for the construction of lines to connect hopeful communities with one of the trunklines or to extend from commercial centers, like Natchez and Vicksburg, into the adjacent interior for the purpose of increasing the business of these towns. Demands for the chartering and construction of such railroads became quite pronounced at the time of the legislative session of early 1867.[75] Economic conditions in the state were especially bleak at this time because of the crop failures of 1866 and the subsequent difficulty of securing capital to continue planning operations. Mississippians envisioned the development of a more extensive railroad system as the first step toward solving their economic problems; in fact, some promoters looked to railroad expansion as a panacea for their difficulties. The editor of the Vicksburg *Herald* exhorted the legislators that it was "the almost universal sentiment of the people of Mississippi that a comprehensive system of internal improvements is the great *desideratum* in our present impoverished condition—the one great thing that is most needed to revive the energies of the people, open up the resources of the State, and put us in the way of growth and general prosperity."[76] The state legislature could aid this work greatly, the editor said, by simply granting liberal charters to groups to construct railroads.[77]

At the same time the Jackson *Clarion* declared that railroad developments were "absolutely necessary to place this section on the high road to prosperity, and give the out-of-the-way and isolated inhabitants a place in the active commercial world."[78] The editor of the Natchez *Democrat* expressed the hopeful belief that the impoverished condition of the state should be no barrier to the construction of railroads. Northerners were anxious to invest in local railroads and businesses, the *Democrat* claimed; therefore "the simple commencement of

[75] Vicksburg *Herald*, January 30, February 17, 1867; Jackson *Clarion*, January 31, 1867.

[76] The editor of the *Herald* associated manufacturing enterprises with "internal improvements" as well as with railroad developments. Vicksburg *Herald*, January 30, 1867.

[77] *Ibid.*

[78] Jackson *Clarion*, January 31, 1867.

a work of this kind will surely bring to [Mississippi] a flow of money and a tide of intelligent men."[79]

Faced with demands from numerous and impatient groups for local railroad charters, the legislature responded with alacrity. In fact, the unsystematic and indiscriminative way in which it passed bills of incorporation brought forth some criticism of its actions. The frustrated but now wiser editor of the Vicksburg *Herald* sarcastically wrote: "We advise our sapient Legislators to incorporate a road from every person's back yard to some point out of the State. Unless they do there is great danger of some point in the State growing to importance."[80]

Notwithstanding the liberal charters secured by local groups, most of the proposed railroads were never constructed. Capital simply was not available for such projects. One interstate company, chartered in 1866 to build the Mississippi portion of a road between New Orleans and Mobile, was more successful. Although faced with financial difficulties, this railroad was completed in 1870. Ten years later the road became a principal link in the Louisville and Nashville Railroad system.[81] Yet, including this line, only 120 miles of new railroad track were opened in Mississippi during the decade following the Civil War.[82]

The restoration legislature also showed its sympathy with the established railroads of the state. Most of the managers of these roads were former Whigs and were active in politics; therefore they belonged to the political group that controlled the state government. Their close association with the legislature worked to their advantage at least on one crucial issue. While this body was in session in early 1867, the presidents of the Mississippi roads met in Jackson for the purpose of lobbying for the repeal of a tax of one half of one per cent per mile on passenger rates. Although this legislature had levied the tax in the fall of 1865, its members were now more sympathetic with the interests of the railroads. Actually, very little of the tax had been collected since a typographical error in the printing of the law had given the railroad companies an excuse to evade paying it. By 1867, however, Governor Humphreys was threatening legal action against the roads unless they made a settlement with the state regarding the tax.

[79] Natchez *Tri-Weekly Democrat*, May 4, 1867.
[80] Vicksburg *Herald*, February 17, 1867.
[81] Watkins, *King Cotton*, 178–79; Stover, *The Railroads of the South*, 147–48.
[82] Stover, *The Railroads of the South*, 59.

Under these circumstances, railroad officials met and were successful in securing the repeal of the obnoxious measure. The fact that Abram Murdock, who represented the Mobile and Ohio company at the meeting, was chairman of the house ways and means committee and that the influential Whig lawyer William Yerger of Jackson was the counsel for the roads was a major factor in this success of the railroad managers.[83]

In general, then, the railroads, the main vehicles of trade for the interior of the state, recovered quickly after the Civil War, despite their apparent prostration when the conflict ended. Their physical restoration was accompanied by relatively lucrative traffic receipts, which paid for the work of reconstruction. Using traffic statistics as arguments that the future of their roads was bright, railroad officials persuaded creditors to grant liberal extensions on the time for the payment of the outstanding portions of their companies' debts. The energetic efforts of these officers, particularly Absalom M. West, Morris Emanuel, and Pierre G. T. Beauregard, in their negotiations with creditors were also significant in the success of these Southern-owned railroads in solving their financial problems. This success enabled local promoters to retain control of the roads, at least for a few years. Furthermore, public sentiment in the state, now directed by business-orientated Whigs, favored the railroads, and this fact contributed to their restoration and to their pre-eminence in the economic life of Mississippi after the war.

[83] Charles E. Hooker to Governor Humphreys, June 18, 1866, in Governors' Correspondence, E-79; Pierre G. T. Beauregard to Humphreys, ibid., E-81; Jackson Clarion, January 29, February 9, 22, 1867.

12

Towns, Commerce, and Industry

THE QUICK restoration of the railroads and the revival of the agricultural economy of the state led to a rapid recovery and growth of towns which in many cases had been damaged or virtually destroyed during the war. The most significant commercial development occurred along the railroads where trade centers and small towns arose to handle the increased business of the interior. The development of a number of these towns had been retarded by the war; but in 1865 hopes were high among people of railroad communities that their villages were destined to be seats of great cities.

Although not many of these railroad hamlets became commercial centers, several experienced a remarkable growth during the first two years after the war. Meridian was an "insignificant village" in 1865, despite its Civil War prosperity prior to Sherman's destructive raid, but by May, 1866, it could boast of a thriving population of fifteen hundred to two thousand.[1] West of Meridian, Newton Station, Forest, and Lake Station on the Southern road were aspiring to the control of the trade of central Mississippi.[2] One traveler reported in 1871 that Okolona, a town on the Mobile and Ohio Railroad in the cotton belt of northeast Mississippi, had recovered rapidly from the effects of the war, and "it is now a well-built town of two or three thousand inhabitants, with a long street of brick stores, and many offshoots on the east, towards the railway depot."[3] Citizens of hamlets along the New Orleans, Jackson, and Great Northern road quickly rebuilt their burnt districts, and one town, Summit, was quite prosperous by 1867.[4]

[1] Jackson *Clarion,* May 1, 1866.
[2] Meridian *Semi-Weekly Gazette,* April 13, 1867.
[3] Somers, *The Southern States since the War,* 144.
[4] Jackson *Clarion,* February 23, 1867.

Prosperity was nowhere more apparent during the first two years after the war than along the Mississippi Central Railroad, and this growth was reflected in the traffic receipts of the road for this period.[5] A correspondent to the Jackson *Clarion*, visiting Winona during the fall of 1866, reported that at least twenty new and substantial commercial houses had been built there during the last few months. "The trade of the place," he wrote, "is five times greater than before the war. The merchants are content to sell goods cheap for cash."[6] Probably the most amazing development occurred at Water Valley. From an estimated population of two hundred in early 1866, this village had developed into a thriving commercial center of two thousand by early 1867. During this period more than two hundred houses were erected in Water Valley. An important factor in this growth was the railroad company's establishment of a large machine shop there. Smaller towns or hamlets, like Vaiden, Durant, and Goodman, on the Mississippi Central road were also growing.[7]

A significant feature of this flourishing commercial activity in central Mississippi was the trade in meats and grains from the Midwest, Kentucky, and Tennessee. One observer traveling on the railroad reported in early 1867, at a time when cotton growers in most areas of the state were finding it extremely difficult to secure advances, that "the quantities of these articles sold [in] a day is perfectly surprising, and the merchants at all the points say that they cannot get their supplies as fast as they can sell."[8] And a correspondent to the New Orleans *Picayune* tied the civil stability of whites and blacks along the railroad to the commercial enthusiasm of the people of the area.[9]

Jackson, at the junction of two railroads and the capital of the state, made little progress toward recovery during the summer of 1865, but during the fall of that year the town experienced a construction boom. In October alone forty stores were completed, and many others were

[5] For brief descriptions of this prosperity, see *ibid.*, November 3, 1866, February 17, 1867; the New Orleans *Picayune*, November 25, December 2, 1865; the Meridian *Semi-Weekly Gazette*, April 20, 1867; and the Vicksburg *Times*, February 19, 1868.

[6] Jackson *Clarion*, November 3, 1866.

[7] *Ibid.*, February 17, 1867; Meridian *Semi-Weekly Gazette*, April 20, 1867; Vicksburg *Times*, February 12, 1868.

[8] Jackson *Clarion*, February 17, 1867.

[9] New Orleans *Picayune*, November 25, 1865.

in the process of being built.[10] Jackson merchants envisioned a period of prosperity as their city developed as a major railroad center and a thriving seat of government. The Southern Railroad, however, was hardly a trunkline, although President Morris Emanuel and the directors of the road believed that it would become an integral part of a great East-West through line. Furthermore, government services at the state level, even during Radical Reconstruction, were not expanded appreciably beyond those that existed during the antebellum period and therefore did not require much in the way of increased facilities or public servants at the capital. The construction fever and commercial optimism soon subsided, and Jackson settled into doldrums of the kind experienced by many other Southern towns of the period. Two decades later Jackson was still a small town of less than six thousand people.

Kosciusko was expected by many of its businessmen to become the commercial center of central Mississippi, once the railroad extension from Canton was completed. In late 1866, months before the road was finished, optimistic merchants and professional men were securing, at inflated prices, properties in Kosciusko on which to establish their offices and shops.[11] But their hopes, like those of the Jackson promoters, were soon dashed, for the completion of the railroad from Canton did not bring the desired prosperity.

Non-railroad communities also succumbed to this speculative mania in real estate. The small Delta village of Friar's Point, which had been burned during the war, showed signs of immediate recovery, despite the fact that a large area of its hinterland was flooded by the Mississippi River. By October, 1865, the local newspaper editor could claim that eight or ten new stores were doing business, and six or eight more were being constructed.[12] Promoters of Lexington, Pontotoc, Carrollton, Paulding, Yazoo City, Raymond, and Hillsboro, all small non-railroad towns and important local centers before the war, were optimistic concerning the postwar development of their communities, but their hopes did not materialize.[13]

[10] Jackson *Clarion*, November 23, December 16, 1865; Reid, *After the War*, 423.

[11] Jackson *Clarion*, September 7, 1866.

[12] Friar's Point *Coahomian*, October 27, 1865. See also *ibid.*, November 17, 1865.

[13] For a contemporary and perceptive analysis of the reasons for the decline of one of these towns, see the Raymond *Hinds County Gazette*, October 14, 1868.

No town in the state felt the impact of postwar commercial optimism as much as Vicksburg, the gateway to the southern alluvial region and to several non-Delta counties in Mississippi and Louisiana.
Actually, there was some justification for this optimism, since, with
the exception of 1867, trade was relatively brisk for Vicksburg merchants during the first few years after the war. The headquarters of
the military district were located in the city, and a great deal of local
purchasing and exchange of national currency occurred there. Several
regiments of Federal troops, both Negro and white, were mustered out
in Vicksburg, and these men had money to spend. Many Northerners
settled in the town, and several of them contributed in an important
way to rebuilding it. Merchants who came there after the war, according to the reliable "carpetbag" editor of a local newspaper, gave new
life and energy to the commercial development of the town.[14]

Probably of equal, if not more, significance in the postwar restoration of Vicksburg was its virtual monopoly of the cotton and provisions
trade of the lower Delta and adjacent areas for a brief period after the
war. This business was largely transported by steamboats on the
Mississippi and Yazoo rivers and on their tributaries. In fact, hopeful
local merchants and packet owners at first believed that steamboats,
with Vicksburg as the center of their operations, would regain their
antebellum pre-eminence in the agricultural trade of the lower Mississippi Valley. This belief was also held by many agents and merchants
of Northern business houses who sought to eliminate competing
factors and jobbers of New Orleans and other peripheral Southern
centers and to sell their goods directly to local stores and planters.
Wholesale stores were established in Vicksburg to distribute Northern
manufactured articles in the valley; and this development was paral-
leled by the arrival in town of cotton buyers to compete for the annual crops.[15] One visitor from the interior of the state in 1868 found
"the city thronged with people, selling cotton and purchasing sup-

[14] Vicksburg *Weekly Republican*, August 31, 1868; Vicksburg *Times and Republican*, October 18, 1871. When regiments were disbanded, local merchants served as agents for Northern firms in the purchase and shipment of surplus army clothing and shoes. L. H. Peirce to Marmaduke Shannon, October 21, 1867, in Marmaduke Shannon and Mrs. William O. Crutcher Family Papers, Mississippi Department of Archives and History, Jackson.

[15] Forest *Register*, December 4, 1869; Vicksburg *Times*, December 19, 1869; Raymond *Hinds County Gazette*, October 14, 1868.

plies."[16] A Northern newspaperman traveling in Mississippi in 1869 reported that Vicksburg was unique among the towns of the state that he had visited, in that there were clear signs of thrift and trade. He believed that the town handled as much business in one day as Jackson did in two weeks.[17]

Although incomplete, population and trade statistics for the period demonstrate the quick recovery and commerical expansion of Vicksburg after the war. The federal census of 1870 shows that 12,443 people lived in the town then, whereas the population was only 4,591 in 1860. The sale of merchandise in Vicksburg in 1870 amounted to $3,450,000, as compared with approximately $1,300,000 in 1860. There are no extant figures until 1871 for the postwar number of bales of cotton handled by Vicksburg merchants; in that year, 34,665 bales passed through the town, as compared with an estimated 2,000 in 1860.[18]

Although Vicksburg's prosperity continued into the 1870's, there was evidence during the early reconstruction period that it could not be sustained for many years. Almost immediately after the war local merchants began to appear along the New Orleans, Jackson, and Great Northern Railroad, and these merchants increasingly drew off business from Vicksburg's eastern trade territory. By 1870 agents of Memphis and St. Louis merchants were penetrating into the lower Delta and seizing the initiative from Vicksburg businessmen in the handling of the area's commerce. St. Louis' success followed the establishment of a line of steamboats by merchants of that city to ply the Mississippi River between Greenville and Vicksburg. These steamboats offered cheap freight rates for local businessmen who traded with St. Louis merchants.[19] Along with periodic inundations of portions of Vicksburg's hinterland in the Mississippi bottoms and the cessation of agricultural production there, competition from St. Louis and Memphis jobbers dealt a severe blow to the town's traffic in the Delta.

Another serious disappointment for Vicksburg promoters was their

[16] Raymond *Hinds County Gazette*, October 14, 1868.

[17] Portions of his report may be found in the Vicksburg *Times*, December 4, 19, 1869.

[18] Except for the population statistics, these figures are taken from the Natchez *Weekly Democrat*, October 2, 1872.

[19] Jackson *Clarion*, February 4, 1866; Vicksburg *Times*, February 16, 1868, September 12, 1869; Vicksburg *Times and Republican*, November 9, 1871.

inability to secure the heralded completion of the Vicksburg, Shreveport, and Texas Railroad. The completion of this road had promised to give them control of the trade of northeastern Louisiana. Then, too, the periodic breakdown of local traffic in Warren County because of impassable wagon roads, which were never adequately repaired after the war, contributed to the end of Vicksburg's prosperity.[20] Thus, it was conditions during reconstruction, not the destructive effects of the war, that brought about the decline of this river port.

Natchez, Vicksburg's sister river emporium in southwest Mississippi, was also favored by prosperity after the war. Yet, unlike Vicksburg's, Natchez' prosperity was not accompanied by an unrestrained boom in business, construction, and population, and a subsequent rapid decline. Furthermore, Natchez' development was based on more solid economic reasons, for its hinterland included a large cotton-producing area free from inundation and competing railroads. Northern merchants, as in Vicksburg, had infused new energy into the community; and these newcomers worked with the old merchant class to develop Natchez along conservative business lines.[21]

Nevertheless, the heyday of Natchez and other river towns had passed, and during the next few decades the rate of growth of interior railroad towns that were strategically located, like Meridian and Corinth, would surpass that of the river ports. To be sure, none of these new towns would become cities, but they would soon replace the river ports as the commercial centers for the people of Mississippi.

Economic needs justified in 1865 a degree of expansion beyond the 1860 levels of these communities. Many white farmers, particularly disabled Confederate veterans, flocked to the population centers seeking employment or hoping to secure sufficient money with which to establish small stores.[22] Because of the need for townsmen to handle the brisk cotton and provisions trade, many of these whites found em-

[20] Vicksburg *Weekly Republican*, May 26, 1868; Vicksburg *Times*, May 4, 1869.

[21] For a brief description of Natchez' postwar prosperity, see Reid, *After the War*, 481.

[22] New Orleans *Picayune*, November 14, 1865; Meridian *Semi-Weekly Gazette*, November 13, 1867. The *Coahomian* reported that even in the non-railroad town of Friar's Point "scarcely a day passes that there is not an applicant for a house, either business or dwelling, and many a man who would make a valuable citizen is driven from town, because he has not capital enough to buy a lot and build a house" in view of the prevailing high prices for real estate. Friar's Point *Coahomian*, October 27, 1867.

ployment or acquired the necessary funds to enter business.[23] At the same time the merchandizing business was given an illusory boost by the activities of Northern wholesalers in flooding Mississippi with manufactured goods.

Northern businessmen at the end of the war foresaw a quick economic recovery for Mississippi and the other Southern states. Northerners believed, with some assurance, that large quantities of cotton, hoarded by planters during the war, were on hand in 1865 and could be used to buy Northern goods. Treasury agents, however, appropriated a great deal of this cotton; and, in short, Northern merchants were too sanguine about the purchasing power of the whites and of the Negroes, whose freedom they believed opened a new market for exploitation.

Railroads provided an excellent means of transportation for the agents and goods of business houses of the North, as jobbers sought to sell their products to people in the interior who in many cases would be buying Northern products for the first time. Approximately one month after the surrender of Confederate forces in Mississippi, one newspaper reported that stores in Grenada, at the juncture of the Mississippi Central and Mississippi and Tennessee railroads, were fully stocked with manufactured goods.[24] The greatest portion of the goods that entered the state, however, were probably shipped there during the late summer and early fall of 1865.[25] After the first three postwar cotton crops failed to sustain this trade, Northern merchants for a time became disillusioned with their efforts to open new markets in Mississippi. Yet, while this trade flourished in 1865, it gave a stimulus to growth in numbers of local merchants, especially along the railroads.[26]

With the extension of merchandising into these interior communities, a commercial revolution occurred. The local merchant, especially after the crop failures of 1866 and 1867, replaced the hard-pressed and reluctant factor as the supplier of provisions for cotton growers.[27] Cotton buyers from the Northeast, bypassing the declining factor, entered the state, established offices in the commercial centers, principally Vicks-

[23] New Orleans *Picayune*, December 2, 1865.
[24] Meridian *Clarion*, June 22, 1865.
[25] Canton *American Citizen*, October 29, 1865.
[26] New Orleans *Picayune*, December 2, 1865.
[27] Loring and Atkinson (eds.), *Cotton Culture*, 158–59; Griffin, "Problems of Southern Cotton Planters," 110.

burg, and dealt directly with local merchants and large planters. It was no mere coincidence that the first Liverpool buyer to appear in Mississippi set up his office at Vicksburg in the largest wholesale house in the state and with easy access to the Delta by water and to the interior of the state by railroad.[28] Soon this wholesale firm, as the supplier of goods for many country storekeepers and planters under the postwar credit arrangement, was handling much of the cotton produced in the southern Delta and a great deal of that of the central interior of the state. Its ascendancy, however, was short-lived.

The presence of middle men in the interior of the state encouraged the opening of new lands for cotton cultivation and motivated subsistence farmers to engage in commercial agriculture. Under the crop-lien arrangement, cotton growers became increasingly indebted to local merchants because of the high cost of credit and their chronic inability to pay off their debts. Significantly, this legal and economic tie with merchants encouraged, if it did not require, them to continue as commercial farmers.

The beginnings of small industrial enterprises also stimulated the growth of towns, primarily along the railroads. Although there were four textile plants and 227 sawmills in Mississippi in 1860, no trend had developed by that time to locate these industrial establishments along the newly constructed railroads.[29] Most of the antebellum sawmills were located near the mouths of streams emptying into the Mississippi Sound, and some were still operating at the conclusion of the war.[30] All of the state's garment factories were destroyed as a result of the war.

Generally unhampered after the war by the need to restore old plants at disadvantageous locations, industrial managers, like James M. Wesson, sought to establish mills along the new lines of transportation. Even before the end of the war, Wesson, the leading textile promoter in the state, had made plans to replace his burnt plant at Bankston with a larger one on the New Orleans, Jackson, and Great Northern Railroad, a few miles south of the capital. Immediately after the cessation of hostilities Wesson went to the North and secured credit for

[28] Raymond *Hinds County Gazette*, October 14, 1868; Forest *Register*, December 4, 1869.

[29] U.S. Bureau of the Census, *Eighth Census of the United States: 1860, Manufactures*, 294.

[30] Nollie W. Hickman, "Logging and Rafting Timber in South Mississippi, 1840–1910," *Journal of Mississippi History*, XIX (1957), 154–55.

the purchase of new equipment and machinery for the plant.[31] Meanwhile, construction of buildings began at Wesson, the company town incorporated by the restoration legislature, and, subsequently, houses for seventy-five operatives were built. The company, capitalized at $500,000, was designed to operate 2,100 wool and 4,032 cotton spindles. One correspondent to the New Orleans *Picayune* optimistically reported after visiting the site of construction that the mill when completed would be "one of the largest manufacturing villages this side of Massachusetts."[32] The mill may not have realized the high expectations of this writer, but the equipment that James Wesson installed in his plant, according to one observer, was the newest and best available at that time in the North.[33] In late 1865 the Wesson mill began operation, producing only cotton yarns at first.[34]

Merchants of railroad towns were inspired by Wesson's example, and with more enthusiasm than financial support they sought charters for fanciful enterprises that would produce in one factory system a variety of articles, including textiles, flour, lumber, cottonseed oil, and iron machinery.[35] Promoters in Holly Springs, on the Mississippi Central road, sought to establish in one industrial complex a large flour mill, a brewery, a tannery, a distillery, and a textile factory.[36] The editor of the Aberdeen *Sunny South,* in explaining the motivation behind this postwar mania for industry, declared that such enterprises "would make us a self-supplying, self-sustaining people. We trust that an era of prosperity is dawning upon us that will make the clang of the hammer, the whirr of the mill, and the buzz of the spindle, as familiar as the shreik [sic] of the shell has been in the years now numbered in the records of the dead past."[37]

The restoration legislature responded to the entreaties of groups seeking charters, and it was especially quick to act to incorporate enterprises after the failure in 1866 of king cotton to restore the expected

[31] Wesson *Weekly Enterprise,* February 1, 1952; Dykes, "Mississippi Industrial Legislation," 29.

[32] New Orleans *Picayune,* November 17, 1865, October 20, 1866. See also *Appleton's Annual Cyclopaedia,* VI, 523.

[33] New Orleans *Picayune,* October 20, 1866.

[34] *Ibid.;* Wesson *Weekly Enterprise,* February 1, 1952.

[35] For example, see the charter granted by the legislature to the Pearl River Manufacturing Company. *Laws of Mississippi, 1865,* pp. 379–80.

[36] Vicksburg *Times,* February 19, 1868.

[37] As quoted in the New Orleans *Picayune,* November 25, 1865. See also an editorial in the Jackson *Clarion,* August 17, 1866.

prosperity of the state. During the brief session of 1867 the legislature chartered fifteen companies, which were to be capitalized at amounts ranging from $10,000 to $500,000.[38] But most of these ventures failed to materialize because of the inability of their promoters to secure the capital necessary to organize and to begin operations. As of 1870 there were only five textile mills in the state, including the relatively large factory at Wesson, and these were using only 3,526 spindles and consuming approximately 1,320 bales of cotton annually.[39] At the same time there were four cottonseed oil mills in Mississippi, with an annual product valued at $165,700, and flour and meal mills with an output worth $2,053,567. Except for lumbering, other small industries were virtually nonexistent. In 1870 there were only 755 more employees in industry than in 1860.[40]

Access to railroad transportation and the timber requirements of the railroads themselves resulted in the development during the postbellum period of a number of sawmills along or near the roads. Lumber was needed to repair and to build houses and stores in the area. The railroads not only served as a means of transportation for forest products but also were consumers of these products. Immediately after the war a demand arose for bridge lumber, ties, and other timber products for use in rebuilding the railroads.[41] Although there were sawmills located along the Mississippi Sound during the antebellum era, the restoration of the New Orleans and the Mobile and Ohio trunklines after the war led to the exploitation of new areas, mainly in the upper piney woods. In Copiah County alone a local newspaper reported as early as November, 1865, that there were forty-two sawmills in the county, with most of these enterprises on or near the New Orleans railroad. The newspaper estimated that these mills were averaging a net profit of sixty dollars per day.[42]

Although the first two years after the war were more prosperous for sawmill operators than the late 1860's because of the heavy restora-

[38] Vicksburg *Times*, October 21, 1866; Jackson *Clarion*, January 23, 1867; Dykes, "Mississippi Industrial Legislation," 33.

[39] U.S. Bureau of the Census, *Ninth Census of the United States: 1870, Wealth and Industry*, 596.

[40] *Ibid.*, 437, 445, 461, 472.

[41] Jackson *Clarion and Standard*, August 4, 1866; Hickman, "Logging and Rafting Timber in South Mississippi," 157.

[42] As reported in the Jackson *Clarion*, November 24, 1865.

tion demands placed on the mills,[43] a review of the census report of 1870, in comparison to that of 1860, gives some indication of the development of this industry during the early reconstruction period. In 1860 there were 227 lumber mills, with an annual product of $1,823,627. These mills employed only 1,420 workers. In 1870 the number of sawmills was 274, with an output worth $2,229,017 annually, and employing 1,992 laborers.[44] Small mills continued to characterize the lumber industry of the state until large syndicates made their appearance in the 1880's.[45]

In essence, then, the development of towns after the war resulted from the needs of an agrarian economy and from the revolutionary changes that were occurring as interior lands were being opened to commercial agriculture. Even the old river port of Vicksburg owed its restoration and brief prosperity to the new trade practices and agricultural expansion in the interior that developed after the war. The small industries that were established during this period, including the lumber industry of the piney woods, had little impact on the economy of Mississippi or on the development of towns. The economy continued to be overwhelmingly agrarian. In fact, the new commercial patterns established during the early reconstruction period virtually insured the fastening of an agricultural, one-crop society upon the people of the state that would serve for the next seventy-five years as an insurmountable barrier to the healthy economic development of Mississippi.

[43] For evidence of this early prosperity, see the following: New Orleans Picayune, November 22, 1865; Jackson Clarion, February 27, 1867; and Morgan, Yazoo, 122.

[44] U.S. Bureau of the Census, Eighth Census of the United States: 1860, Manufactures, 294; U.S. Bureau of the Census, Ninth Census of the United States: 1870, Wealth and Industry, 453-54. The naval stores industry was practically nonexistent in Mississippi at this time. There was only one small establishment in both 1860 and 1870.

[45] Paul W. Gates, "Federal Land Policy in the South, 1866–1888," Journal of Southern History, VI (1940), 313–17; Nollie W. Hickman, "Lumber Industry in South Mississippi, 1890–1915," Journal of Mississippi History, XX (1958), 211–12.

13

Political Readjustment, 1866-67

Political adjustments for Mississippians that occurred after the defeat of the Johnson program in the congressional elections of 1866 were more difficult to make than those of 1865. During the first few months after the war apprehensive and disillusioned secessionists generally chose not to participate in political activities. Expecting the worst at first, these former Confederates were soon pleasantly surprised by Johnson's spirit of moderation, and they had few, if any, misgivings about accepting the changes that the President insisted on as prerequisites for restoration to the Union. None of these changes involved altering the fundamental political structure of the state. Although they might have been disappointed with the President's preference for Union Whigs in the provisional government, secession Democrats soon remembered that Johnson's antebellum political antecedents were the same as theirs.

Whigs, most of whom evidently were original Unionists, also found Presidential Reconstruction quite palatable. Controlling both the provisional and restoration governments, Whigs found themselves the principal beneficiaries of the President's program. The main political adjustment that this group had to make was a pleasant one—the ascension to power after years of occupying the frustrating position of a minority party in Mississippi politics. With the triumph of the Radical Republicans in the fall of 1866, however, both Whigs and Democrats had to face the eventuality of Negro suffrage and its feared consequences.

By 1866 traditional political differences between Democrats and former Whigs became less important as arguments concerning the folly of secession ceased to have their former appeal. Moreover, in-

228

terest in national developments and the call for unity in support of the President tended to confuse and to minimize local differences. The Jackson *Clarion and Standard* somewhat exaggeratedly declared in the spring of 1866, when the Radicals in Congress were making their first formidable assault upon Johnson's program, that party lines in Mississippi had been "completely obliterated, and the masses of the people sustain President Johnson's policy with an unanimity unknown in the past history of political parties."[1] Whigs, however, insisted that the term "Democrat" be replaced by "Conservative," or some other word, to describe the coalition supporting the President. In fact, even before the call for a national conservative convention, editor George W. Harper, a Whig zealot, urged that pro-Johnson Whigs and Democrats, along with moderate Republicans, should unite on the national level under the banner of conservatism. Harper proposed that "old party names, as well as platform be utterly ignored (both north and south), and that a platform be erected upon which every true friend of a Constitution-Union can stand. . . . The adoption of any one of the distinctive names would fail of the object contemplated. It would be quite as hard for the old Democrats to become latter-day Whigs as it would for us old Whigs to become Democrats in 1866."[2]

On June 26, 1866, a call was issued by Johnson supporters in Congress for a national convention of conservatives to meet at Philadelphia on August 14.[3] In Mississippi, both the Jackson *Mississippian* and the *Clarion and Standard*, upon the suggestion of leading Whigs of the capital and of Chief Justice Alexander H. Handy, a former Democrat, published a call for a statewide "Union convention" to meet in Jackson on July 26.[4] From the beginning this movement was dominated by Whigs. Governor Humphreys and Senator-elect Sharkey had early given their support to such a movement. County conventions, held

[1] Jackson *Clarion and Standard*, June 7, 1866.

[2] Raymond *Hinds County Gazette*, June 15, 1866, quoted in Thomas B. Alexander (ed.), "Persistent Whiggery in Mississippi Reconstruction: The *Hinds County Gazette*," *Journal of Mississippi History*, XXIII (1961), 74. The editor of the Jackson *Clarion* was also an early advocate of a national conservative party to counter the Radicals. See the issue of April 12, 1866.

[3] Beale, *The Critical Year*, 127.

[4] Jackson *Clarion and Standard*, July 6, 18, 1866. Rivalry between these two journals was so fierce that an argument concerning which newspaper initiated the call for the state convention was a cause for editors John L. Power and Edward M. Yerger "to go armed for each other." *Ibid.*, July 21, 1866.

in pursuance of the call for delegates to the state convention and for which information on proceedings is available, were controlled by conservative Whigs. Abram Murdock was the most prominent and active person in the Lowndes County (Columbus) meetings, and Whigs George L. Potter, William and Edward M. Yerger, John L. Power, Amos R. Johnston, Fulton Anderson, and Judge John Watts were the leaders in Hinds County (Jackson).[5] Earlier meetings held in Adams County (Natchez) in support of Johnson were dominated by Whigs William Dix, Giles Hillyer, and William T. Martin.[6]

Even more significant was the dominant position that former Whigs assumed when the state conservative convention, consisting of delegates from thirty-two of the sixty counties, met at Jackson. The president of the convention, John Watts, and the other officers were men of the Henry Clay persuasion.[7] Membership in the delegation to represent the state at Philadelphia was reserved for the most prominent Whigs in Mississippi. Of the fourteen delegates originally selected by the convention, eleven have been identified as to their party affiliation. Ten of the eleven were Whigs, with the only Democrat being Hiram Cassedy of south Mississippi. Cassedy, however, declined the appointment and was replaced by a young Whig from Humphreys' home county.[8] William Yerger, Horatio F. Simrall, and Potter were the leaders of this Whig-dominated delegation.

Although a very large majority of the whites of Mississippi supported the National Union movement, not everyone in the state believed that the formation of a new party was advisable. George W. Brooks, a restoration legislator and a Douglas Democrat in 1860, denounced those who were willing to break from the Democratic party to form a new organization. Mississippians, he said, had witnessed the disastrous consequences of splitting the party of Jackson, which had

[5] Ibid., July 15, 18, 1866.

[6] Minutes of a meeting of citizens held at Natchez, May 17, 1866, in Johnson Papers.

[7] New York Times, July 26, 1866. More counties would have been represented in the state meeting if conservatives had had sufficient time to meet and select delegates to the convention. Raymond Hinds County Gazette, July 27, 1866.

[8] Jackson Clarion and Standard, August 2, 1866. One prominent disunion Democrat, Lucius Q. C. Lamar, received a few votes for delegate, but, like Albert G. Brown, David C. Glenn, and other leaders of the secession party, he continued to refrain from political activity. Ibid., July 31, 1866. See also the Jackson Clarion, March 27, 1867.

occurred as a result of the cleavage in the party in 1860 and the subsequent election of Lincoln as President.[9]

The most prominent dissenter from the prevailing political philosophy of 1866 was James Lusk Alcorn. He had formulated his views as a result of observations and discussions in Washington, where he had spent several months as a levee commissioner and as a Senator-elect from the state.[10] And the conclusions he reached were based, he believed, upon considerations of practicality and expediency. From Washington on August 29, 1866, Senator-elect Alcorn issued an address to the people of Mississippi which was subsequently published in the newspapers of the state. He declared in this message that the principal reason for the continual exclusion from Congress of the state's representatives was its leaders' unwise support of President Johnson and the Democrats. With a great deal of political perception, Alcorn argued that

the Republican party has become an overshadowing power in the North. The surrender of the South precipitated it forward toward the end of its mission [abolition of slavery]. Dissolution threatened it thus suddenly in the springtime of its strength. The best political minds of the party felt therefore the necessity of infusing into it a general principle of life [i.e., Negro suffrage].

The Democrats are regarded by the party in ascendancy throughout the North with intense hatred. The passions of faction separate the two in even instances where you would look for the philosophical temper of statesmanship. To you this would be of very little concern, if party blindness had not included you among the objects of this hate. The Republicans have jumped to the conclusion that, if they consent to your political rights, they would be out-voted in the next contest for the Presidency by the Democrats. This consideration underlines the fact of your exclusion from representation.

Party ties have fallen from your limbs charred. They have been consumed like flax in the flames of war. You came back into the Union free from all restraints of party friendships. You have come back nationalists. Your sworn fealty, as well as your interests, pledges you to the Union. Your account with parties of the North commenced from the day that gave to the country the President's policy of "restoration."[11]

[9] Jackson *Clarion,* August 11, 1866. The Jackson *Clarion and Standard,* July 28, 1866, alludes to other opposition to the National Union Convention.

[10] Montgomery, *Reminiscences,* 267.

[11] Alcorn's address may be found in the Jackson *Clarion,* August 21, 1866.

For the moment, Mississippians should make no political alliances but remain neutral in the struggle between Johnson and Congress so that their representatives in the latter body would be accepted by the Republicans. The importance of having their congressmen seated could not be overemphasized, Alcorn declared. If Mississippi and the other Southern states were represented in the national legislature, the cotton tax might be repealed and interference in the state's regulation of its labor system might be eliminated. In this address, designed for state-wide circulation, Alcorn chose not to mention that with the representatives of the affected states in Congress federal aid for levee repairs might also be secured.[12] Restoration of the levees was a vital concern to Alcorn and his Delta associates.

Mississippians did not heed Alcorn's advice to refrain from participating in the Johnson movement, with many preferring to believe that their Senator-elect, long an antagonist of the Democratic party, was motivated in his views by partisan bitterness and by personal ambition to take his seat in Congress.[13] Moreover, they were unprepared to accept reasoning that insisted that Mississippians remain neutral when the President, they believed, was fighting the battle of Armageddon for them.

At Philadelphia, Sharkey and Potter were appointed to the executive committee of the new organization, and William Yerger, as a member of the committee on resolutions, played an important role in the drafting of the platform of the National Union movement.[14] The results of this convention were greeted with a great deal of enthusiasm by Johnson supporters throughout the nation. But in spite of its apparent success, the National Union convention made one fatal mistake. It did not form a party. A conservative group within the old party was formed, but no new party with party machinery or party candidates was organized.[15]

Even before the date of the congressional elections (November 6,

[12] *Ibid.*

[13] For an example of this interpretation of Alcorn's motives, see the Vicksburg *Times,* October 21, 1866. Evidently there were a few in the state, in addition to Alcorn, who as early as April, 1866, urged Mississippians to be neutral in the conflict between Johnson and Congress. See the Jackson *Clarion,* April 20, 1866.

[14] Raymond *Hinds County Gazette,* August 24, 1866. Although Sharkey was selected for the executive committee, he was not a delegate to the convention. L. Marshall Hall, "William L. Sharkey and Reconstruction, 1866–1873," *Journal of Mississippi History,* XXVII (1965), 3.

[15] Beale, *The Critical Year,* 137–38.

1866), it had become apparent to many that the Radicals would win an overwhelming victory and would then be in a position to assume control of reconstruction. At this time Mississippians began to waver somewhat in their support of the President. The Jackson *Clarion* editor now doubted the advisability of a militant stand against the Radicals, believing, instead, that "we should stand by the Constitution and simply ask our rights."[16] On the day of the election, and before the results were known, the editor, now thoroughly disillusioned with politics, declared: "We are disgusted with Northern treachery and corruption, and should stand apart from the political contest now going on in the North, until we can take our place in the councils of the nation. . . ."[17]

The change in the policy of the management of the Vicksburg *Times* was even more abrupt than that of the Jackson *Clarion*. The *Times* had been established in October, 1866, with the announced purpose of supporting the President and with a view that no further concessions should be made on the reconstruction issue.[18] But only a few days after it began publication, and as a Republican triumph appeared inevitable, the editor declared that, in spite of the fact that Negro suffrage was repugnant to his nature, it might not prove too distasteful in practice. Based upon the performance of the blacks since securing freedom, the *Times* editor professed not to believe that the Negroes would support the Republican party, but, rather, would vote with their former masters. "They certainly have as a class shown a wonderful magnanimity in their new sphere, and as proof, witness the thousands who have voluntarily returned to their former places, and are virtually occupying the same positions of servant" as before.[19] At the same time, the prominent James M. Wesson, president of the Mississippi Manufacturing Company and a Whig, believed that it was in the power of the legislature "to head off the Radicals." His plan was for the state to enfranchise "all negroes [who] can read and write and [who] own a free hold of forty acres of land or five hundred dollars worth of town property." Wesson also suggested that white voting be restricted to property owners.[20]

[16] Jackson *Clarion*, October 12, 1866.
[17] *Ibid.*, November 6, 1866.
[18] Vicksburg *Times*, October 23, 1866.
[19] *Ibid.*, November 1, 1866.
[20] James M. Wesson to Governor Humphreys, October 4, 1866, in Governors' Correspondence, E-80.

The overwhelming victory of the Radicals in the fall elections, occurring at a time when economic prospects appeared bleak as a result of the crop failure of 1866, created a feeling of despondency in the minds of the great majority of white Mississippians. Under these circumstances the Jackson *Clarion* editor, and probably most of the whites of the state, chose to ignore political affairs. "We have dabbled in politics enough," he declared. "We have been almost ruined by political agitation, and are now willing to turn our attention to manufactures, agriculture, and commerce."[21] Again, in late December, 1866, the editor advised: "We have seen enough of the valley of humiliation, and must stand aloof, no matter what the pains and penalties of Congress may be." Apparently opposing ratification of the pending Fourteenth Amendment, he declared that "we will wear the manacles of despotism with the best grace possible, but will never [contribute] to the overthrow of the republican theory of government."[22]

During the interim between the fall elections and the passage of the first reconstruction acts in March, 1867, a great deal of debate occurred in Mississippi on the question of ratifying the Fourteenth Amendment. Governor Humphreys in October, and before the elections, had urged the legislature to reject this amendment, since it represented "a gross usurpation of the rights of the State."[23] The legislature, however, preferred to await the outcome of the national elections, and thus it postponed action on the amendment. A few Mississippians already realized that the Republican program, as embodied in the Fourteenth Amendment, was actually a moderate proposal for reconstruction when compared with the demands of many Radicals for outright Negro suffrage.[24] Those persons who sought to explain the amendment in this manner, however, were generally reluctant to recommend that the legislature ratify it. Senator-elect Al-

[21] Jackson *Clarion*, November 8, 1866. See also the Meridian *Semi-Weekly Gazette*, March 23, 1867.

[22] Jackson *Clarion*, December 20, 1866.

[23] *Senate Journal, 1866–1867*, p. 8.

[24] Raymond *Hinds County Gazette*, November 2, 1866. The second section of the Fourteenth Amendment did not provide unequivocally for Negro suffrage; its framers were not yet ready, or able, to take action to divest the states of any part of their control over suffrage. This section declared, however, that where a state denied the right to vote to any of its citizens "except for participation in rebellion, or other crime, the basis of representation" in Congress "shall be reduced" proportionately.

corn, on the other hand, had no misgivings about suggesting a course of action for the legislature to follow. In an address before that body on January 25, 1867, Alcorn declared that, although in principle he opposed the amendment, he would advise the legislature to ratify it for reasons of diplomacy and expediency. He reiterated his earlier statement that "the Democratic party at the North has no power to help us, if they would, and their record shows that they would not, if they could."[25]

Sharkey, the state's other Senator-elect, was quite active in opposing the amendment. He wrote Governor Humphreys that the measure was "a mere effort to force negro suffrage upon us, whether we are willing or not." Furthermore, "should this amendment become part of the Constitution, we shall have a very different Government from that which we inherited from our ancestors."[26] After the triumph of the Radicals at the polls, a somewhat reluctant Sharkey, along with representatives from the Carolinas, advanced a plan that was designed to split the Republican party and to eliminate the obnoxious features of the Fourteenth Amendment. In essence, the proposal provided for qualified Negro suffrage through state constitutional amendments, but, significantly, at the same time it restricted the number of whites who could vote. The plan specified that the ballot should be extended to only those male adults, without regard to race, who could read the Declaration of Independence and the Constitution and who could write their names. An alternative for those who could not pass this literacy requirement was the possession of $250 worth of taxable property. This proposal would not apply to persons who were already registered.[27]

In proposing an alternative plan, Sharkey and his friends had failed to understand the intentions of the Republicans in advancing the Fourteenth Amendment. The amendment was designed by the

[25] Alcorn's speech was reported in the Jackson *Clarion*, January 29, 1867.

[26] Sharkey's letter to Humphreys may be found in the Jackson *Clarion*, September 28, 1866.

[27] Sharkey to Humphreys, February 3, 7, 1867, in Governors' Correspondence, E-81; Vicksburg *Herald*, February 6, 8, 1867; Hall, "Sharkey," 3. The concept underlying this proposed amendment was a forerunner of schemes employed by some Southern states during the late nineteenth and early twentieth centuries to disfranchise Negroes, yet at the same time provide loopholes for whites. For a discussion of the disfranchisement methods later employed by the whites, see Woodward, *Origins of the New South*, Chap. 12.

majority in Congress in 1866 as a compromise to secure the support of all Republicans to a program which would reduce the representation of the former Confederate states in that body unless they were safely under Republican control. The compromise was not entirely satisfactory to either the moderate or the radical wings of the party, but it was ambiguous enough to permit each to support it, and no conservative Southern plan could split Republican unity on this point.[28] Congress therefore summarily rejected the Sharkey-advocated proposal.

It is impossible to determine accurately the prevailing attitude of white Mississippians toward the impending congressional program and toward its chief feature, Negro suffrage. Many leaders in the state may have desired qualified freedmen suffrage as embodied in the Sharkey proposal, but the literacy or property qualification for voting, as the Vicksburg *Herald* editor said, "is as impracticable as it is offensive."[29] The legislature of 1867, asked by Sharkey to give its opinion on the scheme, indicated its disapproval of the proposal. During the same session the legislature overwhelmingly rejected the Fourteenth Amendment but indicated that it would give "respectful consideration" to any plan or amendment by Congress which would represent a final settlement of the reconstruction question.[30] In refusing to ratify the amendment, legislators argued quixotically that they had no assurances that this would be a finality. Others simply wanted no part "in rivetting upon Mississippi and the South the 'Sherman iniquity' and its whole chain of 'enormities.'"[31] To have ratified the amendment out of a sense of expediency, as Alcorn suggested, would have been dangerous politically even for those legislators who may have understood the course of national events and may have desired to placate Congress. Nevertheless, any such action on the part of Mississippians would have had little effect on the process of reconstruction, unless the other Southern states had ratified the amendment.[32]

[28] Randall and Donald, *The Civil War and Reconstruction*, 580–81. Federal protection for the civil rights of Negroes in the South was another and more obvious objective of the Republicans in proposing the Fourteenth Amendment.
[29] Vicksburg *Herald*, February 10, 1867.
[30] *Ibid.*, February 13, 1867; Jackson *Clarion*, January 31, February 9, 17, 1867.
[31] Jackson *Clarion*, February 14, 1867; William L. Harris to Governor Humphreys, March 10, 1867, in Governors' Correspondence, E-81.
[32] David Donald asserts that the failure of the Southern states to ratify the Fourteenth Amendment cost the South the support of moderate Republicans in

After the passage in March, 1867, of the first reconstruction measures, a virtual revolution occurred in the political attitudes of many of the leaders of the state. These leaders, at last recognizing that black suffrage was inevitable, reversed their earlier position toward qualified Negro suffrage and began to argue publicly that the whites of the state should readily accept the congressional program of enfranchisement and, as a result, be in a position to control the Negro vote. Such a policy, they said, would not be inconsistent with their recent repudiation of the Fourteenth Amendment, since the military reconstruction acts, in contrast to the amendment, guaranteed representation in Congress and were designed as a finality in all essentials.[33] In fact, the position of some vocal Mississippians at this time closely resembled Alcorn's public views, which had been denounced as exceedingly repulsive a few months earlier. The new editor of the Jackson *Clarion*, the former secessionist Ethelbert Barksdale, was one who now agreed with Alcorn that the people of the state should accept wholeheartedly Congressional Reconstruction and that they should not unite with any Northern political party until reconstructed.[34] The editor of the Meridian *Gazette*, and a former disunionist also, declared that Alcorn's argument "embodies some very sensible views on the political situation. We fully agree with Gen. Alcorn that it is 'impolitic to unite ourselves at present with any party at the North, only so far as it is a party of restoration.' . . . With restoration and full assurance of civil and political rights to the blacks, to be established in our State Constitutions, the issues of the past would be settled, and new political organizations would arise." Once the reconstruction process had been completed, the *Gazette* editor advised, Mississippians should then align with the party that would reduce the tax on cotton, lower the tariff, and practice economy in government.[35]

Several factors contributed to this swift reversal of views and to the positive way in which many Mississippians at this time accepted

Congress and made possible the enactment of the Radical Republican proposal of universal manhood (Negro) suffrage. David Donald, *The Politics of Reconstruction, 1863–1867* (Baton Rouge: Louisiana State University Press, 1965), 61–62.

[33] Jackson *Clarion*, March 7, 9, May 24, 1867; Meridian *Semi-Weekly Gazette*, March 16, 20, 1867.

[34] Jackson *Clarion*, May 24, 1867.

[35] Meridian *Semi-Weekly Gazette*, May 18, 1867.

Negro suffrage. Of course, most whites, except for intimidated loyalists, had no desire to live under military rule, as provided by the reconstruction acts until such time as the state would be restored to the Union. But military supervision of state affairs had not been too distasteful in 1865, and in 1867 it was probably deplored more than actually feared by Mississippians. On the other hand, many believed that, if Southerners did not indicate a willingness to cooperate with the triumphant Congress, more radical measures than the enfranchisement of Negroes or temporary military rule might be imposed upon them. In urging a policy of cooperation, editor Barksdale exclaimed that the "spectre of sweeping confiscations" haunted the land, and that such a policy as advanced by Thaddeus Stevens would triumph immediately if whites did not willingly acquiesce in the congressional program. Already this "spectre" of confiscation "presses as a mountain of lead upon the energies [of the people], paralyzing energy, destroying confidence, over-throwing credit and forbidding emigration." The great need, both politically and economically, Barksdale emphasized, was for a final settlement of the reconstruction issue.[36]

The Meridian *Gazette* also expressed the belief that the economic restoration of the state depended upon a speedy acceptance and implementation of the congressional plan. Not until the political reconstruction of the state had been completed, it declared, would "business and money stride confidently hand in hand together across the length and breadth of the land."[37] In essence, then, the economic difficulties, experienced by the state as a result of the crop failure of 1866, accentuated the desire on the part of many for the complete reconstruction of the state in the Union, almost regardless of the political requirements involved.

Of equal, if not more, importance in motivating many Mississippi leaders to accept with a show of willingness the new political dispensation was the necessity for quick action to secure control of the new electorate before Radical Republicans could organize it for their own purposes. Many were quite frank in stating this motive in embracing Congressional Reconstruction. Editor Barksdale advised: "Let us accept negro suffrage as an inevitable fact. . . . If the new sufferagan is unqualified for the important duties committed to him, it is the part

---

[36] Jackson *Clarion*, March 16, 1867. For a similar approach, see the Vicksburg *Herald*, March 14, 1867.

[37] Meridian *Semi-Weekly Gazette*, March 23, 1867.

of wisdom that they whose interests are involved with his own, should strive to enlighten his understanding." Unless the old citizens of the state accepted Negro suffrage and influenced the black man's vote, "a wall of separation will be reared between the two races, and the negro will be left to seek counsel from those who are more willing to give it," Barksdale argued in a later issue of the *Clarion.* Then, "rampant agrarianism," in the form of confiscatory state and local taxes on land would be the order of the day.[38] Yet, in their efforts to control the Negro politically, Barksdale called upon whites not to deceive him with false promises or misinformation as to their future policies.[39]

Beginning in March, 1867, a series of letters from influential Mississippians who supported cooperation with Congress appeared in the newspapers of the state. These letters were designed to convince whites that the votes of the blacks might be controlled by a speedy acquiescence in the reconstruction acts and by convincing the Negroes of the state that the native whites were sympathetic to their interests.[40] David C. Glenn, an influential fire-eating secessionist in 1860 and the author of one of the letters, reflected the views of the correspondents when he declared that he abhorred the thought of Negro suffrage, but "if we act judiciously we may make it an element of strength instead of weakness."[41] State supreme court Justice Henry T. Ellett, also a former secessionist, felt that "patriotic and good men" should instruct the blacks on how to vote. "It is not the negroes we have to fear," he declared, "but unprincipled white men who will seek to use them for selfish and wicked ends."[42] The Meridian *Gazette* also expressed apprehension that outsiders might attempt to control the new electorate, yet "if we exert ourselves we can still control the State and give the people a constitution framed by white men and under which all can afford to exist by accomodating themselves to circumstances."[43]

James Lusk Alcorn also urged the necessity for immediate action on the part of conservative whites before the Radicals could win the

[38] Jackson *Clarion,* March 9, June 11, 1867.
[39] *Ibid.,* June 26, 1867.
[40] For several of these letters, see *ibid.,* March 13, 30, April 4, 21, 25, June 22, 1867. See also the Meridian *Semi-Weekly Gazette,* April 6, 13, 20, 1867; and the Vicksburg *Herald,* March 15, 1867.
[41] Vicksburg *Herald,* March 15, 1867.
[42] Jackson *Clarion,* April 25, 1867.
[43] Meridian *Semi-Weekly Gazette,* March 23, 1867.

Negro vote. In a pamphlet circulated throughout the state, Alcorn exclaimed:

The Loyal League is upon you. Even a brief experience of the workings of that voting machine would satisfy you, as it has me, that all which our people claim for the influence of the "old master" on the freedmen is neither more nor less than nonsense. The terrible necessities of our position demand blunt speaking. . . . The "old master," gentlemen, has passed from fact to poetry!

The man who speaks of the policy of the party in power as one actuated by passion, I cannot stoop to notice. Our reason must begin at a higher level. . . . The legislation of Congress is evidently directed more than ordinary by the necessities of party. A sectional organization must necessarily prove short-lived. The republicans deem it, therefore, a necessity to obtain support at the South. Negro suffrage is a logical sequence from that fact: the radicals failed to find, in all this broad section of ours, any hope of support amongst the whites. Opposed to that measure [Negro suffrage] themselves save as necessity of power, they accepted it with fear and trembling as to its effect upon their popularity at the North.[44]

Yet the Republicans were anxious, Alcorn asserted, to mitigate as much as possible the adverse effect that freedman suffrage might have in the North by establishing a cooperating party in the South that would embrace both blacks and whites. Hence a door would be left open by which local whites who cooperated with Congress might exercise political control over the Negroes. With a platform guaranteeing to the blacks all of their rights as citizens, including a program of public education, the whites of Mississippi could maintain "their position as advisers of the old and devoted servants of the South—the colored people." Alcorn concluded by declaring: "The colored man comes, as well as the white man, within the scope of my proposed negotiation. . . . All that Congress has given him I accept as his with all my heart and conscience. I propose to vote with him; to discuss political affairs with him; to sit, if need be, in political counsel with him; and from a platform acceptable to him, to me, and to you, to pluck our common liberty and our common prosperity out of the jaws of inevitable ruin." Such a policy "would save the people of Mississippi from a domestic radicalism infinitely more dangerous to both black and white than that which has triumphed in Tennessee."[45] Soon Alcorn was urging the formation of a new state party, to align with the na-

[44] Alcorn, *Views on the Political Situation*, 2–3.
[45] *Ibid.*, 4–5.

tional Republican party. This party would consist mainly of Union Whigs and Negroes and would specifically exclude secessionists.[46]

Somewhat ironically, former secession Democrats, who had generally refrained from participating in public affairs during the first two years after the war, led the effort in Mississippi to secure the acquiescence of the whites in the congressional plan and to gain control of the Negro vote. Since they had not very actively associated themselves with the Johnson program, these former secessionists were in a better position than Whig leaders to urge cooperation with Congress without appearing to have sharply reversed their earlier reconstruction position. One such secession leader, former Governor John J. McRae, in a letter to the Meridian *Gazette* supporting cooperation with the Republicans, was able to say with little fear of being charged with inconsistency that it would have been best for Mississippi had Johnson submitted to Congress in the beginning.[47] At the same time, Albert G. Brown, the most influential of the antebellum fire-eaters, chose, like McRae, to abandon his policy of abstention from public affairs and began urging that local whites assume control of the reconstruction process. In a speech to a mixed group of blacks and whites in Copiah County, Brown declared that "I am not only willing, but anxious, to instruct" the Negro in the "ABCs of his politics."[48] By returning to the political wars at this time, former secessionists probably saw an opportunity to regain public prestige, since many Whigs, who had dominated state politics during the period of Presidential Reconstruction, hesitated to cooperate with the Republicans.

Even so, the controversial and emotional nature of the Negro suffrage issue made it dangerous politically for aspiring leaders to support such a program. Accordingly, not all secession leaders thought that the time was propitious for ending their political retirement. Lucius Q. C. Lamar, an influential disunionist in the convention of 1861 and a former Confederate colonel, wisely chose to devote his full attention to his duties as professor of law at the University of Mississippi. He remained publicly silent on political matters until 1870.[49] This inaction on the part of Lamar and other ambitious young men, until after political patterns had been formed on reconstruction

[46] Jackson *Clarion*, September 19, 1867.
[47] Meridian *Semi-Weekly Gazette*, April 20, 1867.
[48] *Ibid.*, August 21, 1867.
[49] Mayes, *Lamar*, 121–24.

issues, made it possible for them to re-enter state politics without the stigma of an unpopular position attached to their names.

The dilemma that many influential Whigs faced with the defeat of their patron, President Johnson, by the Republicans, made it difficult for them to change their tactics suddenly and to exhort Mississippians to support the Radical program. Like Giles Hillyer of the Natchez *Courier*, they were "not yet prepared to consent to the sacrifice of constitutional liberty" for reasons of expediency.[50] Sharkey, with Humphreys' endorsement, sought an injunction from the United States Supreme Court to prevent the enforcement of the reconstruction acts. In the case of *Mississippi v. Johnson* the court declined to act on Sharkey's suit, explaining that reconstruction policies were a political matter over which it could not assume jurisdiction.[51] Most Mississippi leaders refused to encourage Sharkey in his efforts, believing by this time that legal attempts to block Radical Reconstruction were unrealistic and would retard the restoration of the state to its traditional place in the Union.[52]

It is unclear whether the rank and file of the whites during the spring of 1867 were willing to follow the advice of Brown, McRae, and other reconstructionists. The Jackson *Clarion* editor believed in June that three fourths of the white people were in favor of accepting the terms of Congress. This estimate may have been somewhat sanguine; yet, if the views of the local newspapers may be used as an index of popular opinion, it is evident that most whites at that time acquiesced in Negro suffrage. Twenty-three journals of the state urged a speedy acceptance of the congressional program, whereas only six newspapers warned against cooperating with the Radicals.[53] Reconstructionists in several counties held mixed meetings, in which the new electorate was courted. In these meetings, whites made promises to protect the political privileges of the Negroes and on several occasions resolved that they would promote the establishment of public schools for both races.[54] Reconstruction newspapers during the spring of 1867

[50] See Hillyer's comments in Ranck, *Brown*, 256.

[51] Sharkey to Humphreys, March 14, 1867, in Governors' Correspondence, E-78; Coulter, *The South during Reconstruction*, 122.

[52] Meridian *Semi-Weekly Gazette*, April 20, 1867; Jackson *Clarion*, May 16, 1867; New York *Times*, April 29, 1867.

[53] Jackson *Clarion*, May 11, 17, June 26, 1867.

[54] *Ibid.*, April 24, 30, 1867; Meridian *Semi-Weekly Gazette*, April 20, May 1, 1867.

optimistically predicted that, once the registration of the new electorate was completed, a conservative constitution was promulgated, and Mississippi and Southern representatives were admitted to Congress, the Radical Republicans would fall from power.[55] But their hopes for control of the freedman vote by native whites were of short duration. Leaders in the Negro communities remembered that all too recently local whites were engaged in a campaign of vociferously denouncing the mere thought of black suffrage, and this suggested that the whites' new acceptance of the political rights of the freedmen was not sincere. The Republican party, organized in the state in 1867, did not find it very difficult, through its Union Leagues, to convince most Negroes that it was the party that had always represented the interests of the blacks.[56]

At the same time, local reconstructionists, or cooperationists, were losing large sections of the white population. By the summer of 1867 such planks in their platform as that advocating public schooling for both races were subjected to severe attacks. A new party arose in the state, the Constitutional Union party, which took advantage of this opposition to the reconstructionists and urged Mississippians to take an uncompromising stand against Negro suffrage. The leadership in this new movement came from four former Whigs, Walker Brooke, a former United States Senator, Edward M. Yerger, George L. Potter, and George W. Shelton.[57] They appeared to delight in associating their old Democratic foes with Northern radicalism. The tables had been turned, they exclaimed. Whigs were now the defenders of Southern rights against an advanced brand of abolitionism, while former Southern nationalists, such as Brown, McRae, and Ethelbert Barksdale, were urging the acceptance of Negro suffrage for reasons of expediency. These Whigs chided Democrats for their inconsistency regarding Southern rights and derisively referred to them as "Assistant Radicals." One Whig editor described the reconstructionists as men "once considered the first men in the State, who are now anxious to pick up the crumbs that fall from radical tables, and [they] are actually

[55] Meridian *Semi-Weekly Gazette*, April 20, 1867.

[56] Abstract of a letter from Mrs. Louisa Flournoy to General Edward O. C. Ord, April 17, 1867, Records Group 98, Fourth Military District, Civil Affairs, Letters Received, 1867, in Records of the United States Army Command, National Archives; Vicksburg *Herald*, April 24, 1867; Jackson *Clarion*, September 19, 1867.

[57] For accounts of this new party and the names of its leaders, see the Jackson *Clarion*, September 5, 1867, and the Vicksburg *Herald*, October 15, 17, 19, 1867.

traversing the State, making negro speeches, getting up negro meetings, and playing second fiddle to Sambo, condescending to act as Vice-President at such meeting, while Sambo submits to act as President of the same."[58] Another Whig editor went further; he charged that "the promise of a little pocket change has induced a few secession leaders in this state to sell themselves to the Republican party."[59]

Actually, the Potter Whigs in their desire to stigmatize their old secession foes with postwar radicalism had oversimplified party alignment on reconstruction and Negro suffrage. Although several former fire-eaters took the lead in urging a willing acquiescence in Congressional Reconstruction, there were also some prominent antebellum Whigs, such as John W. C. Watson, Alcorn, William Yerger, Fulton Anderson, and Amos R. Johnston, who advocated a similar policy. Furthermore, most reconstructionists, whether Whigs or Democrats, did not cooperate with the Republican party in the state, preferring to pursue an independent course in implementing Negro suffrage and hoping that Congress would accept their actions in good faith. Only a few citizens of the state, notably Alcorn, Abel Alderson, Robert W. Flournoy, and Jefferson L. Wofford, dared to face possible political, and even social, ostracism by assisting in the organization of the "Black Republican" party in Mississippi.

Potter and his group of "irreconcilables" were able to exploit effectively the unrealistic hopes of many whites that the Democratic party would triumph in the presidential and congressional elections of 1868, and that all that was necessary to secure redemption from the Radicals was patience, combined with an adamant refusal to compromise on the suffrage issue. By the fall of 1867 even some cooperation leaders had found it desirable to abandon their advocacy of reconstruction under the congressional plan and to join the Potter movement.[60]

Thus, on the eve of the first state election in which Negroes participated, Mississippians returned to an anti-Negro platform and thereby surrendered by default the direction and control of the political revolution that Congress had put in motion. But it probably would

[58] Raymond *Hinds County Gazette,* June 28, 1867. See also a statement by the editor of the Brandon *Republican* in the Meridian *Semi-Weekly Gazette,* May 1, 1867.

[59] As reported in the Meridian *Semi-Weekly Gazette,* July 11, 1867.

[60] *Ibid.,* October 16, 19, 1867.

have been asking too much so soon after the days of slavery for the majority of white Mississippians, who viewed the freedmen as inferiors and unfit for citizenship, much less qualified to vote intelligently, to cooperate for an extended period of time in a program that would guarantee equal political rights for Negroes.

14

Conclusions

THE PRESIDENTIAL plan of reconstruction allowed Mississippians a large measure of freedom in the management of their own affairs, and they were therefore able to react naturally to postwar problems of restoration and adjustment. As a result a familiar pattern of internal divisions developed. In fact, many of these divisions had their basis in antebellum attitudes, party politics, and antagonisms which were only modified or conditioned by the results of the Civil War. A significant change, however, had occurred in the leadership structure of the state since the antebellum period. Whigs, members of the minority party before the war, had assumed control of Mississippi, and they sponsored policies that, notwithstanding their prewar precedents, were generally free of the emotionalism of the sectional conflict of the 1850's. Their ascendancy during the period immediately after the war was due mainly, but not exclusively, to their prewar opposition to secession. As the directors for a time of the reconstruction process, these Whigs not only worked for the quick restoration of Mississippi to the Union but also promoted what they believed to be conservative policies for the economic and social rehabilitation of the people of the state. Nonetheless, Whigs were often divided on specific issues because of the unique problems of the postwar era and their confusion as to the meaning of the forces at work both within and outside of the state. In the end they followed policies more attuned to prewar experiences than those which fully recognized the harsh realities of postwar adjustment. Particularly is this evident in the efforts of the Whig-controlled restoration government to define the freedmen's position in Mississippi and to attract money and capital for economic recovery and development.

For a time the political policies of the new Mississippi leaders contributed in a positive way to the process of restoration and readjustment. The reconstruction activities of these men during the spring and summer of 1865 produced a speedy acceptance by the great majority of Mississippians of the Johnson-defined results of the war. An election was promptly held to restore civil government in the state, in keeping with the President's policy, and original Unionists were sent to Washington to represent Mississippi in Congress. The cooperation of state leaders with Federal officers, notwithstanding occasional altercations, resulted in a virtual cessation of military interference when the restoration government took office. The near anarchy of the spring of 1865 was brought under control, and depredations against the hapless freedmen were largely halted by early 1866, although some lawless elements continued to act with impunity in remote parts of the state. The restoration of effective local governments was by no means a small accomplishment, since frontier conditions existed in Mississippi at the end of the war. The unstable and insecure nature of society under such conditions was accentuated by the presence of approximately 400,000 freedmen, by conflict and confusion over the ownership of valuable cotton, and by the continuation of wartime-engendered bitterness in communities where loyalists and deserters had been active.

Then, too, during Presidential Reconstruction, Negroes were returned to the fields as a result of the work of local whites, of Federal officers, and of natural economic forces. In fact, the freedmen's place in the society of the state was largely determined during this period. Without land and money and with little business knowledge, Negroes soon found themselves again dependent upon the planter for a livelihood and for protection from antagonistic and predatory whites. Under such a paternal system blacks were to be long in rising above the mudsill of society, notwithstanding the political gains that they made during the period of Radical Reconstruction.

Despite early successes, Mississippi leaders of 1865–67 failed to secure the restoration of the state to the Union or the economic recovery of the people. Forces and developments outside of the state were primarily responsible for the defeat of the moderate Presidential plan for the quick political reconstruction of the former Confederate states. But Mississippians, by enacting an excessively comprehensive and discriminatory settlement for the freedmen and summarily rejecting the Thirteenth and Fourteenth amendments, contributed to the discrediting of Johnson's program and to the success of the Radical Republicans in the North. Triumphant Radicals then proceeded to impose military reconstruction and Negro suffrage upon the Southern states, and thereby produced another psychological crisis for Mississippians. Clearly, the mild nature of Presidential Reconstruction had inflated the hopes of former Confederates and specifically caused them to believe that defeat did not carry with it any real political penalties nor any changes in prewar Constitutional forms and practices. It may be said with some assurance that their approach to Congressional Reconstruction would have been more realistic had there been no Presidential Reconstruction and had Negro suffrage been imposed upon the state immediately after the war when they were prepared for the worst at the hands of the victors.

Postwar economic problems proved more formidable, more complex, and more enervating than those posed by the vicissitudes of political reconstruction. These problems might have been solved had money been available in the state after the war. Only through the accumulation of money could Mississippians hope to escape financial bondage to outside impersonal interests, educate their children, diversify the economy of the state, and rebuild the levees that protected the richest farm land in the South. But significant barriers existed to their regaining financial solvency and accumulating money. Some of these obstacles, notably the cotton tax and the discriminatory national banking acts, were the work of the federal government; however, at home the misguided efforts of Whig leaders aggravated the crisis. Particularly, the Whig government's insistence that old financial obligations be met placed an unnecessary burden on debtors, including the levee board, and intensified the difficulties of recovery. The Whig argument that money would not be extended where public respect was not shown for the rights of creditors was unrealistic in view of the economic debacle that the state experienced as a result of the war. Under such adverse economic conditions, debtor relief measures would have been no real deterrent to the extension of money for Mississippi enterprises.

Actually, king cotton was the great, if not the only, hope for immediate economic recovery. Mississippians had not lost their skill or knowledge of the production and marketing of cotton, and during the first two years after the war, with the staple selling for more than thrice the price that it brought in 1860, they were wise in attempting to restore temporarily the cotton economy. Postwar editors and leaders wishfully proclaimed that, once the price of the staple fell and its usefulness for attracting money was gone, cotton could be relegated to a secondary role in the economic life of the state.

But their plans went astray when cotton growers failed to produce sufficient yields to profit while the price was high. Labor problems, the inundation of the Delta, and the general dislocation of the economy of the state were mainly responsible for this failure; and, when the market sharply declined, farmers and local merchants alike found themselves heavily in debt. In order to continue operations they were forced to turn increasingly to outside sources of credit, which they were able to secure only on very unfavorable terms and generally by pledging the future cotton crop in payment. There was always a market for cotton, and therefore credit was extended to produce it. In fact, more people than ever before, due to the expansion of railroads into the interior, became involved in commercial agriculture and its credit arrangement. Under such a system, Mississippians could only hope that farming and marketing conditions would soon be favorable so that they would be able to pay their debts and still have some money left. But their hopes were not fulfilled, and the great majority of them, whether landed proprietors, merchants, yeoman farmers, or sharecroppers, soon found themselves mired in the position of debtors under the debilitating credit arrangement, and commercial centers such as Vicksburg and Jackson became virtually stagnant.

This somber condition, therefore, had its origins in the effects of the Civil War and the expedients that were introduced during the early reconstruction era to overcome them. The most enlightened policies of Mississippi leaders of this period would have been of little avail in solving the postwar economic problems of the state. Only outside financial assistance could have brought about a return of prosperity in Mississippi, assistance that not only would have led to agrarian recovery but soon made possible the diversification of the economy of the state. The need for federal aid specifically is well-illustrated in the frustrating efforts of state leaders to construct a durable levee for the protection of the fertile lands of the Delta. Mississippi, in effect, needed a Marshall Plan after the Civil War if it expected to regain economic parity with the Northern states. It received no such aid—and economic doldrums settled over the state which were not broken until the age of Franklin D. Roosevelt.

Bibliography

Primary Sources

MANUSCRIPTS

B Y FAR the most significant manuscript collection used in this study is the voluminous Mississippi Governors' Correspondence, Files E-68–81, in the state's Department of Archives and History at Jackson. Although a great deal of the material in this collection concerns requests for pardons or office, many of the letters are very revealing in their descriptions of conditions in the state during the period immediately after the Civil War. On the other hand, the executive journals of the governors found in the Mississippi archives were of very little importance as sources for this book. Of special value in the public papers at Jackson are the manuscript election returns for the counties in the Records of the Secretary of State for the State of Mississippi, File F-89, and the Records of the Mississippi Legislature, File 1-119. Included in the Broadsides Collection, 1831–70, in the state archives is the *Tabular View of the Legislature of 1865*, which, significantly, reveals the political affiliation of the restoration lawmakers. The William Whitehurst Papers, a large collection in the archives, contain only a few items that are of importance for the period of Presidential Reconstruction. Although small in size, the Oscar J. E. Stuart and the John L. Power Papers in the same depository are very illuminating for white attitudes in 1865. The Marmaduke Shannon and Mrs. William O. Crutcher Family Papers and the Mrs. Nancy

Richey Papers in the archives give insights into some of the economic changes that followed the Civil War. The Walter Goodman (or Mississippi Central Railroad Company) Papers, another small collection in the state archives, provide valuable information on the difficulties involved in the efforts of the officials of one railroad to make a satisfactory financial arrangement with the company's creditors. Of very little value for the early reconstruction period were the James W. Garner Papers in the archives, but one letter from Adelbert Ames to Professor Garner describes the conditions of the state institutions after the war. A map of abandoned plantations near Vicksburg, prepared by Federal officers in 1864, is also found in the archives.

In the Duke University Library are two small collections that were of especial importance for their descriptions of the economic effects of the war. The Henry M. Crydenwise Papers describe planting conditions and life in the Delta during 1866 from the point of view of a sympathetic veteran of the Federal army. The Francis W. Henry Papers reflect the impoverishment of the people of the state and the resulting feeling of hopelessness on the part of creditors.

Several manuscripts in the Southern Historical Collection, University of North Carolina, Chapel Hill, contain information on the early reconstruction period in Mississippi. Of some significance were the diary and scrapbook of Jason Niles, a Union Whig of central Mississippi. However, very little revealing data was found in either the James Lusk Alcorn or the John F. H. Claiborne Papers at Chapel Hill. A manuscript autobiography of Judge Josiah A. P. Campbell in his papers in this library comments on Campbell's efforts to secure justice for the freedmen in his court.

A very significant collection used in this study was the Andrew Johnson Papers in the Manuscripts Division, Library of Congress. Persons of all classes and reflecting widely divergent views wrote the President offering their advice on how Mississippi should be reconstructed and describing conditions in the state. Especially interesting in this collection were letters to Johnson from Mississippi loyalists. The Salmon P. Chase Papers in the same library contain two letters of unexpected richness from Federal District Judge Robert A. Hill to the Chief Justice on the changing white attitudes toward Negro rights in view of the continued impoverishment of the state and the impending failure of Presidential Reconstruction.

In the National Archives the reports and correspondence of Freedmen's Bureau officers in the Freedmen's Bureau Records, Mississippi, 1865–68, Bureau of Refugees, Freedmen, and Abandoned Lands, Records Group 105, were especially important, not only for descriptions of the difficulties confronting the Negroes in freedom and for the bureau programs to aid them in overcoming these problems, but also for accounts of planting and labor conditions in the state after the war. Helpful in securing information on the political background of several Mississippi leaders during this period and the losses suffered by some members of the planter-lawyer class were the Records of the Adjutant General, Amnesty Papers, Mississippi, Records Group 94, National Archives. Of less value in the same archives were the Military Records, Mississippi District, Office of the Adjutant General, Miscellaneous Branch, 1861–70, Records Group 94, and the Records of the United States Army Command, Fourth Military District, Civil Affairs, Letters Received, 1867, Records Group 98.

Some use was also made of two other collections. The background of one Whig political leader in Mississippi during Presidential Reconstruction is described in a letter in the Rutherford B. Hayes Papers, Hayes Memorial Library, Fremont, Ohio. An accounting record in the Mary Shaw Papers, in the possession of Ann Bowman, Fayette, Mississippi, suggests the difficulties involved in the establishment of a healthy planter-labor relationship after the war.

PRINTED GOVERNMENT DOCUMENTS: UNITED STATES

a. Executive Branch

General and General Court Martial Orders, Circulars and Circulars Civil Affairs, Headquarters, 4th Military District, 1867. Vicksburg: Government Printing Office, 1868.

Report of the Commissioner of Agriculture for the Year 1866. Washington: Government Printing Office, 1867.

Report of the Commissioner of Agriculture for the Year 1868. Washington: Government Printing Office, 1869.

U. S. Bureau of the Census. *Eighth Census of the United States: 1860.* 4 vols.

⸻. *Ninth Census of the United States: 1870.* 5 vols.

⸻. *Tenth Census of the United States: 1880.* 22 vols.

The War of the Rebellion: A Compilation of the Official Records of the Union and Confederate Armies. 73 vols., 128 parts. Washington: Government Printing Office, 1880–1901.

b. Legislative Branch

"Affairs of the Southern Railroads," *House Reports*, 39th Cong., 2nd Sess., No. 34, pp. 1–1057.

"Captured and Forfeited Cotton," *House Executive Documents*, 39th Cong., 2nd Sess., No. 97, pp. 1–95.

"Condition of the South," *Senate Executive Documents*, 39th Cong., 1st Sess., No. 2, pp. 1–108.

"Freedmen's Affairs," *Senate Executive Documents*, 39th Cong., 2nd Sess., No. 6, pp. 1–230.

"Message of the President of the United States and Accompanying Documents to the Two Houses of Congress, at the Commencement of the Second Session of the 39th Congress," *House Executive Documents*, 39th Cong., 2nd Sess., No. 1, pp. 1–14.

"Railroad Property," *House Executive Documents*, 39th Cong., 1st Sess., No. 155, pp. 1–523.

"Reports of the Assistant Commissioners of the Freedmen's Bureau Made since December 1, 1865," *Senate Executive Documents*, 39th Cong., 1st Sess., No. 27, pp. 1–166.

"Report of the Commissioner of Internal Revenue, June 30, 1866," *House Executive Documents*, 39th Cong., 2nd Sess., No. 55, pp. 1–349.

"Report of General Oliver O. Howard, December 1865," *House Executive Documents*, 39th Cong., 1st Sess., No. 11, pp. 1–58.

"Report of the Joint Committee on Reconstruction," *House Reports*, 39th Cong., 1st Sess., No. 30, Pt. III, 1–187.

"Report on the Levee on the Mississippi River," *Senate Reports*, 39th Cong., 1st Sess., No. 126, pp. 1–4.

"Report of the Commissioner of the Freedmen's Bureau," *House Executive Documents*, 39th Cong., 1st Sess., No. 70, 1–403.

"Condition of Affairs in Mississippi," *House Miscellaneous Documents*, 40th Cong., 3rd Sess., No. 53, pp. 1–299.

"Correspondence Relative to Reconstruction," *Senate Executive Documents*, 40th Cong., 1st Sess., No. 14, pp. 1–287.

"Levees on the Mississippi," *Senate Reports*, 40th Cong., 1st Sess., No. 2, pp. 1–8.

"Affairs in the Late Insurrectionary States," *House Reports*, 42nd Cong., 2nd Sess., No. 22, pp. 1–588.

"Report from the Committee on the Levees of the Mississippi River," *Senate Reports*, 42nd Cong., 2nd Sess., No. 170, pp. 1–10.

"Seizure of Cotton," *Senate Executive Documents*, 43rd Cong., 2nd Sess., No. 23, pp. 1–73.

"Statements, Letters, and Testimony Relative to Captured and Abandoned Property, before the Committee on Expenditures of the Treasury Department," *House Miscellaneous Documents*, 44th Cong., 1st Sess., No. 190, pp. 1–180.

PRINTED GOVERNMENT DOCUMENTS: MISSISSIPPI

Constitution of the State of Mississippi As Amended, with the Ordinances and Resolutions Adopted by the Constitutional Convention, August, 1865. Jackson: E. M. Yerger, State Printer, 1865.

Journal of the House of Representatives of the State of Mississippi, October, November, and December Session of 1865. Jackson: J. J. Shannon and Co., State Printers, 1866.

Journal of the Proceedings and Debates in the Constitutional Convention of the State of Mississippi, August, 1865. Jackson: E. M. Yerger, State Printer, 1865.

Journal of the Senate of the State of Mississippi, October, November, and December Session of 1865. Jackson: J. J. Shannon and Co., State Printers, 1866.

Journal of the Senate of the State of Mississippi, at a Called Session, October, 1866 [January-February, 1867]. Jackson: J. J. Shannon and Co., State Printers, 1866 and 1867.

Journal of the State Convention and Ordinances and Resolutions Adopted in January, 1861. Jackson: E. Barksdale, State Printer, 1861.

Laws of the State of Mississippi, Passed at a Regular Session of the Mississippi Legislature, Held in the City of Jackson, November and December 1861, and January 1862. Jackson: Cooper and Kimball, State Printers, 1862.

Laws of the State of Mississippi, Passed at a Regular Session of the Mississippi Legislature, Held in the City of Jackson, October, November, and December, 1865. Jackson: J. J. Shannon and Co., State Printers, 1866.

Laws of the State of Mississippi, Passed at a Called Session of the Mississippi Legislature, Held in the City of Jackson, October, 1866, and January and February, 1867. Jackson: J. J. Shannon and Co., State Printers, 1867.

JUDICIAL DECISIONS: MISSISSIPPI

Coffman et al. v. *The Bank of Kentucky,* 40 Miss. 29 (1866).

Mosely v. *Anderson,* 40 Miss. 49 (1866).

Thomas v. *Taylor,* 42 Miss. 651 (1869).

PUBLISHED LETTERS, CONTEMPORARY ACCOUNTS, REPORTS, AND REMINISCENCES

Alcorn, James Lusk. *Views of the Honorable J. L. Alcorn on the Political Situation of Mississippi.* Friar's Point, Mississippi: n.p., 1867.

Alexander, Thomas B. (ed.). "Persistent Whiggery in Mississippi Reconstruction: The *Hinds County Gazette,*" *Journal of Mississippi History,* XXIII (1961), 71–93.

Annual Report of the President and Directors of the Mississippi Central Railroad Co., to the Stockholders for the Year Ending August 31, 1865. New Albany, Indiana: Norman and Matthews, Railroad Printers, 1865.

Annual Report of the President and Directors of the Mississippi Central Railroad Company to the Stockholders for the Year Ending August 31, 1866. Jackson, Tennessee: W. W. Gates and Co., Printers, 1866.

Barbee, William J. *The Cotton Question: The Production, Export, Manufacture, and Consumption of Cotton.* New York: Metropolitan Record Office, 1866.

[Benham, George C.]. *A Year of Wreck: A True Story by a Victim.* New York: Harper and Brothers, 1880.

Bettersworth, John K. (ed.). "Mississippi Unionism: The Case of the

Reverend James A. Lyon," *Journal of Mississippi History*, I (1939), 37–52.

Fleming, Walter L. (ed.). *Documentary History of Reconstruction: Political, Military, Social, Religious, Educational, and Industrial, 1865 to the Present Time*. 2 vols. Cleveland: Arthur H. Clark Co., 1906-1907.

Fulkerson, Horace S. *A Civilian's Recollections of the War Between the States*. Baton Rouge: Otto Claitor, 1939.

Hilgard, Eugene W. *Report on the Geology and Agriculture of the State of Mississippi*. Jackson: E. Barksdale, State Printer, 1860.

Knox, Thomas W. *Camp-fire and Cotton-field*. New York: Blelock and Co., 1865.

Loring, Francis W., and C. F. Atkinson (eds.). *Cotton Culture and the South, Considered with Reference to Emigration*. Boston: A. Williams and Company, 1869.

Montgomery, Franklin A. *Reminiscences of a Mississippian in Peace and War*. Cincinnati: Robert Clark Company Press, 1901.

Morgan, Albert T. *Yazoo; or on the Picket Line of Freedom in the South*. Washington: Published by the author, 1884.

Morse, John T., Jr. (ed.). *Diary of Gideon Welles, Secretary of the Navy under Lincoln and Johnson*. 3 vols. Boston: Houghton-Mifflin Company, 1911.

Osborn, George C. (ed.). "The Life of a Southern Plantation Owner during Reconstruction, as Revealed in the Clay Sharkey Papers," *Journal of Mississippi History*, VI (1944), 103–12.

Rainwater, Percy L. (ed.). "The Autobiography of Benjamin Grubb Humphreys, August 26, 1808–December 20, 1882," *Mississippi Valley Historical Review*, XXI (1934), 231–55.

Reid, Whitelaw. *After the War: A Southern Tour*. Cincinnati: Moore, Wilstach, and Baldwin, 1866.

Report of President M. Emanuel to the Stockholders of the Southern Railroad Company, March 15, 1866. N.p., n.d.

Richardson, James D. (comp.). *A Compilation of the Messages and Papers of the Presidents*. 11 vols. New York: Bureau of National Literature and Art, 1896–1908.

Sabin, Edwin L. "Vicksburg and After: Being the Experience of a Southern Merchant and Non-combatant during the Sixties," *Sewanee Review*, XV (1907), 485–96.

Schurz, Carl. *The Reminiscences of Carl Schurz*. 3 vols. New York: The McClure Company, 1908.

Silver, James W. (ed.). "The Breakdown of Morale in Central Mississippi in 1864: Letters of Judge Robert S. Hudson," *Journal of Mississippi History*, XVI (1954), 99–120.

Smedes, Susan Dabney. *A Southern Planter*. 4th edition. New York: James Pott and Co., 1890.

Somers, Robert. *The Southern States Since the War, 1870–71*. London: Macmillan and Co., 1871.

Trowbridge, John T. *The Desolate South, 1865–1866*. New York: Duell, Sloan, and Pearce Co., 1956.

Warren, Henry W. *Reminiscences of a Mississippi Carpetbagger*. Worcester, Massachusetts: The Davis Press, 1914.

NEWSPAPERS AND CONTEMPORARY JOURNALS

Bankers' Magazine and Statistical Record, 1866.

Canton *American Citizen*, 1865–66.

Cincinnati *Enquirer*, 1865.

Commercial and Financial Chronicle: Banker's Gazette, Commercial Times, Railway Monitor, and Insurance Journal, 1866–68.

De Bow's Review, 1868.

Forest *Register*, 1869.

Friar's Point *Coahomian*, 1865–67.

Hernando *Weekly Press*, 1869.

Jackson *Clarion*, 1865–67.

Jackson *Clarion and Standard*, 1866.

Jackson *News*, 1865.

Jackson *Weekly Clarion*, 1867.

Macon *Beacon*, 1865.

Memphis *Appeal*, 1865.

Merchant's Magazine and Commercial Review, 1867.

Meridian *Chronicle*, 1868.

Meridian *Clarion*, 1864–65.

Meridian *Semi-Weekly Gazette*, 1867.

Meridian *Weekly Gazette*, 1867.

Mobile *Advertiser and Register*, 1865.

Natchez *Courier*, 1865, 1867–68.

Natchez *Democrat*, 1865–66.

Natchez *Tri-Weekly Courier*, 1865.

Natchez *Tri-Weekly Democrat*, 1866–67.

Natchez *Weekly Courier*, 1866.

Natchez *Weekly Democrat*, 1865, 1872.

New Orleans *Picayune*, 1865–66.

New Orleans *Price Current*, 1865.

New York *Times*, 1865–67.

New York *Tribune*, 1865.

Port Gibson *Standard*, 1865–66.

Raymond *Hinds County Gazette*, 1865–70.

Vicksburg *Herald*, 1865, 1867.

Vicksburg *Herald and Mississippian*, 1867.

Vicksburg *Journal*, 1865.

Vicksburg *Times*, 1866, 1868–69.

Vicksburg *Times and Republican,* 1871.
Vicksburg *Weekly Republican,* 1868.

Secondary Sources

BOOKS

Appleton's Annual Cyclopaedia and Register of Important Events. 15 vols. New York: Appleton, 1861–75.
Beale, Howard K. *The Critical Year: A Study of Andrew Johnson and Reconstruction.* New York: Harcourt, Brace and Company, 1930.
Bettersworth, John K. *Confederate Mississippi: The People and Policies of a Cotton State in Wartime.* Baton Rouge: Louisiana State University Press, 1943.
Biographical and Historical Memoirs of Mississippi. 2 vols. Chicago: Goodspeed Publishing Company, 1891.
Biographical Directory of the American Congress, 1774–1961. Washington: United States Government Printing Office, 1961.
Boyle, James E. *Cotton and the New Orleans Cotton Exchange: A Century of Commercial Evolution.* Garden City, New York: Country Life Press, 1934.
Clark, Thomas D. *A Pioneer Southern Railroad from New Orleans to Cairo.* Chapel Hill: The University of North Carolina Press, 1936.
Clayton, Alexander M. *Centennial Address on the History of Marshall County.* Washington: R. O. Polkinhorn Printer, 1880.
Coulter, E. Merton. *The South during Reconstruction, 1865–1877.* Baton Rouge: Louisiana State University Press, 1947.
Dickey, Dallas C. *Seargent S. Prentiss, Whig Orator of the Old South.* Baton Rouge: Louisiana State University Press, 1946.
Donald, David. *The Politics of Reconstruction, 1863–1867.* Baton Rouge: Louisiana State University Press, 1965.
Ezell, John S. *The South since 1865.* New York: The Macmillan Co., 1963.
Fish, Carl R. *The Restoration of the Southern Railroads.* Madison: University of Wisconsin Press, 1919.
Franklin, John Hope. *Reconstruction: After the Civil War.* Chicago: The University of Chicago Press, 1961.
Garner, James W. *Reconstruction in Mississippi.* New York: The Macmillan Company, 1901.
Gray, William F. *Imperial Bolivar.* Cleveland, Mississippi: Bolivar *Commercial* Newspaper Co., 1923.
Hesseltine, William B., and David L. Smiley. *The South in American History.* 2nd ed. revised. Englewood Cliffs, N. J.: Prentice Hall, Inc., 1960.

Humphreys, Benjamin G., Jr. *Floods and Levees of the Mississippi River*. Washington: N.p., 1914.

Johnson, Allen, and Dumas Malone (eds.). *Dictionary of American Biography*. 20 vols., plus supplements. New York: Charles Scribner's Sons, 1928–.

Klingberg, Frank W. *The Southern Claims Commission*. Berkeley: University of California Press, 1955.

Lipscomb, William L. *A History of Columbus, Mississippi, during the 19th Century*. Birmingham: *Dispatch* Printing Co., 1909.

Litwack, Leon F. *North of Slavery: The Negro in the Free States, 1790–1860*. Chicago: The University of Chicago Press, 1961.

Mayes, Edward. *Lucius Q. C. Lamar: His Life, Times, and Speeches, 1825–1893*. Nashville: Publishing House of the Methodist Episcopal Church, South, 1896.

Massey, Mary Elizabeth. *Ersatz in the Confederacy*. Columbia: University of South Carolina Press, 1952.

McKitrick, Eric L. *Andrew Johnson and Reconstruction*. Chicago: University of Chicago Press, 1960.

Moore, Albert B. *Conscription and Conflict in the Confederacy*. New York: The Macmillan Company, 1924.

Overy, David H., Jr. *Wisconsin Carpetbaggers in Dixie*. Madison: The State Historical Society of Wisconsin, 1961.

Pereyra, Lillian A. *James Lusk Alcorn: Persistent Whig*. Louisiana State University Press, 1966.

Rainwater, Percy L. *Mississippi, Storm Center of Secession, 1856–1861*. Baton Rouge: Otto Claitor, 1938.

Ramsdell, Charles W. *Behind the Lines in the Southern Confederacy*. Baton Rouge: Louisiana State University Press, 1944.

Ranck, James B. *Albert Gallatin Brown: Radical Southern Nationalist*. New York: D. Appleton-Century Co., 1937.

Randall, James G., and David Donald. *The Civil War and Reconstruction*. 2nd ed. revised. Boston: D. C. Heath and Co., 1961.

Rhodes, Marce C. *History of Taxation in Mississippi*. Nashville: George Peabody College for Teachers, 1930.

Rowland, Dunbar. *Courts, Judges, and Lawyers of Mississippi, 1798–1935*. Jackson: Hederman Bros., 1935.

————. *History of Mississippi: The Heart of the South*. 4 vols. Chicago: S. J. Clarke Publishing Company, 1925.

————. (ed.). *Mississippi: Comprising Sketches of Counties, Towns, Events, Institutions and Persons, Arranged in Cyclopedia Form*. 3 vols. Atlanta: Southern Historical Publishing Association, 1907.

————. (ed.). *The Official and Statistical Register of the State of Mississippi, 1908*. Nashville: Brandon Printing Co., 1908.

Saloutos, Theodore. *Farmer Movements in the South, 1865–1933*. Berkeley: University of California Press, 1960.

Sharkey, Robert P. *Money, Class, and Party: An Economic Study of*

Civil War and Reconstruction. Baltimore: The Johns Hopkins Press, 1959.

Simkins, Francis B. *A History of the South.* 3rd ed. revised. New York: Alfred A. Knopf Co., 1963.

Stover, John F. *The Railroads of the South, 1865–1900: A Study in Finance and Control.* Chapel Hill: The University of North Carolina Press, 1955.

Walker, Peter F. *Vicksburg: A People at War, 1860–65.* Chapel Hill: University of North Carolina Press, 1960.

Watkins, James L. *King Cotton: A Historical and Statistical Review, 1790 to 1908.* New York: James L. Watkins and Sons, 1908.

Wharton, Vernon L. *The Negro in Mississippi, 1865–1890.* Chapel Hill: University of North Carolina Press, 1947.

Wiley, Bell I. *Southern Negroes, 1861–1865.* New Haven: Yale University Press, 1938.

Woodward, C. Vann. *Origins of the New South, 1877–1913.* Baton Rouge: Louisiana State University Press, 1951.

Woolfolk, George R. *The Cotton Regency: The Northern Merchants and Reconstruction, 1865–1880.* New York: Bookman Associates, 1958.

Wyeth, John A. *That Devil Forrest: Life of General Nathan Bedford Forrest.* New York: Harper and Brothers, 1959.

ARTICLES

Alexander, Thomas B. "Persistent Whiggery in the Confederate South, 1860–1877," *Journal of Southern History,* XXVII (1961), 305–29.

Anderson, George L. "The South and Problems of Post-Civil War Finance," *Journal of Southern History,* IX (1943), 181–95.

Bowman, Robert. "Reconstruction in Yazoo County," *Publications of the Mississippi Historical Society,* VII (1903), 115–30.

Deupree, J. G. "Colonel R. A. Pinson," *Publications of the Mississippi Historical Society, Centenary Series,* II (1918), 9–11.

Donald, David H. "The Scalawag in Mississippi Reconstruction," *Journal of Southern History,* X (1944), 447–60.

Doster, James F. "The Georgia Railroad and Banking Company in the Reconstruction Era," *Georgia Historical Quarterly,* XLVIII (1964), 1–32.

———. "Were the Southern Railroads Destroyed by the Civil War?" *Civil War History,* VII (1961), 310–20.

Drake, Winbourne M. "The Mississippi Reconstruction Convention of 1865," *Journal of Mississippi History,* XXI (1959), 225–56.

Futrell, Robert F. "Efforts of Mississippians to Encourage Immigration, 1865–1880," *Journal of Mississippi History,* XX (1958), 59–76.

Gates, Paul W. "Federal Land Policy in the South, 1866–1888," *Journal of Southern History,* VI (1940), 303–30.

Griffin, Richard W. "Problems of the Southern Cotton Planters After the Civil War," *Georgia Historical Quarterly*, XXXIX (1955), 103–17.

Hall, L. Marshall. "William L. Sharkey and Reconstruction," *Journal of Mississippi History*, XXVII (1965), 1–17.

Halsell, Willie D. "Migration into, and Settlement of, Leflore County, 1833–1876," *Journal of Mississippi History*, IX (1947), 219–37.

Hardy, William H. "Recollections of Reconstruction in East and Southeast Mississippi," *Publications of the Mississippi Historical Society*, VII (1903), 199–215.

———. "Recollections of Reconstruction in East and Southeast Mississippi," *Publications of the Mississippi Historical Society*, VIII, (1904), 137–51.

Hickman, Nollie W. "Logging and Rafting Timber in South Mississippi, 1840–1910," *Journal of Mississippi History*, XIX (1957), 154–72.

———. "Lumber Industry in South Mississippi, 1890–1915," *Journal of Mississippi History*, XX (1958), 211–23.

Kelly, Arthell. "Levee Building and the Settlement of the Yazoo Basin," *Southern Quarterly*, I (1963), 285–308.

Lee, Stephen D. "Sherman's Meridian Expedition from Vicksburg to Meridian, February 3rd to March 6th, 1864," *Publications of the Mississippi Historical Society*, IV (1901), 37–47.

Magee, Hattie. "Reconstruction in Lawrence and Jefferson Counties," *Publications of the Mississippi Historical Society*, XI (1910), 163–204.

McNeily, John S. "From Organization to Overthrow of Mississippi's Provisional Government," *Publications of the Mississippi Historical Society, Centenary Series*, I (1916), 9–403.

———. "War and Reconstruction in Mississippi, 1863–1890," *Publications of the Mississippi Historical Society, Centenary Series*, II (1918), 165–535.

Miles, Edwin A. "The Mississippi Slave Insurrection Scare of 1835," *Journal of Negro History*, XLII (1957), 48–60.

Pereyra, Lillian A. "James Lusk Alcorn and a Unified Levee System," *Journal of Mississippi History*, XXVII (1965), 18–41.

Rister, Carl C. "Carlota, a Confederate Colony in Mexico," *Journal of Southern History*, XI (1945), 33–50.

Roberts, A. Sellew. "The Federal Government and Confederate Cotton," *American Historical Review*, XXXII (1927), 262–75.

Saloutos, Theodore. "Southern Agriculture and the Problems of Readjustment: 1865–1877," *Agricultural History*, XXX (1956), 58–76.

Sillers, Walter. "Flood Control in Bolivar County, 1838–1924," *Journal of Mississippi History*, IX (1947), 3–20.

Sydnor, Charles. "The Free Negro in Mississippi before the Civil War," *American Historical Review*, XXXII (1927), 769–88.

Walters, John B. "General William T. Sherman and Total War," *Journal of Southern History*, XIV (1948), 447–80.

Zeichner, Oscar. "The Transition from Slave to Free Agricultural Labor in the Southern States," *Agricultural History*, XIII (1939), 22–32.

DISSERTATIONS AND THESES

Breese, Donald H. "Politics in the Lower South during Presidential Reconstruction, April to November, 1865," Ph.D. dissertation, University of California at Los Angeles, 1963.

Drake, Winbourne M. "Constitutional Development in Mississippi, 1817–1865," Ph.D. dissertation, University of North Carolina, 1954.

Dykes, Mary Frances W. "Mississippi Industrial Legislation, 1865–1880," M.A. thesis, Mississippi State University, 1953.

Ganus, Clifton L., Jr. "The Freedmen's Bureau in Mississippi," Ph.D. dissertation, Tulane University, 1953.

McPherson, Milton M. "The Federal Cotton Tax in the South, 1862–68," M.A. thesis, University of Alabama, 1959.

Moore, Ross H. "Social and Economic Conditions in Mississippi during Reconstruction," Ph.D. dissertation, Duke University, 1938.

OTHER SOURCES

Interview with Wendell B. Johnson, Associate Professor of Geology, Millsaps College, Jackson, Mississippi, February 8, 1965.

Index

of state capitol, 3; disbands legislature, 17

Osterhaus, Peter J.: describes need for law and order, 35; attempts to reform cotton confiscation practice, 67; and the militia controversy, 72–73; intervention of, 83; directs Negroes to work, 94; aids in rebuilding railroad, 198

Owen, F. A., 56

Patton, William S.: gubernatorial candidacy of, 106, 110, 115; defeat of, 110–11, 111n

Paulding, 219

Peace movement: beginnings of, 11–12; reasons for failure of, 12–13; restricted to river counties, 13

Pettus, John, 47

Peyton, Ephraim G., 114

Philadelphia, Pa.: meeting of National Union convention in, 229, 232

Piney woods: in October election, 110–11; center of destitution, 164

Pinson, Richard A., 114

Planter-lawyer class: insolvency of, 32

Pollan, William M.: calls for harsh reconstruction policy, 42; hails triumph of Whig principles, 45; leader of Union League in Choctaw County, 49

Ponchatoula, La., 23

Pontotoc, 219

Pontotoc County: vote of legislators of, on civil rights bill, 136

Port Gibson *Standard*: on federal bankruptcy law, 179–80

Potter, George L.: leader of constitutional Whig group, 49; delegate to reconstruction convention, 51; and emancipation of slaves, 53; leads opposition to Negro testimony, 107; defeated for supreme court seat, 114, 115; state leader in National Union movement, 230, 232; leader of Constitutional Union party, 243, 244

Potter Whigs: oppose unconditional abolition of slavery, 48–49, 59; satisfied with Harrison amendment,

54; foes of Congressional Reconstruction, 244

Power, John L.: estimates war casualties, 26–27; in conservative movement, 230

Prentiss, 20

Property exemption law, 176–77

Property losses: in towns, 18; on plantations, 20

Property proviso of civil rights act: debate on, 130–32; repealed, 151

Property tax: imposed by Federal government, 161

Public school system. *See* Common school system

Quitman *Messenger*: on regulation of Negroes, 124

Radical Reconstruction: beginning of, 237; former secession Democrats acquiesce in, 241, 243–44; mentioned, 172, 179, 236, 247

Radical Republicans: critical of reconstruction convention, 58; on Humphreys, 117n; denounce Black Code, 141; triumph over Johnson party, 151, 233, 234; secure enactment of bankruptcy law, 179; struggle with Johnson, 229, Alcorn's view of, 231–32; reconstruction plan of, 234; and imposition of military reconstruction, 248; mentioned 107, 118, 238, 239, 240. *See also* Republicans

Radicals (Mississippi): in legislature, 121 and n, 122–23, 132, 135–36

Railroad creditors: liberality of, 198, 203, 206, 208, 209, 216

Railroad notes: depreciation of, 22; redemption of, 155–56

Railroads: condition of, 22; new lines contemplated, 212–15; promotion of, 214–15; presidents meet on tax issue, 215–16; pre-eminence in economic life of state, 216; distribute Northern goods, 223; new industrial plants located along, 224

Raymond, 219

Reconstruction: desire for, 11; attitude toward, 39